COMPANION TO

2017

Published by Times Books

An imprint of HarperCollins Publishers
Westerhill Road
Bishopbriggs
Glasgow G64 2QT
www.harpercollins.co.uk
times.books@harpercollins.co.uk

First edition 2017

A catalogue record for this book is available from the British Library.

ISBN 978-0-00-826263-1

10 9 8 7 6 5 4 3 2 1

Printed and bound by CPI Group (UK) Ltd, Croydon, CR0 4YY

THE TIMES

COMPANION TO

2017

CONTENTS

Contents

INTRODUCTION

Like its predecessor this volume brings together outstanding writing, photography and graphics from a year in the life of the world's most famous newspaper. It covers an eventful, unsettled 12 months, from September 2016 to August 2017. In a new-year editorial on December 30, 2016 (reprinted here on p125), *The Times* took stock. If 2016 had been a year of "shocks, setbacks and slaughter", the paper thought it would also seem with hindsight "a year of revolution ... part of a rolling transformation of political institutions, and of geopolitical shifts". Britain's EU referendum and the election of Donald Trump had been manifestations of a populist rejection of established elites. They expressed the deep-rooted grievance of millions of voters who felt ill-served by representative democracy and to whom the rapid expansion of global trade had not brought prosperity.

The Times viewed the year ahead with trepidation, predicting that "the many cracks opened up in 2016 will widen in 2017". To a degree they have. Britain, split almost down the middle by the referendum vote, is no less divided over Brexit than it was a year ago. Trump's America is riven by dangerous tensions. Yet in some ways, this anthology suggests, the 2016 revolution may have stalled. Britain is no nearer knowing how Brexit might work or what it will mean, and a general election called to bring clarity had the opposite effect. President Trump's efforts to turn rhetoric into policy have so far largely been frustrated. In France the presidential victory of Emmanuel Macron was no doubt a shock to the country's political system, but the sudden rise of a wealthy, centrist, business-friendly financier hardly feels like a triumph of populism over the establishment. Meanwhile, around the world, elites cling stubbornly to power by whatever means they can.

It's a gloomy picture, perhaps, but it shouldn't – and doesn't – make for gloomy newspapers. In a world of conflict and upheaval readers want accurate, balanced, immediate first-hand reports. They want powerful human stories that bring developments alive, reliable facts on which to base their own judgments, authoritative commentary and analysis to put the news in context and explain why it matters. *Times* readers expect their paper to take them seriously. They need to know the worst, and to understand it. But they expect also to be entertained, by articles on fashion or football or gardens or dogs that are as lively and as expert as the coverage of politics and world affairs.

An edition of *The Times* contains between 150,000 and 270,000 words. It never seems enough. Every night, as deadlines loom, good stories are cut back, held over or dropped altogether when something more urgent or important comes along. There are 110,000 words in this book. To claim such a tiny fraction of the paper's annual output as "the best of" would be absurd. The hope is that the articles included nonetheless give an engaging picture of a momentous year, and show the quality and range of the journalism that *The Times* produces day after day.

Ian Brunskill
Assistant Editor
The Times

ACKNOWLEDGMENTS

Special thanks to Matthew Lyons (production editor), Nasim Asl, Jack Dyson, Josie Eve and Ailsa McNeil (editorial assistants), Sarah Willcox (sub-editor), Mark Grayson and Andrew Keys (designers); and to Gerry Breslin, Jethro Lennox, Karen Midgley, Kevin Robbins and Sarah Woods at HarperCollins. Thanks also to the contributors and to the following *Times* colleagues: Grace Bradberry, Peter Brookes, Becky Callanan, Jessica Carsen, Magnus Cohen, Nigel Farndale, Hannah Fletcher, Richard Fletcher, Rana Greig, Fiona Gorman, Jeremy Griffin, Tim Hallissey, Robert Hands, Suzy Jagger, Nicola Jeal, Alan Kay, Alex Kay-Jelski, Jane Knight, Robbie Millen, Simon Pearson, Monique Rivelland, Fay Schlesinger, Tim Shearring, Mike Smith, Sam Stewart, Matt Swift and the *Times* graphics team, Craig Tregurtha, Emma Tucker, Pauline Watson, Giles Whittell, Rose Wild, Danny Wilkins, Fiona Wilson and John Witherow.

AUTUMN

MERITOCRACY IS THE LAST THING BRITAIN NEEDS

Philip Collins

SEPTEMBER 16 2016

"IT IS NOT ENOUGH to succeed. Others must fail." Gore Vidal's waspish hopes for his friends captures, in an epigram, why Theresa May does not really mean what she says about meritocracy. Meritocracy does not mean meritocracy. At the beginning of their time in office every prime minister has to make the meritocracy speech. The ardour always fades because, looked at straight on, meritocracy is a radical and terrifying idea.

The term itself was designed as a warning rather than an aspiration. Michael Young wrote *The Rise Of The Meritocracy* in 1958 to raise the alarm that a society based on a narrow definition of merit, embodied in an intelligence test at an early age, is a terrible place to live. Young's meritocracy descends into disorder as the sheep and the goats start to fight. There is nothing wrong, of course, with a weaker version of meritocracy in which talent and effort are rewarded to a greater extent than their opposites. This is what every prime minister is initially getting at, translated into the bloodless jargon of social mobility. But even that they cannot really mean.

This is why we have been treated to yet another turn of the wheel for the over-sold hysteria about grammar schools. When Gordon Brown took over from Tony Blair one of his first acts was to reform the royal prerogative powers, such as the declaration of war, that are carried out by the prime minister. Theresa May's exhuming of grammar schools prompted the same thought I had then: is that all you've got? If a few grammar schools is all you're about, then you're not really about much. This will not be the full return of the binary distinction between grammars and secondary moderns. The school system is too diverse for that.

Besides, Mrs May's advisers know all the objections to grammar schools. They know the cause of social mobility in the 1960s was the conversion of Britain, between the end of the First World War and the end of that decade, from an essentially blue-collar economy into a mostly white-collar one. Suddenly there was more room at the top. Grammar schools coincided with this change but did not cause it. At the height of their popularity, of the grammar school children who gained two A levels, less than 1 per cent came from the skilled working class.

This is a point so well established that it enabled even Jeremy Corbyn to get the better of Mrs May at PMQs this week. After the beating, Mrs May's spokesman was unable to cite any evidence in support of her policy. That's because there isn't any.

That has not prevented plenty of Tory MPs and columnists from elevating their autobiographies to the status of policy writ. There really is no more firmly established body of evidence in all of education. So why does it have to be said over and over? Are these Tories so arrogant that they are impervious to evidence? No, they just don't know what they are talking about. They are simply observing that there were more people mobile in their generation and ascribing that fact, wrongly, to schools.

The government's green paper actually admits its own problem: "Under the current model of grammar schools ... there is ... evidence that children who attend non-selective schools in selective areas may not fare as well academically — both compared to local selective schools and comprehensives in non-selective areas." The rest of the document is then an attempt to salvage selection from the jaws of this yawning disaster. The upshot will be that the conditions imposed on schools before they can opt to select will be so severe by the time the bill limps through parliament that there will be little incentive to do so. Most of the large academy chains have no need of selection. Mrs May's speech on meritocracy was a grand vision saddled to a sorry policy.

The fabled popular demand will dissipate too. Grammars were not abolished by Tony Crosland in a fit of socialist envy.

They were closed by Margaret Thatcher because of middle-class parents complaining to local authorities that their children were not getting in. Young put the politics of grammar schools perfectly: "Every selection of one is a rejection of many." Meritocracy has the unfortunate effect of making aspiration a zero-sum game. My very stupid children (well, not mine, yours), with all their good fortune, will have to fall down a snake while your bright poor child climbs a ladder. No ordinary middle-class parent is going to stand idly by while that happens. It therefore follows that the policy meritocrat will have to commit to some policies even more unpalatable than grammar schools.

There is in fact a Meritocracy Party in Britain, which demands that the Queen abdicate and that only those with relevant experience, which would presumably include the Queen (Tory), be permitted to vote. They want inheritance tax at 100 per cent. I may have earned the money but my children have not and if advantage can be purchased, which it can, then the transfer from me to them impairs the principle of merit.

Advantage goes back a long way. In 1693 John Locke wrote a parenting guide, *Some Thoughts Concerning Education.* The best recommendation was that children should eat no vegetables but the rest has worn well. Locke points out that good citizens are created by good parents and it's still true. Educated parents are marrying their own kind and talking to their children. High-income parents talk with their school-aged children for three hours more per week than low-income parents. By the age of three a poor child would have heard 30 million fewer words at home than one from a professional family.

It matters. How children perform in tests when they are three and a half is a strong predictor of how well they do at school years later. The best way to predict a person's social position at the age of 19 is attainment at 16, which in turn is best foretold by attainment at 11. And you can tell who is going to do well at 11 simply by looking up who did well at seven. A meritocracy would therefore withdraw resources from the later years of life and spend earlier in the life cycle. The only government member I recall taking this seriously is a little-remembered person by the name of Andrea Leadsom.

The regime in Young's *Rise Of The Meritocracy* collapses when the government takes the children of the poor into care to ensure equality of opportunity. Every politician wants the soft version of meritocracy in which the poor do well but nobody suffers. It's a fantasy and that is why the pertinent response to Mrs May is not hysteria about a return to the 1950s but simply this: is that all you've got?

JEREMY PAXMAN: 'I'M NOT ASHAMED TO SAY I'VE SUFFERED DEPRESSION'

Interview by Janice Turner

September 24 2016

Jeremy Paxman relished "war-gaming" interviews, a former *Newsnight* producer tells me: debating the research, plotting manoeuvres, setting bear traps into which ministers would tumble. So how do you war-game a man who knows all the moves? After his famous question about whether he prayed with George W Bush, Tony Blair cavilled at his intrusiveness and Paxo threw up his hands in faux innocence: "But prime minister, I'm just trying to work out what kind of chap you are."

What kind of a chap is Paxman, beneath the suits, the elaborate disdain, the position in our culture — vacant since he left *Newsnight* two years ago — as the scary tutor/imposing father who sees through our dissembling and flaws? His memoir, *A Life in Questions*, abounds with great hack yarns about Diana, Princess of Wales, and the Dalai Lama, war reporting, political scuffles and BBC crises, yet personal detail is sketchy. He has declared his three children and partner, Elizabeth Clough, absolutely out of bounds. Indeed, no girlfriend gets more than a single line. While Paxo the man —

what he feels, whom he loves — emerges rarely and fleetingly from his carapace of high snark.

So in 300-plus pages we glean that he sits on the toilet shooting squirrels out of the bathroom window, he's happiest fishing and (thanks to an anecdote about Orthodox Jews) that he is uncircumcised. Yet those who know him well speak of a complicated man roiling with self-doubt who "struggles with existence". Ask about his father, they say, whose approval he sought in vain. Ask about his depression. Ask Paxman if he is happy.

We meet at Galvin La Chapelle in east London and I have bagged us a table alone on the mezzanine high above the shiny City lunch crowd. Paxman is late, caught in cross-town traffic from his Notting Hill flat where he lives three days a week rather than commute from his family home near Henley, Oxfordshire. I watch him walk very slowly up the stairs. He wore out his knee running, is considering replacement surgery and is clearly in pain. (Later, when I see him wincing and offer to carry his suit bag, he splutters and tells me to f*** off.) Otherwise he looks splendid for 66: lean apart from a slight bay-window belly; thick, almost white hair; fine skin with that rich man's holiday burnish. His azure linen jacket with elaborate stitching is very natty.

Old age, however, seems much on his mind and appears to revolt him. His most recent headlines were for blasting the magazine *Mature Times* for its stairlift ads and portrayal of people his age as "on the verge of incontinence, idiocy and peevish valetudinarianism". (He has a rather Alan Partridge-esque vocabulary, calling party conferences the "gallimaufry of our democracy".) I note that his memoir is rather ageist: he refers to "whiffy old wrinklies" and tells an unkind story about John Gielgud needing help to go to the loo. He writes that old people who don't pay "direct" taxes (ie aren't working) shouldn't be allowed to vote.

Does he use his free bus pass? The eyebrows shoot up.

"I don't have one."

Why not?

"Because I'm still earning and I'm very happy if people want to give you a discount because you're over a certain age. But I've just done four weeks filming a series about rivers. The week after next I'm in Washington. Why should I expect others to pay my Tube fare?"

Why do you believe you should be allowed to vote but people who've retired from jobs you can't do in old age — roofers, say — should not?

"I did not say that!"

You said no representation without taxation.

"Yes. And there will come a point of course when no one asks me to do anything. It happens to all of us."

So in the meantime you should be allowed to vote but they shouldn't?

"Sometimes, life is like that, Janice. Unfair."

For the first 20 minutes, after Paxo has ordered "heritage tomato" salad (scorn about what "heritage" means), mutton (scorn about how much "lamb" is really mutton) and a glass of white wine (which he believes doesn't count as real booze), the interview comprises me asking a question and him knocking it down. It feels like a bizarre stress dream in which I'm on *Newsnight* playing Jeremy Paxman while the real Jeremy Paxman harrumphs and sneers. He calls me (humorously, maybe ...) "a silly woman", accuses me of misquoting him, tells me to "cast a more artful fly" and, as if abrading dim *University Challenge* contestants, cries, "Oh, come on!"

How the hell, I think, am I going to ask about his father? In the book, Keith Paxman is a puzzle, a shape-shifter, a domineering presence but also an invisible man, whom his son has clearly spent his whole life trying to fathom. Jeremy, his eldest child, was born near Leeds while Keith, a naval officer, was away at sea, and screamed when introduced to him. "Relations between us never really improved much." His father had a vile temper and beat him for any perceived insubordination with sticks, shoes, cricket stumps or his bare hand. "Did I love my father?" he writes.

"My feelings ranged from resentment to passionate hatred."

Paxman is scathing about his father's social pretensions and evolving accent as he leaves the navy and tries, falteringly, to rise in the world. Keith resents his wife's family wealth, which pays for Jeremy, his two brothers and little sister to attend private schools. He becomes a typewriter salesman then ascends to manage factories across the Midlands. The family home grows to a country house and Keith adopts brass-buttoned blazers, a monocle and plus-fours. Paxman sees him as a try-hard and a phoney who once introduced his son to his golf-club friends as "one of those homosexual communists from the BBC".

Moreover, the family's social standing is precarious: middle class "by our fingernails". Jeremy never feels at ease at Malvern College "with the boys who genuinely belong to the professional classes", and a sense of not truly belonging and a bad case of impostor syndrome have never left him.

Later, when Labour nationalises the steel industry, his father quits and is transformed into a comedy huckster, buying cosmetics from a company called Holiday Magic in a pyramid scheme, then a chain of laundrettes. Finally, Keith reappears at the end of the book, as a coda, having moved to Australia and broken contact with his family. Paxman goes over to find him but the encounter is so vaguely explained, we don't learn if his mother had been divorced or had died. It is as if Paxman, having started to exhume this painful matter, finds it too difficult to finish.

I ask what lasting effect his father had on his life. "There comes a point, about the age of 40, when you have to stop saying how you are is a consequence of how you were brought up. And particularly when you are 66, it is pathetic to say, 'I am as I am because of things that happened in my childhood.'

"I understand what you're digging for. I'm just ... " I'm not digging — I'm asking about your memoir. "Yes, you are digging." It's my job to dig. "Well, you just said, 'I'm not digging.' Make up your mind."

Wouldn't you ask, in my position?

"Well, I might." Eventually, Paxman says quietly, "I will not be portrayed as a 'poor little me' figure."

The "homosexual communist" remark, he says, was "an example of wardroom humour". But it stuck with you? "Oh, I remember it vividly, where it happened."

Did your father ever say he was proud of you? "I expect so ..."

Did you *feel* he was proud?

"It wasn't a terribly ... It wasn't that sort of close, intimate relationship. But I do understand that if I answer your question saying, 'Oh, I never felt he was proud of me,' I know how you will write that. I'm like the boy in the jam factory who didn't eat jam because he knew what went into it."

When his father left, Paxman was about 24, a BBC trainee. He does not report whether his departure was expected or sudden. "I don't recall. I wasn't at home."

Didn't you all wonder over time why he didn't come back? "No."

He sees his siblings from time to time — his brother Giles was British ambassador to Spain — but they aren't terribly close. "If we don't see people very often ... Intimacy is the consequence of familiarity, isn't it?" He assumes his parents divorced, because his father eventually remarried in New Zealand and his stepmother brought Keith's ashes to scatter in England. When I wonder how his father's example influenced his own parenting he is instantly angry, accusing me of asking about his children. Which I wouldn't dare. Then he says, "I think everyone is scared to some extent of becoming their parents and I suppose that would have been the case. The family relationships, I find they don't resonate happily to me."

Paxman's mother, however, barely features in the book, except as quietly running the household. He doesn't even note when she died.

"Both my parents are dead," he says, taking off his glasses and rubbing his eyes. "It's strange, death, isn't it? However old you are, when you've finally lost both parents, there is a feeling of being orphaned. And I think it's very cruel that all the very vibrant memories I have of my mother are now intertwined with the memory of how she looked at the point of death." Was he there? "Yes, the skin kind of collapses on to the skull and you recognise the person, but you don't recognise them. They've clearly passed from one state of being to another ... I remember when she was young and she had this luxurious black hair which she kept pinned back in a bun. And she had three boys within three and half years or something. And boys are quite difficult ... "

I ask how old his mother was when she died.

"I'm ashamed to say I cannot tell you."

After his father had been gone for more than a decade, sending only curt Christmas cards, Paxman went to Australia to find him.

"I was astonished by his lack of curiosity. I mean, there were grandchildren he'd never seen, spouses he'd never met. It seemed as if we were part of a life he'd put behind him."

Was it the journalist in him who wanted to go, or the questing son?

"Both of those things, I think. I wanted to see if he was all right and I was slightly concerned in case I was becoming him."

It is the most revealing thing he's said in an hour. And I recall a childhood incident he describes of his sister finding their father sobbing on the bathroom floor. "I didn't want to feel I was living my life as he lived his life ... I think he was actually a vulnerable man and he probably thought cutting himself off was the only way to survive."

Paxman refers to his depression ("I spent several years seeing a therapist, and several more on antidepressants," he says in his foreword) in several brief incidents. When he was studying at St Catharine's College, Cambridge, friends recall him standing on a bridge saying, "It is completely and utterly meaningless, isn't it?" then going to the pub. Aged 35, after stints in Belfast during the Troubles and as a war reporter in

Zimbabwe and Lebanon, and having lost three good friends, he suffered insomnia and nightmares: "I didn't exactly have a breakdown. But it was pretty like one."

He has refused to talk about it before. "I don't see any reason to be ashamed of saying I've suffered depression, as have a vast number of people. What I'm really not willing to do is try to appear as a victim." As when discussing his father, Paxman's greatest fear is of appearing to whine or look pitiful and weak.

Has he learnt anything during his years of treatment he'd care to pass on?

"The great thing is that unless we are all finished, the sun's going to come up tomorrow. It's always worst in the middle of the night, and what seems insurmountable at 3am, at 8am looks completely different. The critical thing they teach you doing CBT [cognitive behavioural therapy] is there is another way of looking at things. I would really like to learn that skill."

Did CBT help him?

"I don't think I was conscientious enough. But that is the key question: when everything seems black and shrouded in gloom and there seems no way out, is there another way of looking at it? Though," he adds quietly, "if you're in the grip of really serious depression, that's almost impossible."

Before I meet Paxman, I call several senior *Newsnight* colleagues who say many warm things. He is not a sulking prima donna: although intolerant of mediocrity, he would voice his view, then get on with the job. Nor is he a bully who "punches down"; he was patient with junior staff and, says one female executive, "was more receptive to women's voices in the newsroom than most men in the Nineties". But it is his complexity that instils loyalty. "Why he is a great broadcaster, not just a good one, is because beneath that outer shell of suave sophistication, there is an inner vulnerability." This, points out another former colleague, explains his sensitivity when interviewing Terry Pratchett about facing death or the MP John Woodcock about his own mental illness.

In his memoir, Paxman expresses regret about his crueller

questions to Gordon Brown ("Why does no one like you?") and asking Charles Kennedy, "Why does everyone say of you, 'I hope he's sober'?" He believes his famous monstering of hapless junior treasury minister Chloe Smith was needed to bring the government to account, but asking, "Are you incompetent?" was "unanswerable and unkind".

The media, he says, can only accommodate one idea of a person. "I know that I will always be Mr Rude or whatever," he says. "But I know that's not me. It's a small part of any human being." Yet that impenetrable outer shell, his air of not caring what anyone thought of him, created jeopardy. When you switched on *Newsnight* and saw Paxman was presenting, nothing seemed unsayable. And his jaded, nihilistic belief that fame, TV, politics, indeed much of human activity, is basically meaningless can be a useful mindset when dealing with the powerful. "The most striking thing about some of them," he writes of establishment luminaries, "is how unimpressive they all are."

The problem with Paxman is this default position — "You're all lying fools" — solidified into a shtick. He quotes Alan Bennett on irony, the English amniotic fluid "washing away guilt and purpose and responsibility. Joking but not joking. Caring but not caring. Serious but not serious." It encapsulates his father's cruel wardroom humour, his own supercilious sneer.

At times he sounds high-handed, especially when discussing peers. Newsreaders, Jon Snow aside, are failed actors, not proper journalists. Nicholas Witchell is a "rather buttoned-up reporter who had written a book about the Loch Ness monster". He says producers cried of one excitable broadcaster, "Stick a fresh battery in the news bunny." (Is this Huw Edwards? "I have no comment to make.")

Although he doesn't dignify his existence with a mention in the book, he was reportedly most unpleasant to Jeremy Vine, whom he saw as a threatening younger version of himself. In Vine's memoirs, he recalls that if he left a mug or family photo in the newsroom they were removed secretly by Paxman. "Jeremy Vine has written his memoirs?" he spits out with disdain. "I don't know what you're talking about." But you called him your "mini-me" and "the sorcerer's apprentice" on air. Paxman huffs. "Did I? Good."

What interests him now more than the TV ephemera of catching out politicians are the bigger questions. "Is there a purpose?" he says. "What do things mean? What is the right way to live? I would rather spend an evening talking about those than how to manage Vladimir Putin or reform the NHS. My great discovery in the past year or so is that news doesn't really matter." He doesn't watch *Newsnight* — "It stops me having to tell people what I think of it."

Since he left the programme he's kept busy writing this memoir, a column for the *Financial Times* and making several TV series. Work, he finds, keeps the black dog at bay. Yet one question nags him: has he fulfilled his potential? "We all ought to ask ourselves that as we approach the finishing line. Could I have done something else? I haven't got any great talents. Well, perhaps I could have put them to better purpose."

Does this come from his father's view that making things was more worthwhile than just reporting on them? "I think that's a fair observation, and that is what I feel."

The Conservative Party made a tentative approach about him being candidate for London mayor. But he says he'd make terrible lobby fodder. He sees himself as a maverick — "I've never been part of the establishment," he insists — which seems at odds with his membership of the Garrick Club. He tells me, off the record, how it came to pass that, after initially being blackballed, he was allowed to join. But he is not naturally clubbable anyway, likes being alone or in his coterie of wealthy fishing mates including Robert Harris and Max Hastings.

We're already late for the photoshoot and I'm pink in the face from the exertion of interview combat. At the end of a TV interrogation, Paxman always asked his subjects, "Happy enough?" Almost always they said yes. So I ask him.

"I'm going to say no," he cries. "I shall say, 'This is a disgrace!'"

But are you ever happy enough?

"I remember at school," he recalls, "three of us talking about what to do. One chap wanted to be a doctor. I didn't know what I wanted to be. The third fellow said, 'I don't mind what I do, as long as I'm happy,' and I remember saying, 'What a ridiculously superficial ambition,' and he just looked slightly gobsmacked." Then, a few years ago, Paxman heard the man worked for the United Nations and wrote saying their conversation had haunted him all his life: "I want to apologise because you were right and I was wrong." The man responded, "Very nice of you to write, but I've no recollection of this at all."

His friends have called him an Eeyore: "It's always damp in my part of the forest," he says. "But who wants to be Tigger? Who wants to be happy?"

So we head for the photographer's studio where Paxman surveys clothes brought in by the stylist ("Look at these ridiculous trousers!") then reappears in his own dark suit, barely worn since he left *Newsnight*. Seeing him there, back in his old armour, standing legs astride, braced for battle, with ministers to slay, I feel that old tingle of late-night jeopardy. And I miss that fearless, melancholy knight.

BATACLAN: ONE YEAR ON

Adam Sage

October 1 2016

"I can remember thinking, 'This is not the right day for my death.'"

Claude-Emmanuel Triomphe was lying in a pool of blood on the floor of Café Bonne Bière bar in Paris. It was just after 9.30pm on November 13, 2015, and the worst terror attack in modern French history was under way. Triomphe — a balding 57-year-old intellectual who has taught in Paris's most prestigious university, worked in the upper echelons of the civil service and founded a think tank specialising in employment issues — had gone to Café Bonne Bière after a chance encounter with an American traveller.

They had just sat down and were about to order a drink when bullets ripped into the bar and into customers' bodies from the pavement.

"I knew straightaway that I'd been hit. I realised it was serious. I lost an enormous amount of blood, the rescue services had not arrived, and I felt the strength leaving my body. I had time to think — and I can say this very calmly today — I had time to think about death.

"I thought, 'I am going to die.' I would not say I was panicking just then, but I was not in a good way and I was afraid."

Later on, in hospital, Triomphe discovered that he had been hit by three bullets. One stopped 2mm short of his intestine, another cut through his sciatic nerve and a third went through his arm. He tells the tale now with alacrity, almost amusement, as we sit in another bar near his Parisian home.

At the time, the ambulance crew was unsure whether he would pull through.

"I realised they were afraid that I would faint and at one point I really felt a sort of great tiredness, like I would slip into sleep. I realised I had to fight against that, and I made enormous efforts to not slip into that sleep."

Outside there was chaos. The three jihadists who had attacked Café Bonne Bière had sprayed five other bars and restaurants with bullets. Minutes earlier three more had detonated suicide vests outside the national football stadium in the capital's suburbs. A further three were in the process of slaying concert-goers during a gig by the US rock group Eagles of Death Metal at the Bataclan venue.

The French equivalent of the 999 line faced an avalanche of

calls — more than 6,000 to the police alone. Operators struggled to work out who had been shot and where. Ambulance crews wondered whether they would be targeted while tending to the wounded. Police squads were sent to one location, then diverted to another. And journalists — me included — tried to work out what on earth was going on.

The newsdesk asked me to go the Stade de France when the first bomb went off. I ordered a taxi, then discovered that there was a siege at the Bataclan and told the driver to go there. I never reached it. Paris was in lockdown and a line of police blocked me a couple of hundred metres away.

I sat on a bench and interviewed a man whose son had been shot in the foot in a restaurant farther to the east — or that is what he had been told by his son's friend, who had phoned him. Like me, he was stuck behind police lines watching columns of armoured vehicles rumble towards the scene of the shootings. Like me, he had no idea what to do.

For want of a better idea, I took the Parisian version of a Boris bike to cycle through streets deserted by everyone except armed officers. The Rue de Rivoli was eerily empty, the Marais devoid of life. Bars and clubs had closed, and been ordered to lock their customers inside. I got into one — the only place I could find with an internet connection at 1am — and ended up writing my dispatch amid inebriated nightclubbers struggling to comprehend what had happened.

We discovered the next morning that 130 people had died and 414 were hospitalised.

Now, with the first anniversary of the shootings and bombings approaching, I am going back over the events of that night, and they still seem as absurd and macabre as ever.

The people I interviewed for this article — the injured, the bereaved, the emergency service representatives — share anger and pain but also perplexity at the sheer senselessness, the incredible stupidity of it all. The attacks — and those that followed in Nice, where 86 people died on Bastille Day, and in Normandy, where a priest was murdered in his church — have propelled France into a disturbing new era. There is distrust and fear, and a widening gulf between the white majority and the Muslim minority.

Yet among the survivors I met, there was little expression of hatred for the Kalashnikov-wielding thugs who perpetrated the Paris shootings — more a sense of withering disdain. "Cretins" was how the father of one victim described them. Triomphe said they were pawns in a sinister game that they did not understand.

Ten months earlier, 17 people had been killed in attacks on the satirical weekly *Charlie Hebdo* and on a Jewish kosher store in Paris.

Parisians knew another massacre was likely. Islamic State had called on its followers to target the French because of their involvement in the Syrian bombing campaign and their perceived hostility to Islam. The movement had more jihadists from France in its ranks than from any other European country and many had returned from the war zone. Nevertheless, the attack, when it came, caught Paris by surprise.

"We heard loud noises but we didn't pay any attention. We just said to ourselves, 'They're Americans, they are putting on a show, they've got out some bangers.'"

Sophie is among 1,500 people who experienced at first hand the blind callousness of Islamist fanaticism when it struck at the Bataclan during a concert. She is a 32-year-old rock music fan who works in a baby-sitting agency, and we meet in her studio flat, which is decorated according to her distinctive tastes. There are several model Tardises that bear witness to her passion for *Doctor Who*.

On the back of the front door Sophie has stuck tickets from countless concerts and films she has seen. But there have been hardly any additions since last November. Sophie and Léa, her friend, had found a vantage point on a platform at the back of the Bataclan and the band was playing *Kiss the Devil*, one of its hits, when Foued Mohamed-Aggad, 23, Ismael Omar Mostefai, 29, and Samy Amimour, 28, burst into the venue.

First came the noise. Then the confusion and panic.

"All of a sudden, I had a big pain in my leg, it was like I'd been hit with a hammer, and that's when I realised what was happening," says Sophie. "I turned my head and saw three people with guns in their hands who were shouting at us, who were shouting that they were doing this for Syria and for Iraq."

The majority of the 90 people who died in the Bataclan were killed in the first 7 minutes, when the terrorists sprayed the crowd with bullets. That, probably, is when Sophie was hit.

Then, for a quarter of an hour, Mohamed-Aggad, Mostefai and Amimour walked through the crowd cowering on the floor and executed people, apparently at random.

Sophie saw them approach. "They were three metres from me, and then I was really, really frightened because when they made eye contact with someone, they shot them.

"I had a T-shirt with skeletons and tattoos on my arms and I was afraid they would see me, so I quickly put on my jumper and thought if they don't see me, if I don't exist, I'll survive."

Earlier — before the killings — a young man had caught her when she stumbled. Now he had been shot and was lying beside her. "I saw his chest stop moving — he was right next to me — and with Léa, we put him on us to protect ourselves." The terrorists went past without noticing them under the now lifeless body.

At about 10pm, two local police officers entered the venue and shot dead Amimour. Mohamed-Aggad and Mostefai fled upstairs, and silence descended upon the Bataclan. Sophie and Léa — and hundreds of other terrified rock fans — ran for the exit and carried on running until finally she sank to the ground by a door in Boulevard Voltaire.

"In fact, I was really hurting, but it was only when I saw the mass of flesh on my leg — it was absolutely horrible — that I realised I had been hit with a bullet. I smelt the smell of blood, and my shoe was full of blood," says Sophie. Léa stopped a minicab and told the driver to head for the nearest hospital. Sophie had been hit twice, in the calf and the thigh, and was almost unconscious when she got there. She was bloodied, terrified, shocked — but alive.

At about the same time — 10.10pm — Chief Superintendent Christophe Molmy was entering the concert hall. Molmy, 47, is a tough cop — powerfully built, exuding understated authority and with a nose that looks like it has been flattened by a baseball bat. He heads the elite Parisian police Research and Intervention Brigade (BRI) and is accustomed to arresting hardened gangsters.

Shoot-outs are his bread and butter. He had been involved in one two days before November 13 when kidnappers had got jumpy during a ransom handover. He recounts the incident as you or I might recount the breakdown of a photocopier in the office. An ordinary problem in an ordinary day's work. The Bataclan was different: haunting, traumatic, life-changing, even for him.

Molmy had created a rapid intervention unit after the *Charlie Hebdo* killings: 15 men who take their guns and stun grenades home at night so they can scramble within minutes. Now they were picking their way across a mass of bodies in a silence interrupted only by the sound of phones ringing as relatives sought news of their loved ones. Some were dead, some injured, some too frightened to move.

"We were destabilised because we had the wounded pulling at our trousers and asking us to help them while we were advancing. The members of the team all have medical training and tried to do what they could, applying tourniquets and talking to people, but you advance nevertheless. If you don't do things with method they do not work out well."

His unit had to make the venue safe for medics, rescue workers and forensic scientists. Molmy had no idea if the terrorists were still there. Perhaps they had fled with the 900 or so spectators who had left with Sophie and Léa. Perhaps they had booby-trapped the hall.

The team took 50 minutes or so to check the ground floor as survivors emerged from the toilets, the cupboards, the electrical cabinets, the suspended ceilings where they had been sheltering. Each one had to be checked in case they had explosives strapped to their bodies — a common Islamic State tactic in Syria. None did.

But of Mohamed-Aggad or Mostefai there was not a trace. "There was no noise, no shots, nothing," says Molmy. "I said to myself that they had probably left, but we advanced prudently just in case."

At about 11pm, the unit went upstairs. Still there was silence. Still they went on.

Suddenly a petrified voice shouted, "Stop. Don't advance. They have taken us hostage."

Molmy realised that Mohamed-Aggad and Mostefai had not fled. They were hiding in a corridor, and dozens of people were trapped with them: 15 to 20 behind the door, equal numbers in rooms off the corridor, and about 40 on the roof. Among them was a pregnant woman and a boy of 12.

Shouting through the door to the corridor, officers persuaded the terrorists to give them the number of one of the hostage's phones so the brigade's negotiator could call them.

The negotiator talked five times to them, at 11.27pm, 11.29pm, 11.48pm, 12.05am and 12.18am. "They were very nervous and tense and a bit incoherent," says Molmy. "They were saying, 'We want you to leave,' but obviously we weren't going to.

"They recited the jihadist diatribe, 'It's your fault — you've come to wage war in Syria so we are bringing the war to you.'"

The negotiator asked the jihadists to release the child. They refused. He asked them to release the women. They refused again.

The negotiator said he was getting nowhere — how could he with people determined to die and to kill? — and Molmy came to the conclusion that an assault was inevitable. The corridor was 1.35m wide and 8.5m long, it was full of hostages and at the far end were Mohamed-Aggad and Mostefai. "It didn't look good to us. We thought there would be damage for us — dead and wounded — and deaths among the hostages."

As soon as the officers entered the corridor, Mohammed-

Aggad and Mostefai opened fire. Bullets flew everywhere: 27 hit the bulletproof shield on wheels (nicknamed the Ramses) behind which the officers were sheltering. Others hit the ceiling, the walls. A ricochet flew into the left hand of one of the officers.

Astonishingly, that was the only injury. For 90 seconds — an eternity, says Molmy — hostages were crawling under the shield or slipping beside it amid constant gunfire from the terrorists, and none was hit. "My colleagues at the front did an extraordinary job," says Molmy. "They are heroes: they were being shot at all the time and they hardly responded. Throughout the intervention, from beginning to end, we fired a total of just 11 shots."

When all the hostages had been pulled out of the corridor, Molmy's team advanced on the terrorists behind the thud of stun grenades. But in the smoke-filled corridor, the two officers pushing the Ramses did not see the stairs at the end. The shield — 80kg of it — escaped their grasp and fell down the steps, and the terrorists sprang forward, guns pointed at the officers. The two men at the front of the police column reacted faster. Mohamed-Aggad and Mostefai were shot dead before they could pull the triggers on their Kalashnikovs.

It was 12.20am and the siege had ended.

An hour or so later Professor Philippe Juvin, head of the accident and emergency department at Georges Pompidou Hospital, learnt that the wounded were being evacuated. He was told to expect a large number of casualties.

Juvin had already asked the usual Friday night array of patients waiting in A&E — the drunks, the hypochondriacs, the footballers who had sprained their ankles — to go home unless they were critical. All but two did. He had summoned all available staff and put out a Twitter message asking for help from doctors or nurses in the vicinity.

Juvin, 52, is a slim, energetic doctor who speaks with a quietly reassuring certainty. He does not look like the sort to panic in a crisis and he is used to dealing with bullet wounds inflicted by combat rifles. Not only did he spend eight months with the French army in Afghanistan, but his A&E department regularly receives gangsters injured in gunfights.

The wounds are not pretty — "If a pistol bullet hits the foot it goes in and out," he says. "With a Kalashnikov bullet, there is no foot left" — but at least they rarely get more than one victim at a time.

That night, his department treated 53 patients with Kalashnikov wounds. "The big difference is that the people we get with bullet wounds are usually the bad guys. We treat them because it's our job but we don't necessarily have much sympathy for them.

"On November 13, we were getting people like you and me, or like our children. We could identify with them. There was an emotional load."

It was a frantic night. There were too many ambulances — 30 or so — for the A&E reception area. No one had imagined so many turning up at once. They created a traffic jam and Juvin had to go into the street to cast an eye over the casualties in the ambulances. Signs of an internal haemorrhage? He waved the ambulance on. A bullet in the arm? He told the patient to do the last 50m on a stretcher.

Juvin and his improvised team — the hospital's doctors and nurses and those who had turned up to help — checked pulse, blood pressure, wounds. Who needed an immediate operation? Who could wait until the next day?

They flew down corridors, bandaged injuries, made rapid life-or-death decisions. Yet Juvin's abiding memory of that night is of silence. "They had debilitating wounds that were probably very painful, and nobody spoke.

"Usually people tell you when it's hurting. There, everyone was in a state of stupefaction. I went into a cubicle and there was a man with a badly damaged leg. I think he was in pain, but he was saying nothing. I said to the doctor treating him to give him morphine anyway.

"He was somewhere else and could not express his pain.

When you have experienced something like that, you enter a dimension that no one can describe."

By 6.30am A&E was empty, the patients all having been dispatched to operating theatres or to other departments. None had died in care during the night.

Juvin went home to sleep. He couldn't. He came back to the hospital. There was a queue of people waiting to give blood and families turning up to ask whether their relatives had been hospitalised at Georges Pompidou. Among them was Georges Salines, a doctor who heads the Environmental and Health Office at the Paris council. He had gone to bed the previous evening unaware that Lola, his 28-year-old daughter, was at the Bataclan. He had not watched the television and had no idea that anything untoward was going on.

At midnight Lola's brother called. He knew about her plans and knew what had happened at the concert hall. He had tried to call her. There had been no answer.

Salines, 59, a slender, fit-looking man with a welcoming smile and a precise discourse, telephoned the emergency helpline set up by the authorities after the attacks. He could not get through. He phoned again, and again, and again. The operator who responded at last — hours later — had no information about Lola and advised him to get in touch with the Paris hospitals. Hospital receptionists said they would phone back. None did.

Somebody told Salines that Georges Pompidou Hospital had patients whose identities had not been established. But when the family arrived, managers said that was untrue. The patients had been identified. Lola was not among them.

"It was only at the end of the afternoon that we discovered her death in very painful circumstances," said Salines. A friend had telephoned the emergency helpline, which was functioning correctly by now, and the operator disclosed that Lola's name was on the list of the dead.

Word got around. It appeared on the internet. There was a denial and confusion. Salines called the emergency number himself. The operator confirmed Lola's death.

"My daughter died for nothing, for an illusion, for a folly. It's absurd," Salines said in *L'Indicible de A à Z* (*The Unspeakable from A to Z*), a book about his reaction to the attacks.

In it, he describes Lola, who worked in the children's books department of a publisher, in these terms: "You liked books, films, drawing, travelling, rock music, children, Billy the Cat, lemon tart, Belgian beer, brunch at the Bouillon Belge bar, singing while playing the ukulele, roller derbies, your friends, your mum, your brothers, your boyfriend, your girlfriends, a kiss on the cheek, making love. You loved life. And all those who knew you liked you."

The months have passed and the scars remain — physical or psychological — for those involved.

Sophie needed two operations, three general anaesthetics — the third to change her bandages — and 43 stitches. She has a bullet in her pelvis and fears that grip her day and night.

"When I go to sleep, I still see what happened almost every night. Either I see them or I hear them. There is the fear. For a long time it was very complicated to leave home. I still don't take the métro or commuter trains. I only take the bus.

"Before, it was simple to make plans. Now I advance day by day. When I go to bed I wonder what will happen tomorrow and what will I see on the news."

Christophe Molmy has been affected, too: "You don't emerge unscathed from an intervention like the Bataclan. It's impossible."

He organised sessions with psychologists for his brigade and gave them and their families the opportunity to make appointments on a one-to-one basis. Some did; the majority did not. "We are still in a macho culture where we say, 'Nah, I don't need that,' but in fact we need it," he says. "I saw the psychologist."

We meet in his office at the end of a warren of corridors in the 19th-century building that is the Parisian equivalent of Scotland Yard. He had never confronted terrorism before 2015.

Now he lives permanently with the threat — a phone at his side at all times, in the shower, everywhere — and admits it has changed his job. "We always used to intervene against gangsters whom we tried not to kill. Today if we go in against terrorists, we go to kill the terrorists. We won't manage to get them to put their hands up.

"We are becoming a little like paramilitaries. We are training and equipping ourselves like soldiers to fight a war."

He talks about the old days of fighting criminals with a certain fondness. "We arrested them; they behaved well; we understood each other. We could have a bite to eat together. But what am I supposed to do with people who come to die? The human relationship is not the same. I don't even know if there is a human relationship."

Surprisingly, perhaps, Georges Salines seems almost the most sanguine of all, despite the loss of his daughter. When we meet in his office, he looks bright-eyed, and says in his book, "I am sad from time to time, I sometimes cry, but I sleep, I work, I talk and I sometimes laugh. You can't avoid the suffering but resilience is possible, particularly in a family whose members love each other."

Salines is head of 13 Novembre: Fraternité et Vérité, an association set up by victims two months after the attacks, and he has used the post to denounce the shambolic organisation faced by relatives of victims in the aftermath of the attack — some being shown the wrong body in the morgue. But he is not vindictive, and insists on the need to heal the split in French society, to avoid marginalising Muslims and pushing them into the arms of the terrorists.

He says in his book that he has no hatred for the jihadists. "I have never experienced this feeling," he says. "I cannot hate the sinister cretins who took my daughter's life and lost theirs in this business. They are victims, too."

Antoine Leiris, a French radio journalist, has written a book, too, after losing a loved one — Hélène Muyal-Leiris, his 35-year-old wife — at the Bataclan. As with Salines, the book is more about love than hate: *Vous N'Aurez Pas Ma Haine* (*You Will Not Have My Hatred*) is the title.

Leiris recounts his love for his wife, and for Melvil, their 17-month-old son — and his fear, uncertainty and pain at the realisation that he will have to bring up Melvil on his own. Of the killers, he has little to say. "I don't know who you are and I don't want to know. You want me to be frightened; you want me to look at my fellow citizens with suspicion; you want me to sacrifice my liberty for security. I won't."

Claude-Emmanuel Triomphe, who had two operations and a month in hospital after being injured in Café Bonne Bière, says much the same thing. "I feel indifference for them. I feel no hatred. I tried to have hatred; I thought it's not normal after all they did to me. If I must express a feeling it is rather pity — pity in the sense that these guys have massacred their own lives: 'Not only have you massacred the life of other people but you have messed up yours as well.'"

He says he has no nightmares, no worries about going out. After months of lethargy he has rediscovered some of his old intellectual energy, too. Nothing is quite the same now, however.

Having given up his post as head of a think tank, he wants to specialise in the estates that are home to a generation of second-generation immigrants, among whom a handful have turned to radical Islamist violence.

"I need to understand why my country is affected by terrorism, why my country has manufactured more jihadists than any other in Europe. It's not to say that other countries are not affected, but France is particularly so."

The incomprehension is widespread in France, and it is Sophie, perhaps, who sums it up best. "You ask yourself questions: what was in their heads when they did that? The youngest terrorist at the Bataclan was 23. Me at 23, I was in Lyons, in university and thinking how I was going to dress the next day and not going to a concert hall to kill people. These are questions that remain and to which we will not have an answer."

YOU CAN'T TRUST THE PEOPLE WITH DEMOCRACY

Roger Boyes

October 5 2016

It must have seemed like a shoo-in for the Colombian president Juan Manuel Santos. After four years of negotiation with Farc guerrillas, a peace deal was unveiled to the accompaniment of a choir singing Beethoven's *Ode to Joy*. After half a century of debilitating war, how could anyone vote against peace in the subsequent referendum? In the end, though, he set himself up. It was a bit like the US civil war general whose last words, glancing at the enemy lines, were: "They couldn't hit an elephant from that dista ..."

It wasn't just the Colombian referendum that went awry. There is a quiet revolt under way across the globe. In vote after vote, people have been rejecting the guidance of political establishments, baffling elites and adding to the sum of anger in the world. In the age of rage, direct democracy is a risk. Referendums are infallible only for dictators — think of Napoleon, master of the strategic plebiscite — when instructions are handed down to voters, when ballot boxes are stuffed and there's a secret police snitch living next door.

The fact is that in free societies a government should not abdicate its responsibility to govern by using a single-issue vote to demand guidance from ordinary punters. Clearly if you want to avert a populist avalanche you should keep capital punishment or mosque-building off the ballot paper. And by now leaders should have learnt too that referendums are not a suitable vehicle for deciding on war, peace or immigration. Viktor Orban, the Hungarian prime minister, has just asked his citizens the impossibly loaded question: "Do you agree that the European Union should have the power to impose the compulsory settlement of non-Hungarian citizens in Hungary without the consent of the National Assembly of Hungary?"

Of those who voted, 98 per cent rejected the idea, as was intended. But most voters stayed at home, perhaps sensing that the vote wasn't about migrant quotas at all (since they are more or less off the table anyway) but rather propelling Orban to a new level in his gladiatorial contest with Brussels. Many Hungarians are quite comfortable inside the EU.

The problem with referendums is that they become a receptacle for grievances and bear little relationship to the question posed. Take Mark Rutte, the Dutch prime minister, who earlier this year was saddled with a referendum on the ratification of an economic deal between the EU and Ukraine. The treaty had been agreed by the government, ratified by all other EU states and was 2,135 pages long. The Dutch rejected it, not because they had done their homework but because they were railing against weak government, against EU dogma and against the possibile eastward expansion of the union. Rutte was ambushed and called the No vote "disastrous". Vladimir Putin rubbed his hands with glee and called it a truly democratic act.

The fact is that voting in a referendum can, without knowledge and preparation, become an almost random transaction between leaders and led. The political philosopher Jason Brennan calculates that the probability of your individual vote changing policy is about as low as winning the lottery. You could of course win hundreds of millions but it is still irrational to buy a ticket. And so it is with direct democracy. Voters, he says, "have no incentive to be well informed. They might as well indulge in their worst prejudices — democracy is the rule of the people but entices people to be their worst."

Most democratic governments that deploy referendums do so out of weakness. In doing so they fool themselves that the wisdom of the people must inevitably support their world view. That's how Juan Manuel Santos and David Cameron ended up in the same leaky canoe without a paddle. The Brexit referendum was a way of pacifying the Conservative Party. Cameron failed to grasp the potency of a national vote that fused mild dissatisfaction with the EU and the seeming inability of the government to get a grip on immigration or shield British jobs from a global slowdown.

By the end of this year there will have been eight major referendums — the next crucial one is Matteo Renzi's attempt to secure backing for his constitutional reforms in Italy. It's too late for the Italian premier to call it off now. If he loses in December, he could also lose office. If the Five Star movement and the Northern League take power in the resulting election they are promising a referendum on Italy's membership of the euro. Few analysts would now rule out an Italian No vote. But whatever the verdict, the uncertainty of a referendum campaign would bring chaos to Italy, where the banks are already wobbly, and speed the unravelling of the eurozone.

The watchword has to be: listen to the people at your peril. Referendums can act as the safety valves of democracy but never as their engine. If legislators run away from their responsibility to consider and scrutinise complex questions, then power will seep away from the centre. The biggest risk posed by Donald Trump is surely that he could undermine or circumvent instititutions that keep America on an even keel. James Madison, the fourth American president, identified the problem: democracies endanger the right of minorities and must therefore devise solid institutions to protect those rights, civil liberties and free trade. Referendums, over-used and cynically steered, can end up subverting rather than enhancing democracy.

It is too late for the Colombian president and for David Cameron, but let's declare a five-year moratorium on referendums. And yes, that means you too, Scotland.

BURNT AND TORTURED MIGRANTS FILLED DECKS AS WE RUSHED TO HELP

Bel Trew

OCTOBER 8 2016

Saturday, October 1

"*Dignity* is a dancer," jokes Captain Louis Ferres when the floor lurches sideways as we drop off a 2.5m wave. The battered ship that can hold up to 450 people is one of three that Médecins Sans Frontières uses to patrol the Mediterranean, searching for migrants in distress. Everyone on board, including Carla the cook, works on the rescues. *Dignity* pirouettes her way to the search and rescue zone 20 nautical miles off the Libyan coast where most migrant boats run into trouble. Huge waves wash over the deck. Half the non-sailors aboard are in their bunks throwing up.

We are told we may not see a rescue as even the most ruthless smugglers don't force migrants into the sea in bad weather. But we still spend the afternoon putting together 450 emergency care packages — socks, nutritional biscuits, water and a towel. There is a strict cleaning schedule to prevent disease spreading through the ship. On Saturday night it's my turn to scrub the inner decks, which I manage without vomiting.

Sunday, October 2

We are woken by news that there will be a rescue at 9am. More than 100 migrants in a rubber dinghy called the Maritime Rescue Co-ordination Centre in Rome by satellite phone at dawn but it takes *Dignity* four hours to reach the position. By the time we arrive the dinghy is nowhere to be seen. Courtney, the ship's nurse, begins to worry. They would have been at sea now for at least ten hours.

Likely weakened by months of starvation and ill-treatment in Libya, many don't last a couple of hours exposed to the blistering heat of the sun. A co-ordinated effort with helicopters and nearby warships finds the dinghy. I jump aboard the rescue speedboat, which cuts through choppy waves to the dinghy. The terrified faces of women and children peer up from the bottom of the waterlogged tub, where they are crouched in lines as if on a slave ship.

This is the dangerous part. Desperate and delirious, people may try to jump aboard and risk turning the boat over. "Try to stay calm, we will rescue all of you," urges MSF's Nicholas over a megaphone while we hand out life jackets. The sickest — including an emaciated Ethiopian boy of 16 — are hauled aboard in the first round. When everyone is on deck and registered, people open up about the hell they escaped in Libya: floggings, rape and kidnappings for ransom. They are transferred to a Save the Children vessel returning to Italy.

Monday, October 3

The shriek of the rescue alarm wakes us. It's 6.30am and a drifting boat has bumped the *Dignity*. The rescue goes well but the MSF team is told of a second, third and fourth boat in the area. The smugglers spotted a break in the storms and packed thousands into life rafts then scuttled home to make more quick profits before the winter ends the crossing season.

The stink of fuel knocks the breath out of me as the survivors of the second rescue stagger on board, their skin coming off in strips. The medics rush to treat a few who have stopped breathing. One pregnant woman grabs my arm and, pointing at a raw strip of flesh, screams. Another woman writhes on her back on the floor, screaming too. A third points to her shredded calf. Then it hits me: these are chemical burns from boat fuel.

"Get their clothes off and shower them now," a voice shouts. We strip most of the 90 men, women and children and hose them down. I carry semi-conscious women to the showers. "We need to support a woman in the hospital to sit upright so she can breathe," says Irene, grabbing me. I end up, covered in blood and faeces, cradling Lovett to keep her breathing.

I hold the hand of her pregnant sister, Joy, who dies on the bed beside us. Her body is packed in ice and placed in the bow. Lovett and the little boy are airlifted to hospital by the Italian coastguard, who won't take Joy's body.

Tuesday, October 4

The soft sobs of the Nigerian woman who lost her two boys, aged four and five, the day before are heard on deck. With nearly 420 migrants on board, including toddlers and a corpse, *Dignity* sails back to Italy. We are posted in shifts as guards to defuse any arguments, spot medical problems and regulate the endless queue for the toilet.

In French, Arabic and English, the men on deck, fleeing Ivory Coast, Mali, Nigeria and Sierra Leone, tell their stories. In the evening I check on the Nigerian girls from Monday's horrific sinking. They giggle at photos of my stupid cat and tell me about their favourite sugar-cane recipes.

Peace, who is spattered with torture scars, asks: "Do white people in Europe like black people? I'm afraid. We're always treated like animals." At night, while on watch on the men's deck upstairs, I listen to Michael, 17, from Nigeria, talking of "making [his] mother proud" in Italy. "Do you think they will let me study? I want to be a doctor."

Wednesday, October 5

Overnight the Italian coastguard again refused to take Joy. Her corpse is beginning to smell. In the morning we dock and the ship goes quiet. Everyone is split into groups depending on their injuries and their ages. They go ashore for medical check-ups and registration.

The UN says that more than 80 per cent of Nigerian girls landed in Italy are trafficked into prostitution. I warn the girls to keep together and stay in the reception centres. Hope is mortified that she has only a blanket to wear. I wash and dry my pyjamas to give to her.

Hours later, as I leave the boat, I hear my name called. The girls are still being processed. Hope, wearing my pyjamas, is grinning. We hug and they board buses, promising to stick together.

Thursday, October 6

More than 10,000 people were pulled from the water in 48 hours this week. We have no idea where people have gone or if Lovett and the others made it. I add as friends the few who have Facebook. Kougan, 23, from Cameroon, who kept me company on night watch, pops up on Messenger: "I very grateful to become your friend Bella, take care for ur self."

'TANTRUMS AND SHOCKING RACISM' OF INQUIRY'S DYSFUNCTIONAL DAME

Andrew Norfolk, Sean O'Neill

OCTOBER 14 2016

ON A SUMMER afternoon this year Dame Lowell Goddard stood at the doorway of her Westminster office and shouted in anger. Unless she got her own way, she is said to have declared, "I'm going to pack my bags, go back to New Zealand and take this inquiry down with me."

A visitor to the headquarters of the national child sex abuse inquiry might have been shocked, not least because the threat was made by the judge paid £500,000 a year to lead an investigation forecast to run for a decade at a cost of £100 million.

Dame Lowell's staff, however, barely flinched. They were used to her tantrums, and worse. Multiple senior sources have told *The Times* that the judge peppered her 16 months at the helm of Britain's biggest public inquiry with racist remarks and expletive-ridden outbursts. Insiders say that Dame Lowell, 67, also appeared to have memory lapses and failed to grasp legal concepts.

She allegedly said that Britain had so many paedophiles

"because it has so many Asian men" — a comment that left colleagues stunned. "I was so shocked to see the number of ethnic people," she is said to have told a colleague, while she allegedly commented that she had to travel 50 miles from London to see a white face. Her home in the capital was a smart, taxpayer-funded flat in Knightsbridge.

Several sources described Dame Lowell's reluctance to question the propriety of the royal family. Discussing the Prince of Wales's friendship with a bishop jailed last year for sex offences against young men, the judge is said to have insisted: "Prince Charles couldn't possibly have had anything to do with that, not with his breeding." The source added: "For someone who claimed not to understand what the establishment was, she had a reverence for it that was quite astonishing."

On the 23rd floor of Millbank Tower, where the Independent Inquiry into Child Sexual Abuse (IICSA) has its offices, staff soon realised that they had a problem. They were supposed to be putting in place the foundations of an investigation into suspected abuse at dozens of institutions, including schools, care homes, the church, the armed forces and parliament.

Since being launched by Theresa May in 2014, IICSA has hired more than 150 staff, opened three regional offices, started the Truth Project to allow abuse victims to give testimony anonymously, commissioned an academic study and begun a legal disclosure exercise demanding that institutions under investigation hand over millions of pages of documents.

Yet it was so dysfunctional under Dame Lowell's leadership that work often ground to a halt because senior staff felt "totally paralysed", one said.

Former colleagues, who have asked not to be named, were puzzled then increasingly troubled. One said that staff who were committed to the inquiry's success felt trapped in "an impossible situation". They felt they were led by someone who at times behaved "like a very angry child".

"The pressure was immense. She was rude and abusive to junior staff, she didn't understand the issues and, worse than that, she used appalling terms all the time. It was almost intolerable," the insider claimed.

Senior staff held furtive meetings to discuss their options. It was agreed that the best hope lay in sharing their concerns with the Home Office. Mrs May, then home secretary, hired Dame Lowell. Only she could fire her.

Whitehall's instinct in the face of calamity is often to hide it, however. Until now, the true picture remained secret. Observers have pointed to the irony of a body established to dissect a culture of institutional secrecy, denial and cover-up becoming an exemplar of the problems it was designed to expose. The inquiry's senior team were all complicit, said one insider. "Goddard should never have been appointed and she should have been removed so much earlier than she was. She was catastrophic."

Dame Lowell arrived in the UK from New Zealand after two false starts in the search for someone to lead the inquiry. Its first two chairwomen were forced to step down in quick succession over their alleged closeness to the British establishment, and the home secretary could not afford a third mistake. When the appointment was announced in February last year, it was claimed that Dame Lowell had been selected after 150 nominees were put through an exhaustive vetting process. The lead counsel, Ben Emmerson, QC, hailed a due diligence exercise of "unprecedented depth and detail".

Insiders tell a different story, of the Home Office's "blind panic" after the resignation in October 2014 of the inquiry's second chairwoman, Dame Fiona Woolf. She survived a month; her predecessor, Baroness Butler-Sloss, had lasted six days. "They were desperate. It couldn't be a judge from England and Wales so they decided to look at the Commonwealth, but they also wanted a woman. There wasn't much choice. Then Goddard's name popped up. It was all signed and sealed very quickly," a source said.

Doubts over Dame Lowell soon emerged. She spent six weeks negotiating a pay deal that eventually included a £360,000 salary plus a £110,00 annual housing allowance, a chauffeur-driven car and four return flights a year to New Zealand with her husband, Christopher Hodson, QC. One senior source viewed such perks as "completely inappropriate for a public servant". Dame Lowell, however, is said to have been outraged that the deal only entitled her to business-class not first-class seats.

"We all had to tiptoe around her. It set the tone for an organisation that became secretive," said a source who accused the judge of behaving like an "autocratic and dictatorial" monarch.

Sources described her regular use of racist language as like "going back to the 1950s". One described a sense of shame that no complaints were made. "You've got someone making racist comments who clearly has a racist attitude, and nobody says anything because we're all bloody pussy-footing around."

Dame Lowell was heavily reliant on Mr Emmerson, 53, a leading human rights QC who is not renowned for his emollience or team-working skills. In early 2015, before he began working with her, he described Dame Lowell as a woman of "courage, independence and vision". Within weeks of her arrival he is understood to have thought differently. In tandem, said one observer, their impact was "utterly toxic", adding: "So many people were devoted to trying to make the damn thing work, to getting to the bottom of some really egregious societal problems. They all deserved so much better."

In public, every senior figure stayed silent, including Professor Alexis Jay, then a panel member, who won praise for her leadership of the Rotherham child abuse inquiry. She became IICSA's fourth chairwoman after Dame Lowell abruptly stood down.

Mr Emmerson resigned last month, 24 hours after being suspended for undisclosed reasons. His departure came two weeks after the unexplained resignation of his junior counsel, Elizabeth Prochaska, 35.

Professor Jay, 67, and others may yet be asked to explain why they did not challenge Dame Lowell. Insiders insist they took the only course of action open to them and prayed for an intervention from Mrs May.

Sources described many months of behind-closed-doors discussions during which panicked staff were assured their concerns were being shared with the Home Office, yet officials "sat there and did nothing". *The Times* has been told that those "kept in the loop" included Mark Sedwill, the Home Office permanent secretary, and Liz Sanderson, Mrs May's special adviser.

Eventually the concerns entered the public domain. At a hearing in late July, the judge's stumbling performance did not go unnoticed. When she admitted her unfamiliarity with "local law", the inquiry was exposed to ridicule. Finally, insiders made their move. On August 4 *The Times* revealed she had been overseas for three months of her first year in office. Within hours, she resigned.

The events of that final day have remained secret until now. That morning she was approached by senior colleagues and informed that her position was no longer tenable. Her response was a two-sentence resignation letter that she sent to the Home Office before leaving for lunch. Amber Rudd, the newly installed successor as home secretary, swiftly accepted it. After lunch, the judge tried to withdraw her resignation. Her reversal was not accepted, and the inquiry lost its third head. That loss should have come many months earlier, her colleagues believe.

Dame Lowell's lawyers denied all the allegations last night.

MIDDLE-AGED VIRGINS: JAPAN'S BIG SECRET

Richard Lloyd Parry

October 26 2016

EVERYONE HAS AT least one bad date story, but few have the twist in the tale told by Takeshi Yokote. It was 1995 and the 21-year-old Yokote was a student at a prestigious Japanese university. His companion was a young woman from his drama club on whom Yokote was painfully keen. He was nervous in the cinema and tongue-tied over dinner. His date's boredom and discomfort were obvious, and it was no surprise that he did not see her again. Yokote shrugged it off, returned to his studies (ancient Greek philosophy was his field) and set about looking for another girlfriend.

Then the unexpected happened: nothing at all. There was no doubt that Yokote liked girls and he met plenty of them as a student and, latterly, as a teacher. He had no difficulty forming friendships with women and he was, and remains, a man of above average looks: neat, slim, articulate and gentlemanly. However, that awkward evening 20 years ago was not only the worst date of his life, it was the only one. At the age of 42 he has never touched or kissed, let alone been to bed with, a woman. And in Japan he is one among millions.

A recently published survey by a government institute provides the latest evidence of what has become increasingly clear over several years — the loveless lives led by more and more young Japanese. As it does every five years, the National Institute of Population and Social Security Research polled 5,300 single people aged 18 to 34 about their sex lives, past and present, and their romantic aspirations. One of its findings was at first glance encouraging: 86 per cent of men and 89 per cent of women hoped to marry. However, 70 per cent of men and 60 per cent of women in the sample were not in a relationship.

Most striking was the answer to the question about sexual experience. The results showed that 42 per cent of single young men and 44 per cent of single young women were virgins, several percentage points higher than when the question was last posed. The survey has been criticised because it inquired only about heterosexual experience — sexually active gay men and women who took the pollster's question at face value will have gone down in the data as chaste. Even allowing for this bias, it reveals a population of millions of adults who have no romantic attachments, no sexual experience and whose numbers have been growing for a decade.

"It's very common," says Yokote. "In any crowd of people I can see them — the ones who don't give any thought to what they wear, who look withdrawn, who look down rather than looking you in the eye. There are lots of people like me."

This is not a collective moral choice, by which young people are consciously "saving themselves" for a future husband or wife. It is more as if an entire generation is losing the knack of intimacy. "As a student I didn't know what to do to take it to the next stage," says Yokote. "I didn't have anyone who could teach or advise me. I still don't know now." And apart from the personal loneliness and isolation experienced by Japan's virgins, they are part of a demographic and economic catastrophe.

Japan is farthest along a path, on which many developed countries also find themselves, towards inundation by the "silver tsunami". About 1.3 million Japanese died last year, but only a million were born. The total fertility rate, the number of children the average woman will bear in a lifetime, is 1.43, far below the "replacement rate" of 2.1. Old people are living longer and longer but the bill for their pensions and medical bills falls to a shrinking number of taxpayers. If the decline in population continues the Japanese will become extinct in the next century. Long before that happens the country will be bankrupt.

High among the reasons for this crisis is the difficulty of being a Japanese parent. Working mothers are still treated as an aberration; inadequate nursery care and lack of flexibility in the workplace often enforces a choice between career and family; many people, especially women, choose the former.

However, there is something more mysterious going on: a growing distaste among the young for relationships.

"The research is consistent," says Masahiro Yamada, a professor of sociology at Chuo University in Tokyo. "Japanese young people are losing interest in, and a desire for, relationships and sex."

Yokote's story goes some way towards illuminating the reasons. He was on the shy side as a boy, but had plenty of friends, girls among them. In his later years at school, the more confident students formed couples, although Yokote's mild crushes never led anywhere. One thing he remembers distinctly is the poor quality of Japanese sex education, which Yamada cites as one of the causes of the problem. "It invariably emphasises the negative aspects of sex," he says. "The risks of pregnancy and disease. Sex education in Japan means scaring people off sex."

After his undergraduate degree, Yokote moved to Tokyo to start a PhD; he packed it in after a few years partly because of the isolation imposed by the scholarly life. As his academic career petered out, he embarked on the life of what the Japanese call a *freeter*, a casual worker in low-paid, low-status jobs. He earned two million yen a year (then about £12,000), just enough to live on, but with nothing left over.

"I got jobs working at the university: washing dishes, putting out rubbish, fetching and carrying," he says. "There were girls around me and I badly wanted a relationship, but I felt that I just couldn't ask them out because of my financial situation. It didn't seem an odd life — there were lots of people around me doing the same kind of thing."

Fifteen years earlier, at the peak of Japan's inflated "bubble economy", a bright graduate such as Yokote would have been eagerly snapped up by a big Japanese company; now they were cutting recruitment to save the jobs of existing employees.

There are other factors that have given rise to the virgin generation, according to Yamada, among them the ease and availability of internet pornography. The decline of traditional matchmakers, who used to arrange unions between young single people, has also played its part, as has the habit among young Japanese of socialising in groups, making it harder for men and women to break off as couples.

A great deal of the problem, he believes, simply comes down to money — for restaurants, entertainment, presents and the other accoutrements of romance, but also to establish a life of self-respect and independence. Eighty per cent of single Japanese live with their parents; Yamada's research shows that while salaries among male workers have declined, women's expectations of income in a potential mate remain unrealistically high.

"The physical aspect of sex is not the problem," says Shingo Sakatsume, who more than anyone else is tackling Japan's virginity crisis head on. "Most people, once they get to that point, can work out that for themselves. It's the social part that is most difficult." Sakatsume is a social worker and the founder of Virgin Academia, a correspondence course for unwilling celibates. It originated in his specialised work providing counselling on sexual matters to people with disabilities. He quickly recognised that a large number of the able-bodied also needed help.

The year-long course is based on his textbook *Virgin Breaker*, which attempts to guide its students towards "graduation" from their virginity. Students follow the book, write essays based on its contents and correspond with Sakatsume by email (most are too shy to meet in person). Month by month Sakatsume attempts to build their confidence, encourages them to create opportunities to meet potential mates and guides them through the niceties of online dating. In three years, 40 people aged 20 to 42, all of them men, have taken the £400 course. Only six have successfully graduated. "It's hard to get past the first step," Sakatsume admits. "Some of these men get to the end of the year and they still haven't signed up to a dating site."

His organisation, White Hands, also organises life classes in which naked models, male and female, pose for an audience of virgins with paints and pencils. The point is to show real human bodies to people whose only experience of them may have been the stylised and aggressive universe of online porn. Yokote went to one and was mesmerised. "Each body was different," he said. "Each one had such beauty. I had never seen a naked woman before. It gave me the impression of such freshness and such life."

Inspired by the experience, Yokote has made a conscious effort to seek out more opportunities to meet women, and to open up — with a certain, hesitant success. A friend introduced him to a woman he likes very much; they meet as often as once a week. "I don't yet have the confidence to say that we are dating," he says, "but I am very fond of her and I want to see more of her. The first time we met, I told her that I was a virgin. I felt I could be so honest with her and it seemed very natural to talk about it." How did she respond? "She said, 'You could practise with me.' "

ROYAL FAMILY ARE MORE SECRETIVE THAN MI5

Ben Macintyre

October 29 2016

A vast splurge of royal history is coming our way with the release next week of *The Crown*, the dramatised story of the Queen from her wedding to the present day. Spanning six seasons, in 60 episodes, it is the single biggest and most expensive bio-epic ever made.

Yet it is an incomplete story because the royal archives remain closed to the public, accessible only to approved scholars, rigorously controlled by unaccountable royal archivists: a glaring, profoundly undemocratic anomaly in an age of supposed openness.

MI5 now regularly reviews and releases its files to the national archives; the royal family feels no such obligation.

The most prominent family in the world remains more secretive about its past than the Security Service.

Held in the Round Tower at Windsor Castle, the royal archives consist of more than two million documents covering 250 years of royal history. "The Royal Household is committed to transparency," declares the royal website, "and to making information available, where appropriate." The royal household alone defines what is "appropriate".

For decades, academics have chafed against the way the archive is run, which allows only selected scholars access to certain parts of the collection, and suppresses royal history that might reflect badly on the institution of monarchy. There is no publicly accessible catalogue, so researchers can only request files already identified in the footnotes of works by "authorised" writers. Fishing without a permit in royal historical waters is strictly forbidden.

This restricted access is justified by royalists on the grounds that this is a private archive and that the royals have a right to defend their privacy like any other family. The royal household is not defined as a public body, and therefore is not obliged to release its files under the 2000 Freedom of Information Act.

Therein lies the central ambiguity of the Queen's position, being at once a constitutional figure and a private person. The monarchy infused and deeply influenced British public life throughout the 20th century, most emphatically in its first half. Successive monarchs and other members of the royal family have played crucial political roles in our past.

The history of the royals is also the history of Britain, and it belongs to the British people; what the royals regard as their history is truly ours and of overwhelming public interest. The royal household has never seen the archive that way, and the story of the sometimes stumbling royal progress through the 20th century has been heavily edited by the royals themselves.

"I am much against destroying important letters," wrote Queen Victoria, yet ordered her youngest daughter Beatrice to rewrite her journal, deleting "painful passages" and burning each original volume as she went. Virtually all the private papers of Edward VII were burnt on the orders of Queen Alexandra. Princess Margaret destroyed hundreds of letters collected by the Queen Mother.

However, there is still much inside those archives that should be fully opened to the light of scholarship. They undoubtedly contain revealing information on Prince John, George V's mentally disabled and epileptic youngest son, who was removed to a farm on the Sandringham estate and died young. Similarly, papers relating to Edward and Mrs Simpson and the abdication crisis remain inaccessible to the public.

The most controversial part of the archive, though, relates to the interwar years, when members of the royal family, in common with others of the British ruling class, were great admirers of Hitler. Some of the more embarrassing material is believed to have been filleted out and destroyed in 1945, but undoubtedly a great deal survives that would elucidate, once and for all, the complex relationship between the royals and the Third Reich, a key to understanding British foreign policy in the run-up to war.

The royal family needs to take a leaf out of MI5's book and open up its past to public scrutiny. In the wake of the Spycatcher scandal, the Security Service came to the realisation that excessive secrecy was damaging its credibility. In the absence of documentary evidence, historians were forced to rely on snippets of gossip and rumour, occasional explosions of scandal and the semi-reliable accounts of disgruntled former employees. (These are precisely the same sort of sources that tend to inform royal stories.)

Starting in the 1990s, MI5 began to release its files to the National Archives on a systematic and logical basis: releasing nothing that could affect national security, compromise the secrecy of other organisations or embarrass living individuals, but everything else, warts and all. MI5's extraordinary role in the Second World War is now largely declassified, but last year the Security Service also released files on the spies Guy Burgess and Donald Maclean, whose escape to Moscow in 1951 was one of the most spectacular cock-ups in spy history.

The royal archives should be placed in the public domain in the same transparent way: material genuinely distressing to living persons could be excluded, but everything of political relevance should be released under the 30-year rule. This would hugely benefit the royal family too, by enabling its 20th-century history to be written on the basis of hard evidence rather than speculation and rumour.

That seems unlikely to happen soon, for the royal archivists seem more concerned about brand management, secret-keeping and damage limitation than history. Last year's discovery of home-cinema footage showing a very young Elizabeth performing the Nazi salute (which any historian worth their salt would publish) prompted outrage among royalists and a promise to investigate how the material had been obtained from the royal archive.

The results of that investigation, if one ever took place, have never been revealed: a secret inquiry, into a secret archive, by a most secretive organ of state.

INSIDE BRITAIN'S ONLY TRANSGENDER CLINIC FOR CHILDREN

Louise France

November 5 2016

Nine-year-old Ash skips across the main road, a blond ponytail swishing from side to side. She — Ash was born a boy but has wanted to be known as a girl since she was four — has just emerged from an appointment at the Tavistock and Portman Hospital's Gender Identity Development Service (GIDS) in north London and what she really fancies is chicken and fries from the local KFC.

She's jittery. A cocktail of relief and adrenaline. Ash is bright and she's researched the facts (Google is useful like that). She knows about hormone blockers: monthly injections that will, if she is prescribed them, put her puberty on hold. She enjoys talking to the child psychotherapists and family therapists. They understand where she's coming from. But sometimes they want to know how she feels, and that is tough to articulate when you're not ten yet. You're being asked to talk about big, embarrassing stuff like puberty when you don't want to look at your body in the bath; when you've convinced yourself you are developing breasts although this is biologically impossible.

At least for now.

She tells the consultant that when she's older she'll have a womb transplant and have a baby. (She's read about it online. "They do it in Sweden," Ash says.) The consultant explains that it isn't always straightforward, but that's not what she wants to hear. When the questions feel too difficult, Ash, who wants to be a trans model when she grows up, gets teary and asks to leave the room.

It's at home in southern England where she lets rip and it's her mother, Terri, on whom she takes out the fear and confusion. Shouting, slamming doors. In the past she's been taunted at school, beaten up, called a "she-male". When she was seven she sent her mother suicidal texts. Sometimes family life revolves around how Ash feels from moment to moment.

GIDS at the Tavistock and Portman NHS Trust (or Tavi, as it's known by locals in the leafy, affluent streets near by) is Britain's only multidisciplinary clinic specialising in children and adolescents who are concerned that they were born the wrong sex. Eighteen years ago, when GIDS began, a team of five received about 30 referrals from children a year. By 2009 referrals totalled 96. In 2014 it was 697. This year about 1,419 children came for help, referred by GPs faced with a condition that they'll most likely have very little experience of.

While, to put the figures into perspective, these numbers account for only 1 in 10,000 young people, the service is under huge pressure. Sixty new members of staff are about to start. Builders have been employed over the summer to carve up the office space in the Tavistock building, an incongruous, anonymous block with a statue of Sigmund Freud in the car park.

The average age of the young people who arrive in reception, with its gender-neutral toilet, is 14, but they are increasingly receiving inquiries from parents of children at primary school. Occasionally there are referrals for children as young as three. One concern is that if these children socially transition — dress as the opposite sex, change their names — at this age, what happens if they change their minds?

I meet Ash and Terri again at home two weeks later. Ash is just back from school, quiet and hungry. She desultorily kicks a football about in her uniform (T-shirt, short grey skirt) and disappears to her bedroom (cluttered, shocking pink). Make no mistake, she looks like a girl. I catch myself staring at her, searching for clues to her biology. Ash is one of the main characters in the first episode of an ambitious and revealing new Channel 4 documentary series — three years in the making — about the Tavistock. It's directed by Peter Beard, who won awards for his last documentary, *My Son, the Jihadi.* The first episode focuses on GIDS. It's the first time they have allowed cameras inside.

We sit in the back garden and her mother explains why she's decided to let Ash appear on television. "I wanted people to see that my kid is not a freak," she says. Terri has wholly taken on board Ash's feminine identity: she lets her wear nail varnish and crimp her hair, although she draws the line at lipstick on school days. "She is not a boy in the wrong clothes; she is actually a girl in the wrong skin. I wanted people to see how hard this is — this is a massive thing for a little kid."

Ask Ash about being born a boy and she makes sense of it by splitting off her masculinity. She says the male part of herself was an older brother "that died or fell off a cliff".

"From the moment Ash could talk, she has been like this," Terri says. "She wanted to have dolls and wear princess dresses."

At first she was not concerned. She had other children and they'd wanted to dress up. "It wasn't an issue."

At nursery Ash wore dresses. "I've never seen her play with a boy," her mum tells me. She sat down to pee despite having brothers. When her father, a scaffolder — Ash's parents split up when she was two — gave her trains for Christmas she refused to play with them. (Recently he has begun to accept Ash's trans status, to the point of accompanying her to a meeting at the Tavistock. "I wouldn't have her any other way," he says in the documentary.)

Did Terri ever think, maybe my son is simply a girlie boy? Yes, she tells me. Her hunch was that Ash would grow up to be gay. "She just seemed to be an extremely camp gay man. And that was fine. We're an open family. We have a lot of gay friends. It wasn't an issue."

Then, when Ash was four, she said: "Why do you keep calling me a boy? Why do you keep saying he? I am a girl. I am a she." Terri remembers the moment vividly. Her distressed son was sitting on her lap in the living room, dressed in a Rapunzel dress with a wig. "She asked me, 'Who is going to take my willy off?' She wanted to know if I would take her to the doctors or would it fall off? That's when I thought, this is a bit more than dressing up."

Might Ash's behaviour just be a phase? It's common for children to experiment with gender roles. Terri explains that she has never once wavered. When school started, every morning was a battlefield. (Start talking about gender and you realise how traditional schools still are about the sexes: boys told to go on one side, girls on the other, unisex school uniforms uncommon.) "For the first year I tried to get her into the boy's uniform, but she hated it. She'd be punching me, biting me, scratching me." In the end, Terri asked the head teacher if Ash could wear a skirt and he agreed.

Any ambivalence has been around whether to tell strangers. Is it better to be taken for a girl and carry the burden of the secret, or to be open about what is happening, with all its complexities? But what Terri would like are answers. "I'd really like to know why," she tells the consultant at the Tavistock. "Where did this come from? She can't have made it up, because she was too small. We didn't know anyone who was trans. She'd never even heard of it. I know it's normal for little boys to play with dolls but to never be interested in one car? To never be interested in Spider-Man? I'd like a reason. But it looks like I'm never going to get one."

There is just one photograph left of Ash as a boy. It's on Terri's phone. All the others have been deleted or shredded. "We did it together," Terri tells me.

What would Freud make of Ash, born Ashton Andrew, name changed by deed poll this year to Ashley Julianne? In a very short space of time the idea that someone can be born into the wrong body has become mainstream. The word "trans" — short for transgender — has become part of our language. So much so in the LGBT world (lesbian, gay, bisexual and transgender), it can seem as though it's the T that's taking up all the oxygen. And now it's trans children who are making the headlines. The award-winning US drama series *Modern Family* has introduced an eight-year-old trans character. Last month CBBC aired an online drama about a boy who wants to be a girl. Tumblr and Reddit have become a virtual space where children share their treatment options.

Yet I'd suggest that Dr Polly Carmichael, the consultant clinical psychologist who leads the GIDS unit, has one of the most challenging jobs in the NHS. Until now she has turned down media requests, concerned that their work will be misrepresented. (The most common misconception, she says, is that the service's main job is to prescribe hormone drugs.)

Carmichael is a softly spoken, cheerful woman, who laughs easily. Watch her in the consulting room and she has a stillness about her that is calming. She also chooses her words carefully. This is an area where even the language used is hotly debated. (For instance, a trans teenager who was born a boy is referred to as a "natally assigned male". An outsider can start to tie themselves up in verbal knots.)

On the day we meet Carmichael has to choose the new colour scheme for the department's revamp. Much trickier is the task of negotiating the demands of a vocal trans community together with meeting the needs of children with complex emotional lives. Not to mention parents coming to terms, or not, with a child who says they are trans.

At the same time there is another group gaining ground: people who argue that we are at "peak trans", that we're living in a sexualised culture within which there is enormous pressure on children to fit gender stereotypes and where being trans has become a glamorous "lifestyle choice". There is a view that this is a generation for whom, unconsciously perhaps, becoming the opposite sex is actually more acceptable than being gay, or not fitting clichéd ideas of what it means to be male or female.

No one can agree on what causes gender dysphoria. And why so many children now say they are experiencing it, or even what it is exactly. Is it a biological condition? A psychological one? Is it genetic or learnt behaviour? Is it nature or nurture? Nor is there one reason why there has been such a dramatic rise in cases — a 100 per cent increase in the past 12 months in Britain. Research is patchy.

What is indisputable is that this is an area that is moving faster than anyone might have imagined, even two years ago. "We are all learning," says Carmichael. "There is no certainty in this area. Certainty is about being closed, which is unhelpful. It's all about being thoughtful, and careful, and treating everyone individually. We don't take a view on the outcome of a young person's gender identification. Our job is not to presuppose anything about what they are going through."

She goes on: "Some adolescents come here who are very troubled. They have only just told their parents." There are a few who contact the unit directly, without having told their parents or their GP. "There is a feeling that you have to act as quickly as possible, often because of fears of self-harm." According to a survey by the trans charity Mermaids 48 per cent of trans people under 26 say they have attempted suicide. "But on the other hand," she says, "there are many young people we see who are doing really well. It's all about promoting resilience in these young people."

The difficulty is that building emotional confidence takes time and for some young people whose bodies are developing — and their parents who may just want this "sorted" — time feels like the enemy. "For families it can be very difficult because they are seeking certainty, but the reality is that we don't have certainty."

The explosion in the figures has led to the impression in the media that there are swathes of children gaily changing gender. The reality is more complicated. About 80 per cent of the children who come to the service before adolescence eventually change their minds. Most decide that they are gay, or bisexual. Conversely, for those who come during adolescence, the figures are reversed and about 80 per cent do pursue sex reassignment.

I'm allowed to sit in on a staff meeting where therapists bring along cases they want to discuss. Young children like Ash may be unusual, but they are not rare. Some have been coming to the unit for 12 years. Many of them, like Ash, will have been living as the opposite gender since they were at nursery and have built up long-standing relationships with their case workers. But one of the therapists mentions the case of a "natally assigned girl" who has been taken by his parents to America for a mastectomy. Children in a hurry to change gender — and parents who fear for their psychological wellbeing — are making potentially traumatic life-changing decisions that cannot easily be reversed.

This is what Carmichael and her team must grapple with. The increase in demand means that children who used to be seen within 18 weeks currently have to wait nine months (although it is hoped that the recruitment drive will change that). Transgender groups complain about the delay and argue that experts at units like the Tavistock are too cautious. Much of the debate swirls around hormone injections: both hormone blockers — prescribed at puberty to inhibit the development of secondary sexual characteristics such as breasts or facial hair — and cross-sex hormones, which the Tavistock prescribes at 16 to masculinise or feminise the body. Thus, a girl who wants to be a boy (a natally assigned girl) will be given testosterone (or "T", as it's known in the chat rooms). It's after this that, when the person is 18 and goes into the adult service, they can opt for surgery.

Hormone blockers are seen as a chance to put the brakes on development, to pause and think about the future. However, 90 per cent of patients go from hormone blockers to cross-sex hormones, hormones that leave teenagers infertile. And it's these cross-sex hormones that cause the most controversy. In America they are prescribed at private clinics to patients as young as 12. There are some in the trans community who argue that the age limit is too high in the UK.

Helen Webberley, a GP in Wales, has set up a private gender clinic and recently started treating children, a "handful" of whom, according to news reports, she has started on cross-sex hormones, including a 12-year-old. Meanwhile, the internet means that there is little to stop under 16-year-olds from buying cross-sex hormones online.

"Currently the zeitgeist is that you go with the child, following the child's lead and wish at every step," says Carmichael. "There has been a large decrease in the age at which cross-sex hormones are available, particularly in the US.

"The big debate at the moment is the pressure to introduce cross-sex hormones earlier and earlier. We have done so at around 16 and we might introduce some flexibility around that. But 12? That is a big departure. The reality is that for some young people, things change all the time. For example, starting a relationship with someone can be associated with them thinking very differently about their gender. This isn't straightforward.

"If young people are being given the strong message that it is the end of the world if they don't get hormones immediately — perhaps the suggestion you should fast-track people who are self-harming — that is potentially damaging." As she says, with some understatement, "It is tricky, really tricky."

Matt, born Matilda, is one of the increasing numbers of natally assigned girls who wish to change gender. The trend at the Tavistock used to be more boy to girl by 3:1, but in the past five years the ratio has reversed.

Matt is also on the autistic spectrum, which complicates the issues (according to the documentary, as many as 30 per cent of male-to-female cases are on the spectrum, a link no one can explain). Matt's diagnosis means that he finds it especially hard to talk about his emotions and the therapists must try to work out if the gender dysphoria is real or an obsessional fantasy. As Carmichael says, "We know he has an incredible imagination. Might it be a story he has created for himself?"

Rachel, Matt's mother, was clear when she agreed to take part in the Tavistock series that she didn't want to sugar-coat what Matt and the family has been — and continues to go — through. They live in Wales. It's fair to say that in their part of the world transgender rights are not on many people's radar. Sometimes it's the small things that resonate. Matt, who loves swimming, was recently disqualified from a competition for being in the boys' team. "I said to my partner, Pete, 'Don't flower it up.' I want it as gritty as it gets so people see what it's like."

At the Tavistock, Matt's caseworker, Dr Charlie Beaumont, encourages him to unpick his feelings, but Matt finds it painfully difficult to talk. His caseworker is concerned there "is a lack of consistency of gender presentation". On the other hand, if not prescribed blockers, might Matt self-harm? Matt is 12. There are signs that breasts are beginning to develop. It's not long now before periods will start.

There is a sense that time is running out, but Rachel tells the doctors tearfully: "I'm not quite ready to lose Tills." She struggles with the impression that has come from Hollywood that being transgender is easy. "I hear all the stuff about people being gender fluid and think, this isn't a fashion thing. There are people in the media who make this all look easy: a man one day; a woman the next. But the reality is it's hard work. I wouldn't wish it on anybody. This isn't left-wing parenting. I'm not somebody going, 'Look how fluid I am with everything.'"

Matt, who loves writing stories and is a massive fan of David Walliams (who wrote the children's book *The Boy in the Dress*), is round-faced, with short hair and expressive big brown eyes. At passport control the authorities often cast around for a girl — "Where's Mathilda?" — and don't believe his mum when she points to Matt. So much so, the family has a letter from GIDS for whenever they go abroad.

As early as aged two and a half, a health visitor commented that Matt — then known as Matilda, or Tills, which is what Rachel still frequently calls him, perhaps betraying her own bewilderment at the turn of events — had an unusually deep voice. "As she got older I always thought she was just a very strong tomboy," Rachel says, looking back. "Detested wearing dresses, didn't want to have her hair combed. I remember buying her knickers and thinking, why on earth does everything have to be covered in princesses? Aged five, she told me she wanted hair that didn't move. In other words, she wanted me to shave her hair off.

"I wasn't too bothered. Not until she started telling everyone she was a boy. At that point, I thought I'd better go to the doctor." Hormone tests were carried out and the assumption was that this was a child who was intersex. When the tests came out negative, Rachel was referred to the GIDS unit.

What was that like? "Oh, they make you question everything," she says. "I think they are trying to find out if this has been nurtured at all. Is this the child or is this the parent pushing their child to be something they don't want to be? But I think they identified quickly that I wasn't happy about it. Why would anybody want their child to face the kind of prejudice that was likely to come her way?"

Matt struggled with his education and being bullied until he got a place at a specialist school where he is accepted as male. "At the old school I'd beg them not to be so gender specific. Now I worry that I sent him to the wolves every day." Despite his being happier at school, Rachel still checks on Matt through the night because she is worried he might hurt himself. She has got rid of anything that could cause harm — the cords on a blind, dressing-gown ties.

In the documentary we watch Rachel weighing up the pros and cons of hormone blockers. "My concern is that it suppresses things. Maybe if she did go through puberty, she'd click into girl mode and be actually, 'I want to be a girl now.' I don't think that will happen, but my worry is that I really am interfering. Now this isn't nature, it is nurture. On the other hand being able to press the pause button could be a good thing."

What does Tills/Matt think? "Tills thinks the rest of the world has gone mad. Just leave me alone. What's wrong with me? I'm just me."

Stephanie Davies-Arai is a parent coach behind a website called Transgender Trend, concerned about the rise in the number of children referred to gender clinics. She argues: "We are setting children off on a path towards sterilisation: medicalisation. It is an experiment that has no precedent ... Are we really willing to so readily accept that a child is the 'wrong' sex at this age rather than address the bullying and the culture that tells him so?" It's a view, she says, that has lost her friends — "There's a feeling that if you don't go along with current trends, you are transphobic."

At first I presumed Transgender Trend was religiously or politically motivated, but that doesn't seem to be the case when we meet. Her view, thoughtfully argued, is that when she was a teenager she, too, would have questioned her gender. "I would have been trans. Because I was not only a tomboy; in my head I was a boy. My sister and I went through our pre-pubescence calling each other Mike and Bill. Until my mid twenties, I didn't want to be a woman. I was a rebel. I look at what is going on and think, I would have gone for this." She doesn't think children can make a decision about gender until their mid twenties when the brain has reached maturity, and that living as the opposite sex at a young age means "you are changing that child's brain, you are building a new identity and by the time you are 12, puberty is the enemy".

Her concern is that, with the help of social media, there might be more awareness around trans, but we're ignoring the issue of social contagion. Davies-Arai argues that it's become cool to be "trans", more accepted than being a lesbian, for example, which is one possible reason why referrals of teenage girls have increased so dramatically. She has heard of clusters of girls binding their breasts and saying they are boys; that parents complain their children are coming home saying, "I'm not sure if I am a boy or a girl," after a class talk about transgender. "Any kid who is like I was — outside the crowd, a bit awkward, the ones who don't fit in — all 'gender non-conforming' kids are included under the trans umbrella now and they are being given no alternative way of understanding their feelings of distress."

But what would she do if her traumatised seven-year-old child announced he/she wanted to change sex? "I would say, be quite casual about it. Don't make a big fuss. Take it away from gender. Parents are advised now to take it very seriously — and I think that is the last thing you do. Address the bullying instead."

If Davies-Arai does have an agenda, it is a feminist one. Almost 1,000 natal females were referred to the Tavistock last year. Might this be more about girls struggling with puberty and their bodies? "There's nobody asking, why do so many teenage girls not want to become women? I think that's what we should be asking, rather than accepting the least likely answer, that they are really boys. It seems a way for us not to seriously look at the culture we are bringing our girls up in."

To some degree, Carmichael might have sympathy with this last argument. What she and her team try to figure out, over months and years, is, "How far are the physical changes one seeks motivated more around feeling that you fit in and are accepted by others?

"You might think, gosh, what are we doing?" says Carmichael. "But there isn't a right and a wrong. No one has the answers. It is an evolving picture with many voices contributing. All we can go on is that people who have taken this route feel this was the right thing to do."

In the documentary, Beard, the director, says to Ash: "Some people change their minds ... "

"Some people. Not me," she responds. Do you think you'll be a girl for ever, he asks. "Yes," she replies. And turns a cartwheel.

A BARE-KNUCKLE FIGHTER IN THE BLOODIEST CONTEST EVER

Rhys Blakely

NOVEMBER 8 2016

IT BEGAN WITH a ride down a golden escalator in the marble atrium of a New York skyscraper. It was June 16, last year, and Donald Trump was announcing a run for the White House. America had no idea what was about to hit it.

Some of the crowd had been paid $50 apiece to turn up at that first campaign event and Mr Trump made headlines with a 40-minute speech in which he praised his golf courses, promised to build a "great wall" along the southern border and called Mexican immigrants rapists. The most wildly unpredictable US election in living memory had begun.

In the months to come, Mr Trump would feud with the family of a fallen Muslim soldier, a Hispanic beauty queen, the leadership of his party, and the Pope. Defying the pundits, this former reality TV star, whose divorces and sex life had kept New York's tabloids entranced for decades, would become the first presidential nominee of a major US party to have no experience in office since Eisenhower and the very first to have boasted about the size of his manhood in a presidential primary debate.

On the Democratic side, Hillary Clinton would face another populist. The former secretary of state announced her candidacy in April last year. She set off on an image-softening road trip to Iowa. The path ahead was rockier than she imagined. The rivals she feared most — Joe Biden, the vice-president, and Elizabeth Warren, the Massachusetts senator — stayed out of the race. But Bernie Sanders, a septuagenarian socialist senator from Vermont, would electrify Democrats suspicious of Mrs Clinton's ethics, her ties to big business and her support for free trade.

She endured a bruising primary while the FBI investigated a secret email system she used while leading the State Department. In February Mr Sanders effectively battled her to a tie in the Iowa caucus, the first primary contest, and then trounced her in New Hampshire. Mrs Clinton was running to be the first woman president, but young women shunned her candidacy.

As the primary race headed to the South, black voters saved her campaign. But questions lingered over whether she could animate Obama voters. She emerged as the second most unpopular nominee of a major US party since polling began. The silver lining? She was running against the first.

It was often predicted that Mr Trump's candidacy would fade. Seventeen Republicans had thrown their hat into the ring: it was a good year to run as a member of the Grand Old Party. A Democrat had occupied the White House for two terms, and rarely has a party kept it for three. Most voters thought the country was on the wrong track. There were six past and current Republican governors and five senators in the race.

Few thought that a brash, twice-divorced celebrity could make a mark. Early on, though, Mr Trump displayed two skills. The first was for attracting media coverage. His mastery of Twitter and of insults bamboozled his rivals. It was estimated that he garnered "free" media coverage worth $2 billion.

The second skill was reaching voters who felt overlooked and left behind, especially white men without a college education. His candidacy coincided with a new scepticism about what he called "the siren song of globalisation".

Mr Trump's diatribes against political correctness, free trade and illegal immigration electrified a section of the right. Supporters quickly forged a consensus on what made him special: his outspokenness, his business acumen, wealth that made him immune to cronyism and his outsider status.

At his first "town hall" event, in the critical early voting state of New Hampshire, Jim Donahue, 65, a maths teacher, thought that Mr Trump could be "America's Vladimir Putin — a nationalist to make the people think that the country could be great again".

It was not until the first Republican primary debate, on August 7 last year, that his rivals realised that Mr Trump was a threat. He was leading the polls and placed at the centre of the stage. His demeanour was glowering, his tan a striking shade of orange. In the opening seconds, the moderators asked the ten men who had qualified to participate if any would refuse to rule out running as an independent in the election.

A theatrical pause — then one hand crept up: Mr Trump's, of course. The crowd booed this challenge to Ronald Reagan's 11th commandment: thou shalt not turn on a fellow Republican. The atmosphere was somewhere between game show and a bare-knuckle boxing match. It was riveting television. The audience broke records.

That evening, aides of Marco Rubio, the Florida senator whom the Clinton campaign feared the most, realised something: untethered to an ideology, unburdened by a respect for facts, and willing to say things no other candidate would dare, Mr Trump was unmanageable.

But that first debate also highlighted his flaws. Megyn Kelly, a star presenter, confronted him on how he had called women "fat pigs, dogs, slobs and disgusting animals". Later that evening he was swarmed by a mob of reporters. Amid the mêlée, Mr Trump fumed. "I think Megyn behaved very nasty to me," he said. That night he retweeted a message that called her a "bimbo". He later suggested that she had asked him unfair questions because she had been menstruating.

That pattern would recur: Mr Trump could not let slights slide. Fourteen months later, when they met for three presidential debates, Mrs Clinton, apparently on the advice of psychologists, baited him. In Las Vegas she said he would be a "puppet" of Vladimir Putin. Mr Trump could barely contain his fury. "No puppet. No puppet," he spluttered. "You're the puppet."

Voters were already worried about his temperament. In the final days of the campaign his aides had blocked him from Twitter, to stop the acts of self-sabotage that frequently cost him support. His treatment of women would come back to haunt him, too.

The summer of last year, however, became known as the "summer of Trump". While the Clinton campaign churned out thousands of words of policy proposals and dodged press conferences, Mr Trump did things no candidate had ever done. At a fair in Iowa he gave children rides on his helicopter. He spent more money on "Make America Great Again" baseball hats than on polling. He demurred when he was asked to denounce a leader of the KKK. He did not release his taxes. He had fun: "We will have so much winning if I get elected that you may get bored with winning," he said.

Last February a second place in the Iowa caucuses for Mr Trump was followed by a victory in the New Hampshire primary. As the primaries headed first to the conservative Deep South and then north to the rust-belt states of the upper Midwest and the industrial Northeast, Mr Trump kept on winning. May 4 marked the Indiana primary. Mr Trump started his day by alleging without a shred of evidence that the father of Mr Cruz, one of only two rivals still standing, had helped to assassinate President Kennedy. By the end of the day the contest was over: Mr Trump was the Republicans' presumptive presidential nominee.

Mrs Clinton, meanwhile, was making campaigning look like solemn work. In July the FBI said it would not recommend charges after investigating whether she had broken the law by using a private email server. The revival of that investigation ten days before the election would send Democrats reeling, and the unflattering inner workings of Mrs Clinton's campaign were revealed when private emails were hacked, probably by Russia.

Time and again, though, Mr Trump defied the laws of political gravity. He won the votes of evangelical Christians despite saying: "I'm not sure I have ever asked God's forgiveness." He said: "I could stand in the middle of Fifth Avenue and shoot somebody and I wouldn't lose voters."

He called the voters of Iowa "stupid". He said that women who had abortions should be punished. The leaders of his own party denounced his attacks on a Hispanic judge as racist. He made remarks some interpreted as promoting violence against Mrs Clinton. He was forced to fire his second campaign manager over alleged links to Kremlin-sponsored strongmen, praised Mr Putin and asked Moscow to hack Mrs Clinton. In the final presidential debate, he suggested he might keep the country "in suspense" and not accept the results of the election.

America has seen populists before. None, though, rose as far or as fast. US politics will never be the same.

LEONARD COHEN

Obituary

NOVEMBER 11 2016

FOR SOMEONE WHOSE songs earned him the epithet "the godfather of gloom", Leonard Cohen had a highly developed and mischievous sense of humour. "I don't consider myself a pessimist," he noted. "I think of a pessimist as someone who is waiting for it to rain — and I feel soaked to the skin."

The subject of his songs over a career that spanned half a century was the human condition, which inevitably led him into some dark places. He suffered bouts of depression and his mournful voice and the fatalism of his lyrics led his songs to be adopted by the anguished, lovelorn and angst-ridden as a personal liturgy.

However, there were also what Cohen called "the cracks where the light gets in". Despite his image as a purveyor of gloom and doom, the inherent melancholia of his songs was nuanced not only by deep romanticism but by black humour.

A published poet and novelist who was in his thirties before he turned to music, Cohen was the most literate singer-songwriter of his age. With Bob Dylan, he occupied the penthouse suite of what he called "the tower of song". Together Cohen and Dylan not only transformed the disposable, sentimental métier of popular music into something more poetic and profound but, for better or worse, made the pop lyric perhaps the defining form of latter 20th-century expression. In an era in which anyone who warbled about "the unicorns of my mind" was liable to be hailed as a poet, Cohen was the genuine article.

Many of his best-known songs — *Suzanne, So Long, Marianne* and *Sisters of Mercy* — were romantically inspired by the women in his life. In *Chelsea Hotel #2*, the theme of longing, love and loss turned to pure lust as he described a liaison with the singer Janis Joplin as she gave him "head on the unmade bed/ While the limousines wait in the street".

Story of Isaac and *The Butcher* touched on religious themes, and war and death loomed large, particularly after his experiences during the 1973 Arab-Israeli war when he offered to fight for Israel and ended up performing for Jewish troops in a tank division that was under fire in the Sinai desert.

Depression and suicide also informed several songs, including *Seems So Long Ago, Nancy* and *Dress Rehearsal Rag*. This tendency to lapse into morbidity led one critic to wail, "Where does he get the neck to stand before an audience and groan out those monstrous anthems of amorous self-commiseration?" Yet if his writing had a philosophical stock-in-trade, it was more stoical perseverance than the abandonment of hope.

Many of his compositions shared a search for self and meaning and were driven by a restless quest for personal freedom, nowhere more so than on *Bird On The Wire,* which opened with probably his most quoted lines "*Like a bird on the wire/ Like a drunk in a midnight choir/ I have tried in my way to be free*".

The song was covered by dozens of artists, including Johnny Cash, Willie Nelson, Judy Collins and Joe Cocker, and was once memorably described as a bohemian version of *My Way,* sans the braggadocio.

Even at his darkest, the prospect of redemption and perhaps even a glimmer of salvation was evident. He described *Hallelujah,* perhaps his best-known composition — and certainly his most covered, with some 300 versions performed or recorded by other artists — as an affirmation of his "faith in life, not in some formal religious way but with enthusiasm, with emotion".

The song took him years to write as he pared back 80 draft verses until each line felt right, as with the second verse: "*Your faith was strong but you needed proof/ You saw her bathing on the roof/ Her beauty and the moonlight overthrew you/ She tied you to a kitchen chair/ She broke your throne, and she cut your hair/ And from your lips she drew the hallelujah.*"

It was characteristic of the meticulous way he worked to make every word count and led to a well-documented exchange with Bob Dylan, who expressed his admiration for the song: "He asked me how long it took to write, and I lied and said three or four years when actually it took five. Then we were talking about one of his songs, and he said it took him 15 minutes."

Unfailingly courteous and possessed of an unfashionably old-world charm, Cohen's intellectual coming of age predated the advent of rock'n'roll. His early cultural heroes were not Elvis Presley and Chuck Berry but the beat writer Jack Kerouac and the poet Lorca, after whom Cohen named his daughter.

His artistic leanings were liberal and bohemian, but he was never a hippy. Dressed in dark, tailored suits and smart fedoras, he had an elegance that was perhaps the legacy of his Jewish father, who owned a clothing shop. Sylvie Simmons, his biographer, reckoned he looked "like a Rat Pack rabbi, God's chosen mobster".

He spoke in a sonorous voice that was full of a reassuring calm and yet animated at the same time. If it was a great speaking voice, it was perhaps not a natural vehicle for a singer, although he developed his own idiosyncratic style to overcome its limitations, one which was compared by the critic Maurice Rosenbaum to a strangely appealing buzz-saw: "I knew I was no great shakes as a singer," Cohen said, "but I always thought I could tell the truth about a song. I liked those singers who would just lay out their predicament and tell their story, and I thought I could be one of those guys."

He was handsome in a rugged and swarthy way, and women found the combination of his physical attraction and the sensitivity of his poetic mind to be irresistible. In turn he described love as "the most challenging activity humans get into" and took up the gauntlet with prolific enthusiasm. "I don't think anyone masters the heart. It continues to cook like a shish kebab, bubbling and sizzling in everyone's breast," he said.

Yet whether love ever bought him true happiness is debatable, and in his 2006 poetry collection, *Book of Longing*, he mocked his reputation as a ladies' man as an ill-fitting joke that "caused me to laugh bitterly through the ten thousand nights I spent alone".

He never married but perhaps came closest to contentment with Marianne Ihlen, the inspiration behind several of his early songs and with whom he lived on the Greek island of Hydra in the 1960s. Their relationship lasted a decade through numerous infidelities. He also had a long relationship with the artist and photographer Suzanne Elrod, with whom he had two children. His son, Adam Cohen, is a singer-songwriter who produced his father's 2016 album *You Want It Darker*. His daughter, Lorca, is a photographer, who gave birth to a surrogate daughter for the singer Rufus Wainwright and Jörn Weisbrodt, his partner.

For all his protests to the contrary, his love life was complicated, almost Byronic in its profligacy. As well as his assignations with Janis Joplin and Joni Mitchell, for example, he rested his head on the perfumed pillows of the fashion photographer Dominique Issermann, the actress Rebecca De Mornay and the songwriter Anjani Thomas. Mitchell, who once said the only men to whom she was a groupie were Picasso and Cohen, celebrated their year-long relationship in several songs, including *A Case of You*, in which her lover declares himself to be as "constant as a northern star". He certainly was not, and yet she sang that he remains in her blood "like holy wine".

Summing up Cohen's lifelong serial inconstancy, his biographer, Simmons, wrote that his "romantic relationships tended to get in the way of the isolation and space, the distance and longing, that his writing required".

Yet he was as fixated on metaphysical matters as he was on carnal pleasures, and many of his best lyrics fused the erotic and the spiritual. In the 1990s his search for enlightenment resulted in him disappearing from public view to live an ascetic life in a Zen Buddhist monastery on the snow-capped Mount Baldy in California. Although he remained a practising Jew, he was ordained as a Buddhist monk in 1996.

He came down from the mountain three years later and returned to civilian life, only to find that while he was sequestered he had been robbed by his longtime manager (and, perhaps inevitably, former lover), Kelley Lynch. He issued legal proceedings against her for misappropriating millions from his retirement fund and swindling him out of his publishing rights. Left with a huge tax bill and a relatively modest $150,000, he remortgaged his home. He was awarded $9 million by a Los Angeles court in 2006.

When Lynch — who was later jailed after violating a court order to keep away from Cohen — was unable to pay, he undertook his first concert tour in 15 years to replenish his funds. It was estimated by *Billboard* magazine that he earned almost $10 million from the 2009 leg of the tour alone.

A golden period of late creativity followed. After releasing a parsimonious 11 studio albums in 45 years, he released three in four years between 2012 and 2016, including *Old Ideas*, which became the highest-charting album of his career, when he was 76.

Leonard Norman Cohen was born in Montreal in 1934 into a prosperous and middle-class Jewish family. His father was already approaching 50 when his son was born, and died when Cohen was nine years old, leaving him with a small trust fund income. His mother, Masha, was the daughter of a rabbi and brought him up steeped in Talmudic lore and the stories of the Old Testament. He later recalled a "Messianic" childhood.

In an era before rock'n'roll he was drawn to the folk and country music he heard on the radio. He learnt to play the guitar as a teenager "to impress girls" and formed a group called the Buckskin Boys. Women also loomed large in his adolescent life. After reading a book about hypnosis, he tried out the technique and persuaded the family's maid to disrobe. He was 13 at the time.

At the age of 15 he stumbled on a volume by the Spanish poet Federico García Lorca in a second-hand bookshop in Montreal. Inspired by Lorca's erotic themes, he decided to become a writer and adopted his lifelong credo that his creative muse was best served via the entanglement of heart and limbs.

At McGill University he chaired the debating society and won a prize for creative writing. His first book of verse, *Let Us Compare Mythologies*, appeared in 1956. A second volume, *The Spice-Box of Earth*, was published five years later and put him on the literary map. By then wanderlust had set in and he travelled widely, spending time in Castro's Cuba before buying a small house without electricity or running water on the Greek island of Hydra. There he wrote further books of verse and the novels *The Favourite Game* and *Beautiful Losers*, as well as conducting a decade-long romantic relationship with Ihlen.

His books were critically acclaimed and one enthusiastic reviewer gushingly likened *Beautiful Losers* to James Joyce. But good reviews don't put food on even Greek tables and his books initially sold fewer than 3,000 copies. In need of cash, he returned to north America in 1966, planning to try his luck as a singer and songwriter in Nashville.

"In retrospect, writing books seems the height of folly, but I liked the life," he recalled. "It's good to hit that desk every day. There's a lot of order to it that is very different from the life of a rock'n'roller. I turned to professional singing as a remedy for an economic collapse."

He never got as far as Nashville. After landing in New York, he was "ambushed" by the new music he heard all around him. "In Greece I'd been listening to Armed Forces Radio, which was mostly country music," he said. "But then I heard Dylan and Baez and Judy Collins, and I thought something was opening up, so I borrowed some money and moved into the Chelsea Hotel."

Collins became the first to record one of his songs and invited him to sing with her on stage. His first live performance caused him to flee with stage fright, but his shyness appealed to the audience who encouraged him back and set him on his new career as a troubadour. Already in his thirties, he was described by one critic as having "the stoop of an aged crop-picker and the face of a curious little boy".

His singing, too, provoked mixed reactions but John Hammond, the legendary Columbia A&R man who had already signed Bob Dylan to the label, was not one to be put off by an unconventional voice. "He took me to lunch and then we went back to the Chelsea," Cohen remembered. "I played a few songs and he gave me a contract."

He spent two years living in the Chelsea Hotel, fell in with Andy Warhol's set, became infatuated with the Velvet Underground's German chanteuse Nico and released his debut album. Sales in America were initially modest but the record found a cult following in Europe and Britain, where he was dubbed "the bard of the bedsits".

Among his most memorable concerts from this time was his appearance at the Isle of Wight Festival in 1970. Unpromisingly he had to go on after an electrifying performance by Jimi Hendrix, yet instead of bringing down the mood he managed to win over the pumped-up, 600,000-strong crowd by telling them gentle self-deprecating anecdotes in a hushed voice, in between his equally low-key numbers.

Although his early records sounded austere, centred around little more than his voice and a softly strummed guitar, in later years he expanded his musical palette, adding a full band and chorus of backing singers. Initially he appeared to be a literary aesthete, aloof from the hurly-burly of rock'n'roll, but by the mid-1970s his life was unravelling in a midlife crisis in which LSD experimentation featured. "I got into drugs and drinking and women and travel and feeling that I was part of a motorcycle gang or something," he admitted 20 years later.

His confusion led him to record with Phil Spector, whose production banished the simplicity of his earlier recordings in favour of melodramatic rock arrangements. One grotesque track, *Don't Go Home With Your Hard On*, featured a drunken chorus of Cohen, Dylan and Allen Ginsberg repeating the title line over and over again.

Working with the volatile Spector was a fraught process. "I was flipped out at the time and he certainly was flipped out," Cohen recalled. "For me, the expression was withdrawal and melancholy, and for him, megalomania and insanity and a devotion to armaments that was really intolerable."

At one point during the sessions, Spector locked Cohen out of the studio, put an armed guard on the door and would not let him listen to the mixes. When Cohen protested, Spector threatened him with a gun and a cross-bow.

The resulting album, *Death of a Ladies' Man* in 1977, was a career nadir that horrified his fan base, and he swiftly returned to something closer to his old style. When five years passed between the release of albums it appeared that his inspiration had dried up, a blockage that he later attributed to having become addicted to amphetamines. *Various Positions* in 1984 was a triumph and included *Hallelujah.* It sparked a revival both creatively and commercially as Cohen adopted the mode of a fashionable boulevardier.

With an increasingly sardonic humour he surveyed the wreckage of the modern world in songs such as *First We Take Manhattan, Democracy* and *Everybody Knows* and painted an apocalyptic picture of the world. It was a vision that struck a hellish chord with the film director Oliver Stone who included three of Cohen's songs from the period in his horrifyingly violent, dystopian movie *Natural Born Killers.* Shortly after the film's release, Cohen retreated to his Zen Buddhist monastery.

When he returned to recording and live performance after a decade-long break, he was treated more like a guru than a peddler of popular songs. Seated on a stool, guitar in hand, or cupping a microphone ("as Hamlet held Yorick's skull", one critic suggested), his concerts became acts of communion, with reverential audiences treating his every utterance as if it were holy writ.

Age seemed to suit him, uniquely emphasising his sagacity, while the advancing years simply made other fading rock stars appear irrelevant. Eschewing make-up, surgery and denial, he embraced getting old as "the only game in town". That he was still writing compelling songs and releasing records into his eighties was "the ash" that showed his life was still "burning well".

Despite continuing his recording career until his final months, Cohen stopped touring in 2013 and hinted at his preparedness for the end in the summer of 2016. After the death of Marianne (obituary, August 27), a letter from Cohen was released in which he said goodbye to his muse and former lover. "Our bodies are falling apart and I think I will follow you very soon," he wrote."Know that I am so close behind you that if you stretch out your hand, I think you can reach mine."

Leonard Cohen, poet and songwriter, was born on September 21, 1934. His death, aged 82, was announced on November 10, 2016

LET'S STOP BEING SO PARANOID ABOUT ANDROIDS

Matt Ridley

November 21 2016

The tech industry, headquartered in Silicon Valley, is populated largely by enthusiastic optimists who want to change the world and believe they can. Yet there is one strand of pessimism that you hear a lot there: the robots are going to take all our jobs. With artificial intelligence looming, human beings are facing redundancy and obsolescence. However, I think this neo-Luddite worry is as wrong now as it was in Ned Ludd's day.

"Any job that is on some level routine is likely to be automated, and if we are to see a future of prosperity rather than catastrophe we must act now," warns Martin Ford, a Silicon Valley entrepreneur, in his book *The Rise of the Robots*.

"With the technology advances that are presently on the horizon, not only low-skilled jobs are at risk; so are the jobs of knowledge workers. Too much is happening too fast," says a Silicon Valley guru, Vivek Wadhwa.

"Think of it as a kind of digital social Darwinism, with clear winners and losers: those with the talent and skills to work seamlessly with technology and compete in the global marketplace are increasingly rewarded, while those whose jobs can just as easily be done by foreigners, robots or a few thousand lines of code suffer accordingly," says Tyler Cowen, an economist at George Mason University, Virginia, in his book *Average is Over*.

Yet we have been automating work for two centuries and so far the effect has been to create more jobs, not fewer. Farming once employed more than 90 per cent of people, and without them we would have starved. Today, it's just a few per cent. Followers of the mysterious "Captain Swing" who destroyed threshing machines in 1830 were convinced that machines stole work. Instead of which, farm labourers became factory workers; factory workers later became call-centre workers. In both transitions, pay rose and work became safer, less physically demanding and less exposed to the elements.

In 1949 the cybernetics pioneer Norbert Wiener warned that computers in factories could usher in "an industrial revolution of unmitigated cruelty". In 1964 a panel of the great and the good, including the Nobel prizewinners Linus Pauling and Gunnar Myrdal, warned that automation would mean "potentially unlimited output ... by systems of machines which will require little co-operation from human beings". This hoary old myth just keeps coming round again and again.

This time it's different, I hear you cry. Those were just peasants or factory hands: now it's software developers, accountants and perhaps even lawyers who face obsolescence through automation. Or academics and journalists! People — oh horror! — like us. Yet if we could lose most of the jobs in farming and manufacturing to automation and still have a record proportion of the population in employment, even while bringing women into the workforce in vastly higher numbers, why should we be unduly alarmed if some white-collar folk now suffer the same fate?

The argument that artificial intelligence will cause mass unemployment is as unpersuasive as the argument that threshing machines, machine tools, dishwashers or computers would cause mass unemployment. These technologies simply free people to do other things and fulfil other needs. And they make people more productive, which increases their ability to buy other forms of labour. "The bogeyman of automation consumes worrying capacity that should be saved for real problems," scoffed the economist Herbert Simon in the 1960s.

Yes, but what if there are no more needs to fulfil? Might there come a point when all the work we can ever need is done by machines, leaving nothing for us to do? When even pet-grooming salons and yoga teachers have been replaced? If so, and if the machines belong mainly to the wealthy, then the economic problem will be one of distribution, not of scarcity, so we may need to consider such radical ideas as the "basic income", in which everybody gets a salary from the government.

It is not going to come to that. There are infinite new ways we can think of to fulfil each other's needs and desires in exchange for reward. Look at the way in which modernity's spectacular productivity has allowed the revival of crafts or the resurgence in live performance.

And in the unlikely event that this end point were ever reached, so what? A world in which machines do literally everything we can ever think of needing done ("Take me to Mars, Hal, and on the way rewrite Shakespeare as rap") is a world in which we can spend our entire time consuming the products of those machines' work. After all, the purpose of all work is consumption, as Adam Smith nearly said. The economist Tim Worstall puts it this way: "There will continue to be jobs for humans as long as there are unsatisfied human wants and desires. Once all of those are satisfied then jobs don't matter, do they?"

We are sharing out less work already. In 1856 an average British man worked 149,700 hours over his lifetime. By 1981 that had dropped to 88,000 hours — despite the fact that he lived much longer. He now spent more time in education, on holiday, in retirement or leaving work early. In 1960 a British worker spent nearly 12 per cent of his or her life at work; by 2010 that number had dropped to less than 9 per cent (and I bet he or she spends some of the "work" time on home life, reading emails, paying bills).

The final argument of the pessimists is that automation is "hollowing out" the workforce by replacing the jobs of the middle-skill professions, so we will be left with a world of hedge-fund managers and their maids. There have been some disproportionate losses of middle-income jobs in the US and Europe since 1980, but as the MIT economist David Autor argues, it's as much to do with competition from China as with automation per se. You cannot outsource maids. And he thinks it is running out of steam anyway.

Journalists, he says, "tend to overstate the extent of machine substitution for human labour and ignore the strong complementarities between automation and labour that increase productivity, raise earnings, and augment demand for labour".

Cheer up. Far from a mass of unemployed Morlocks living miserably poor lives while the digital Eloi monopolise the few well-paid jobs, automation is granting us ever more time, as well as more goods and services.

WINTER

GAME'S SOUL IS NOT AT LORD'S. IT IS HERE

Mike Atherton, Mumbai

DECEMBER 8 2016

IT CALLS ITSELF the home of cricket, by Twitter handle and common consent, but it isn't really. Not when there are 12ft gates and a huge brick wall keeping the public at bay, and when you need the fattest of wallets to watch an international match there — if you can get hold of a ticket — or buy a beer or sandwich. It's a commercial powerhouse, a successful brand and, of course, it has the history, but Lord's is not the home of cricket.

South Mumbai is about as close as you get to the heart and soul of the game. A mile or two square, from the pukka gymkhanas at the north end of Marine Drive to the Oval Maidan, just inland from the southern tip of it at Nariman Point. An area that teems with cricketing history, has produced some of the greatest players, and remains home to the ordinary cricketer, no matter how wealthy or privileged, how poor or unconnected.

Let's head out from the Trident hotel, then, where both sets of players are staying, along with tour groups and assorted journalists, pausing briefly to gaze out beyond Chowpatty Beach to the swanky Malabar Hill, the birthplace of one of the greatest England captains, Douglas Jardine. (What tactics would Jardine devise for Virat Kohli?) It's early, barely light, but the honking of the cars has already begun, the kites are flying overhead and the walkers and runners are out, using the three-mile stretch along Marine Drive to keep their lungs in decent order, not always easy in Mumbai.

We'll turn right, past the charmless Air India building, heading down through a nondescript quarter dominated by dreary government constructs and on towards the first great expanse, the Oval Maidan.

It's Sunday morning and the market traders are setting up their stalls, the street-food sellers are firing up their equipment, ready to prepare the vada pavs, misal pavs, dhalpuri, bhelpuri, idlis and all manner of biscuits and teas. A handful of boys sprint past us, dragging their cricket bags along the floor, sturdy wooden bats to hand. They are dressed in coloureds, with their names on their backs, and they are in a hurry.

Ahead of us and to our left stretches the Oval Maidan, named because of its shape, which is actually more of a rectangle, more than 20 acres, running north–south, and already teeming with players of all ages, all abilities, crammed so close together you wonder how matches are regulated, and why there are not more injuries. This is the prettiest of the maidans, with the University of Mumbai and the great Rajabai Tower and the ornate High Court framing one side, and palm trees shading the circumference.

Around the edges, informal knockabouts are happening; on the main parts, where there are cut pitches, more formal matches are taking place. The standard varies: it is already warm, the early morning sun has burnt off the haze and the dew, and so it is no place for a fast bowler. Some fancy their chances, and they chuck rather than bowl the ball, but mainly wiry arms and flexible wrists send the ball spinning towards the batsmen. Even here, Indian spinners look more natural, more born to it, less rigid and manufactured. It is in the blood.

What are a young cricketer's needs? Sun and space, mainly. Cricket on the maidans bursts into life after the monsoon rains give way, although there is the Kanga League that is played through rain and shine. With sun and space, though, often the most rudimentary pitches and equipment will suffice. From the townships of South Africa to the beaches of the Caribbean, the back alleys of Dhaka to these maidans, cricketers emerge, self-taught and self-motivated.

We're walking north now, staying on the western side of the Oval Maidan, so that we can peek through the railings at the matches taking place, maintaining the view offered by the university and High Court in the background, and occasionally stooping to throw back a ball that has come through. At the end, instead of carrying straight on to the next green expanse, we'll take a short detour left, past the Oxford bookstore, and towards the old Brabourne Stadium, home to the Cricket Club of India, pentangular tournaments between 1937–46 and Test matches in Mumbai regularly until 1973, when the Wankhede Stadium supplanted it.

It's a good place to stop, sit in one of the planter chairs on the veranda, grab a cool drink and soak in the atmosphere of an old colonial-type club, with its swimming pool, billiards room, library and lush green outfield. The most recent time England played a Test there was almost 44 years ago, when they were plundered by Farokh Engineer, who scored what was, for the time, a rapid hundred. Engineer was one of four players from the Parsee Cyclists Cricket Club who once played in the same Test team for India in 1961 and their home, the Azad Maidan, is our next port of call.

Up towards the Central Telegraph Office, then, turning left on Mahatma Gandhi Road and towards the Cross Maidan, so named for the cross, situated at its north end, that still attracts religious devotees, but this morning is home to a football match, not cricket. On then, quickly, heading north until we get to a crossroads where we can turn in and on to a path that heads through the Azad Maidan. We are struck immediately by the contrast: one genteel game at the Bombay Gymkhana, with its green-baize outfield, to our right, and hundreds of matches being played on the scrub of the Azad Maidan to our left.

The black and gold-coloured flag is fluttering above the Bombay Gymkhana pavilion, a magnificent building that stretches along almost one entire side of the ground. The Bombay Gymkhana was home to the first Test in India, in 1933, and with government edicts dictating that no wall or boundary can surround the western side, it hasn't changed that much in appearance. It is still exclusive, despite the flimsy rope and pathway, which are the only things that separate it from the democratic happenings on the Azad Maidan.

Azad means free in Persian, and this ground is host to 22 clubs, with their tiny, canvas-covered makeshift pavilions, and numerous other games after hours, when anyone can use its vast expanse. Of all the maidans, this is perhaps the most famous as a result of the gluttonous feats of run-scoring in school matches. It was here that Sachin Tendulkar and Vinod Kambli put on a 664-run stand in a Harris schools' competition almost 30 years ago. In his autobiography, Tendulkar relates that his scores in the 1987–88 Harris Shield quarter-final, semi-final and final were 207 not out, 326 not out and 346 not out. After his effort in the semi-final, he wandered across to the other end of the maidan and played in another match, scoring 178 not out.

He would have needed some food and drink after that, and so do we, so we'll retrace our steps and head down one of the food lanes that bisects the Azad Maidan and the Cross Maidan. If you're brave, you can give the street food a go — I'll leave you to it. We're close to the Wankhede Stadium now, so close that on thrumming nights in the IPL, or after the World Cup final here in 2011, the noise would have carried to these neighbourhoods. International cricket, with its facilities, superstars and wealth, is so close but so far away.

Because of the railway line, we'll have to turn left, head back to Churchgate and get on to Marine Drive again, wander past the InterContinental hotel, which has one of the best rooftop bars, and be guided by the floodlights of the stadium, looming before us. We'll pass the Brabourne again, then turn right and head through the Vinoo Mankad gates — Mankad being far from Mumbai's most celebrated cricketing son, but the one whose name is still given to a cricketing act — and walk down towards the Vijay Merchant pavilion.

I've got an accreditation, so I'm going to leave you now, and head out on to the middle where the groundsman is finalising his preparations for the Test pitch and take a peek. Away to the left is the Sachin Tendulkar stand and opposite that the Sunil

Gavaskar pavilion, the two most revered members of the Mumbai school of batting. However, neither averages as many in first-class cricket as its founding father, Merchant, who, with an average of 71.64, stands behind only Donald Bradman.

Many of the greats started on the maidans before graduating to international cricket at Gymkhana, then the Brabourne and now the Wankhede — a seamless link. It's all there, within a morning's walk. Follow that path and you'll feel closer to the heart and soul of the game than anywhere else.

CONFESSIONS OF A MIDDLE-AGED MAN

Jonathan Gershfield

December 10 2016

Peter sits down in the chair next to mine, looking a little hesitant. "Before we start," he says. "I need to ask you a question. Would you feel comfortable if a trainee nurse sits in on our session?" He clears his throat. "A male nurse, of course."

Now, I'd had intimate medicals before. Plenty of them. And with 60 years of prodding and poking behind me (and in front), I'm quite laissez faire these days. But this is new territory for me. Because I'm here at the urology clinic for my induction. My injection-therapy induction. To treat the "dysfunction" I'd experienced since parting company with my prostate six months earlier.

OK, if you want me to spell it out — my "erectile dysfunction".

The session will involve an injection and, with any luck, an erection — my first in six months. Now, an erection is a rather personal condition and, call me old-fashioned, until today I'd only shared mine with one person at a time. And that person, invariably female and invariably someone with whom I have been in a relationship, has been generally prepared to bare all, too — them's the rules. So flaunting my tumescence in the presence of not one but two total strangers, both fully dressed and fully male, is not something I'm ever going to "feel comfortable" about.

On the other hand, I'm a Brit. So I can usually muster a stiff upper lip, even if other parts of my anatomy remain temporarily flaccid.

"Of course," I say, doing my best to put the poor man at ease with a genial sweep of my hand and a sanguine smile. "No problem."

Peter thanks me and opens the door. An earnest young man shuffles in, introduces himself a little stiffly (no doubt there's another word, but that's the one that infiltrates my consciousness) and pulls up a chair to make a cosy threesome.

Peter outlines how the injection will work. Perhaps because of the worldly air I'm trying to adopt, he assumes prior knowledge. But ever since my first brush with a vaccination at the age of four, when I'd bolted, terrified, out of the doctor's surgery and into the high street with my ageing GP and my hysterical mother in hot pursuit, I'd studiously avoided ever eyeing a needle. Or an episode of *Holby City* come to that. So I haven't a clue how to do it.

We go back to first principles. How to break off the ampoule. How to draw the solution into the syringe with the long needle. How to expunge the air bubbles. How to switch needles. And finally, how to inject. To demonstrate, Peter opens a drawer and produces — arrgghh! — a large fibreglass penis. I shaft uneasily in my chair. *Shift*, I mean, *shift*. (My brain's really messin' with me now.)

Then he asks if I'm ready. "Sure," I lie. I am to inject myself, it seems, under Peter's watchful eye. And the trainee's, of course. Four watchful eyes, peering unblinkingly at my privates. I carefully prepare the instruments of torture. But as I grip the ampoule and draw the solution into the syringe, the needle jolts and (just like in the fairytale) pricks — I mean *stabs* — the tip of my finger. Blood oozes out and the trainee reaches for a plaster, visibly relieved to have a role beyond that of spectator.

The moment is a rude awakening. The last thing you'd want is to put one of those things anywhere near a sensitive area, let alone an erogenous one. Yet that is precisely what I have to do. And sure enough, with the needle now locked and loaded, Peter gestures to the bed. "You'll be more comfortable there," he says. I wouldn't bank on it.

With my sanguine smile now more of a hardened — *fixed*, I mean — grimace, I duly lower my kecks to half-mast, perch on the edge of the bed and take myself in hand. I glance up at those four watchful eyes. The trainee's fresh face is now as red as a radish as Peter points to the target.

My hand is trembling, furiously, like a leaf with the DTs. No wonder surgeons don't operate on themselves. I take a deep breath to steady my nerves, take aim ... and fire. In it goes, first the needle, then the solution ...

I am all set to swear like the mother of all mothers in childbirth, but the procedure is amazingly painless. Peter congratulates me (On what? Not swearing? Not bolting for the high street? Not hitting a main artery?) and says they'll leave the room so I can massage myself in private.

Massage myself? There's no mention of that in the booklet.

"We'll be back in 15 minutes," he says. "We should have a result by then."

"Touch wood," I say, instantly regretting it.

I shuffle over to the window to make sure the venetians are fully closed. Then I text Cathy. "*OMG. You'll never guess what I'm doing.*" She guesses. "*I hope you're thinking of me,*" she texts back.

In all honesty it's hard — I mean *difficult* — to think of anything even mildly erotic in this brightly lit, clinical room. If TripAdvisor had a page on the subject, I'd suggest Barry White, scented candles, internet access. Although Hippocrates might not approve.

Within minutes there's a stirring, like a slowly rising soufflé or a cobra charmed from its dormancy. By the time they return, I'm fully charged. Peter nods his approval, like a queen proudly inspecting her Home Guard, and produces a plastic ruler, mounted with four rubber buttons. For a moment I wonder if

I'm meant to kneel while he places it on my shoulder, or stand so he can pin it to my lapel like a medal. But he explains that it's merely a way to measure the strength of my erection. I press No 3: "Firm enough for penetration but not completely hard." That'll do for starters. Peter's compliments are tempered with a health warning, however. If it lasts more than one hour, I'm to vigorously run up and down some stairs. Two hours, take a cold shower. Three, an ice pack. Four, call an ambulance.

With those cautions ringing in my ear, I quickly get dressed, take my injection kits, say goodbye to the two men with whom I now feel a strange connection and head out towards the Tube, grateful that I had the foresight to wear boxers and loose-fitting trousers.

But if that standout moment marked the end of a turbulent year, this is how it had all started ...

The silence is suffocating.

We're driving back from a "make or break" weekend in the New Forest and ... let's just say it wasn't a "make". In all honesty, if months of counselling couldn't save our marriage, then a weekend away with the ponies was never likely to. So now there really is nothing more to say. All the home truths and dirty washing have been aired, and wisps of thin grey smoke are the only signs of life in the tangled wreckage of our 30 years together. We sit in silence in the bank-holiday traffic. The engine's thrum and the air-con's whirr form a sorry soundtrack to what had once been an extremely happy union, full of love and hope and joy.

So how did it all go wrong? The stresses of urban living? The strains of work-life balance? The challenge of bringing up kids? Or is it merely that human beings were never designed for such long-term arrangements.

I can't take the suffocating silence. I switch on the radio. On most other days Adele would have been a welcome accompaniment to our journey home. But right now my missus and I would rather listen to the sound of our own fingernails scouring a blackboard.

Tears are gonna fall, rolling in the deep ...

We sit stony-faced for the first few bars. I am the first to blink, switching over to a radio sitcom. An audience guffaws. That's more like it. Laughter is the best medicine. Except there's nothing more profoundly irritating than guffawing when the jokes aren't funny. Not to us they aren't anyway, not today.

When we arrive home, my missus breaks the silence. She's staying with a friend tonight and wonders if I'd mind fetching her suitcase from the loft. There's an unfamiliar hollowness to her voice, a kind of polite brittleness she normally reserves for traffic wardens. She could have just used the case we'd taken to the New Forest, but technically that's mine, and maybe this is her first stab at dividing our assets.

Either way, I'm glad of the opportunity to demonstrate my dignity under duress.

Still in shorts and trainers, I climb the ladder and open the hatch. But as I reach inside for her red Samsonite, I feel a sudden searing pain in my left buttock, as if I've been speared by the Devil's trident. A thousand volts fuse buttock to brain in a millisecond. Jesus Christ! Has she taken leave of her senses? This may be our lowest ebb, but we've never resorted to violence.

I collapse on the landing, writhing. My missus stands over me, eyebrows shaped like question marks. But she isn't holding a skewer, a pitchfork or a branding iron. Just a Cath Kidston toilet bag. Nonetheless, my backside's on fire. And as I wrestle my shorts to the floor, out it plops. The culprit. The perpetrator. A wasp.

I scramble to my feet, spewing expletives, grinding the little bastard to a pulp under my size 11s.

My missus tells me to calm down or risk anaphylaxis. She's not a medic, but she has watched a lot of *Casualty*. Plus, she hates bad language. And as the family's official first-aider, she does at least know of an antidote for wasp stings.

So two minutes later I am lying face down on our marital bed and she's basting my bum with balsamic. A moment of exquisite tenderness in the midst of our Armageddon.

My relief is palpable. I hug her in gratitude. She smiles uncertainly ... then heads off to pack her things.

It's a strange thing, waking up single again after such a long time. *Thirty years*! I mean, that's longer than Nelson Mandela spent on Robben Island. Which I realise is a cheap joke and totally unanalogous to my situation, and the very fact that I still find it funny, whereas my wife almost certainly won't, perhaps goes some way towards explaining our split in the first place.

But whatever the reasons and however resilient you may be, it's hard not to feel reduced, diminished and depleted. It's a basic law of mathematics — your "other half" has gone. At night, for example, you find yourself sleeping on the same side of the bed, despite the circuitous route to the bathroom. In the morning, on autopilot, you still take two cups from the cupboard when you make the tea. And you're constantly referring to "us" when what you actually now mean is just "me".

Because we're creatures of habit, aren't we? And after half a lifetime, "adjustment" doesn't come easy. Especially with that maelstrom of mixed emotions to muddle through. Exciting, challenging, liberating, yes ... but at the same time, disconcerting, lonely, sad. And arguably a whole lot worse when, deep down, you genuinely still like each other. Break-ups are surely much easier for people who hate each other's guts.

Still, one way or another, you just have to get on with it. So your first preoccupation is who to tell and how. Each family member presents a different challenge. Each set of friends needs to be assured there's no acrimony — no sides. (And even then, as no one enters Noah's Ark without a plus-one, it will be a while before either of you gets invited to dinner.) Then there's the change to your domestic arrangements. Dividing your bank accounts. Splitting your worldly goods. Who gets the photo albums? Who gets that honeymoon sculpture? Who gets to spend Christmas with the boys? Every last detail in your life, recalibrated, recalculated, redefined.

The fact is, nature did not intend you to reinvent yourself at 60. So it's tempting just to draw the curtains and hunker down with your Sky box and a hot toddy. But when it does finally dawn on you that you don't have to conform or compromise any more, that you can now make radical changes to your life without having to refer or defer, it's quite an empowering feeling. Hey, you can leave the toilet lid up if you want to! You can paint the living room purple! Upload heavy rock to your iPod! But why stop there, for God's sake? What about the Big Stuff? Live the dream. Indulge your fantasies. Buy a flash car, for example. How about a Corvette Stingray? An Aston Martin? Something with gull wings? Cruising down Barnes High Street with the wind in your hair and Dire Straits pulsating from the speakers. That'd cheer you up, right? Sure it would. It does!

Until reality kicks in and you remember two things. The first is that flashy cars cost a fortune to run. And your impending divorce is going to plunder your bank balance. And the second is that you're 60 and, not to put too fine a point on it, you'd look like a twit.

But don't be disheartened. There are loads of other options. How about a nubile young girlfriend? You still have all your faculties, or most of them, so it's certainly not out of the question. We older guys have our allure. Look at Bernie Ecclestone. Donald Trump ... Hmmm. OK, scratch that. In any case, deep down you know damn well you'd prefer someone who's been around the block a couple of times herself. Someone who's actually heard of Dire Straits. Someone who's so busy worrying about her crow's feet and laughter lines that she fails to notice your ineluctably expanding bald patch and your dad-dancing. Besides, if 60 is the new 40, then 55 is the new 35. And 35 will do me fine.

But hang on a minute. This is freedom, man! *Don't* throw it away. Don't waste this golden opportunity. How about a tattoo? It's cheaper than a flashy car. Plus you can design it to order. Give vent to your inner id. Get a flashy car splashed across your pectorals. Get a supermodel spread across your stomach. Why not get both? There again, wearing your heart on your sleeve is one thing; having it indelibly inked on your actual skin quite another. Far better would be to get a girlfriend with a tattoo instead. They're much easier to remove.

Fair enough, no flashy new car then, no girlfriend half your age, no tattoo. What about some funky new clothes? A sleek designer suit. Some groovy shoes. A tailored coat. And you can join a gym. Work those glutes, crunch those abs, get that six-pack back. Yeah, that makes much more sense. Until you remember that you have a pathological aversion to gyms and you can't abide shopping.

So perhaps this reinvention thing is overrated? Perhaps by the time you hit 60, you're simply too set in your ways to change anything. Maybe just making the most of what you've got is the answer?

Several months on, and still reeling from a wretched summer in which I had to say goodbye to my lovely dad and very nearly my mum, too, I am sitting in a coffee bar waiting for a hot date. Although how hot she is remains to be seen because we haven't actually met before. I'm early; she's late. So there's plenty of time to run through the usual catechism. Will she look anything like her photo? Will there be chemistry over the cappuccinos? And (inevitably) what the hell am I doing here? Well, the answer to that one is simple. I've succumbed to the new social norm and "gone online".

I mean, how else do you meet someone when you emerge, semi-institutionalised, from a long-term marriage, defined (even by yourself) as half-a-couple?

Not that there's a dearth of singles out there. If 42 per cent of marriages end in divorce, the odds get even shorter when the kids fly the nest, and the glue that's held things together starts to crumble. But any "appropriate" single women I know seem far too familiar somehow. It would feel a bit, you know, like incest. My friends seem reluctant to introduce me to anybody they know for fear of upsetting my ex. At least I *think* that's the reason.

Besides, it's not just "how" you meet someone, it's "how quickly". A fella in his twenties or thirties has all the time in the world. But in your sixties, it's a different story. "*At my back I always hear/ Time's winged chariot hurrying near.*" Andrew Marvell could have put it another way: "*Better get your arse in gear/ Before you need a Zimmer, dear.*"

The great thing about online dating is that it speeds things up. So, encouraged by Bridget, my dating guru, I logged on to Encounters, the *Times* singles website. Window-browsing only, of course. But with that tingle of single women smiling beguilingly from its pages, I was soon won over.

I chose my user name — *WingedCharioteer* (natch) — wrote my profile, found some photos and pressed send. Within hours there was a steady trickle of respondents. Within days, a barrage. There's a healthy appetite for fresh meat, it seems. And, according to Bridget, men "of a certain age" with their own teeth and hair are at a premium. The website has a chart showing the 20 most popular men and women, based on "hits" from other members. And to my amazement, within a couple of weeks, I was topping it. The 2015 Christmas No 1!

It's a curious thing, this online mating dance. A member clocks your profile, ticks a box, makes you a "favourite". You receive an alert, then check out theirs. If you like what you see, you respond. Then, buoyed by this reciprocity, you exchange a flirty message or two and, if the vibe feels right, suggest a phone call. By now you'll have dropped your disguise — and so will she. You just have to pray she's not a bunny boiler. So you have your chat and, if the voice doesn't set your teeth on edge (or vice versa), you arrange a date. A drink or dinner if you're feeling bold. A cautious cappuccino if not.

I sip my cautious cappuccino and glance around. Still no sign. Perhaps she's clocked me through the window and done a runner. I glance at her photo on my phone. She doesn't look the running type.

So I revert to my catechism. What exactly are you looking for when there's no longer that pathological imperative to "go forth and multiply"? Someone to sit in the rocking chair next to yours and watch the sun go down with? Someone to knit your bedsocks and make your Ovaltine just the way you like it? Someone who reminds you to take your pill every morning? Yeah, right. The irony is, you're looking for the same things you were looking for back in the day. Only now they're much harder to find.

A woman appears at the doorway, suited, booted, slapped and coiffed. I don't actually recognise her from the photo, but she's agitated enough to be on a date. And before I know it, *TangerineDream* is beside me with her skinny macchiato.

But say you do find a person who ticks all the boxes. What about "the baggage"? Sure, you want someone who's lived a life, who's loved, travelled, has children she adores, a career she enjoys, a circle of friends who actually matter to her. Because you have those things and you want that symmetry. You just have to hope that none of the above will stifle a new relationship. Or that life hasn't left her too cynical, suspicious and cagey.

On the other hand, it pays to be circumspect. Because when you're "a certain age", investing six months in another failed relationship means you emerge six months older, six months greyer and six months closer to the departure gates. It's a biological time bomb of a very different kind.

My new companion's a chatty one all right. She hasn't drawn breath since she sat down. No danger of an awkward pause, at least. I'm really not sure if it's there though, that "indefinable something". The "chemistry" that can sweep you off into the deep unknown. On the other hand, how the hell do you know if you have that "connection" unless you at least try to connect? As a refugee from a very long marriage, those instincts can get rather rusty.

So I smile warmly across my cold cappuccino and, without interrupting her flow, *TangerineDream* smiles back.

One of the benefits of online dating is that you can set your radius wherever you want. I found that 60 miles was about my limit. If you're a true romantic, prepared to comb the planet for the perfect partner, you would doubtless set yours to infinity.

Although that first cappuccino would set you back a bit. Plus, there's the carbon footprint to think about.

I wasn't thinking about my carbon footprint when I first clapped eyes on my new neighbour. It was a few months later and I'd popped over with a parcel I'd taken in for her that morning. What to Cathy, I'm sure, was no more than a brief how-do-you-do across the doormat, was to me more like a Christmas epiphany. At that point, of course, I had no idea we had anything more in common than a shared postcode. All I knew was that she had a smile that could have lit up Oxford Street.

Perhaps things were looking up at last?

TERRIBLE TEACHING IS WHAT MAKES OXFORD SPECIAL

Giles Coren

DECEMBER 10 2016

YOU'LL HAVE SEEN the story last week about a graduate of Brasenose College, Oxford, suing his alma mater for a million pounds because "appallingly bad" and "boring" teaching in his third year led to his getting a second-class degree in modern history when he felt he deserved a first. This in turn led to his not becoming a big-shot commercial lawyer but only some other kind of lawyer, which led to his having less money, a smaller house, a shabbier car, a worse life, a shorter penis and issues around sleeplessness, much of it to do with recurrent stress dreams about the exam result that doomed him to a life of misery.

Faiz Siddiqui took the exams fully 16 years ago. And the case raises so many questions that my own tiny mind has been boggling ever since.

We all have moments when we lie awake at night, wondering

about the life we might have had if certain things had not gone wrong. For me it was not going to Nick Rayne's 13th birthday party in 1982 because I was scared there would be girls there, and subsequently finding out that there had been girls there and that everyone had snogged them and I'd totally missed out on the chance to begin my sex life, a setback from which I have never fully recovered.

Also not taking up the offer of an exchange year at an American high school when I was 17 and then finding out that the guy who went instead of me was beating hot chicks away with a muddy stick because of his English accent.

Also going up to Oxford with a girlfriend and then staying with her for two years when I should have been shagging around like every other student in the world, with the result that I got to my 21st birthday having shagged almost nobody.

But that's sex, which is very important. Whereas to lose sleep in adulthood regretting the teaching you got in your third year? That is stone-cold mental. I can't even remember the name of the mad old coot who supervised my third-year special paper. It was meant to be on WB Yeats but he spent eight weeks and 14 bottles of sherry trying to persuade me to change over to TS Eliot, whom he had known well, and then that was the end of term. "Appallingly bad" and "boring" do not even begin to cover it. But I have scarcely given it a thought since, let alone worried what kind of lawyer I might have made if the lazy old bastard had been better at his job.

Who even knew there was more than one kind of lawyer? Or that the class of degree you get affects which kind you become? Do they not all lead lives of quiet photocopying in dusty offices, commute from the suburbs and then retire at 50 to play golf? What on earth has the quality of Oxford teaching got to do with it?

Maybe the problem stems from Mr Siddiqui being of foreign origin and somehow mistakenly equating Oxford University with "learning" and "teaching" and getting value for money. We British johnnies who make up the majority of undergraduates, or did in my day, never gave that a second thought. One goes to Oxford precisely *because* the teaching is rubbish, nothing is compulsory, tutorials are optional after the first week and nobody ever, ever talks about careers.

If you want to be "taught" and pass exams and become a lawyer, don't you go to a red-brick? Or Cambridge? Oxford is for drinking and playing tennis and nicking books out of the Bod under your cricket jumper and lobbing them at punting tourists from Magdalen Bridge. If you ask me, Mr Siddiqui got the wrong end of the stick altogether with his tertiary education and is now just embarrassing himself. After all, if it comes to suing the old place for getting you the wrong exam results I would do the same: take them to the cleaners for having, quite ridiculously, awarded me a first.

Complete farrago. I never read a book in three years, just flicked through some Coles Notes during the summer term whenever our chaps were batting and got lucky with the questions in the old summer quiz. And it cursed me for life: everyone for ever afterwards expecting me to be some sort of genius when I am in truth — as you, dear readers, know better than anyone — a total moron.

"Oh here comes Giles with his big shiny First Class Degree From Oxford," people go. "We'll ask him what he thinks about this weighty matter." And then it turns out I have nothing between my ears but sawdust and can only respond with silly faces and fart noises.

Great things were expected of me as a young man on account of my wholly inappropriate degree, but look where I have ended up: in a job where most of the better-known proponents — your Caitlin Morans, your Clarksons and Charlie Brookers and AA Gills — barely even went to school, let alone got as far as the Oxford University Summer Term Spelling Bee.

You think that you never got to be a big-shot commercial lawyer, Mr Siddiqui, because bum teaching diddled you out of a first. But what's my excuse? I endlessly tell people that finals are all down to luck, getting the right questions and not having too bad a hangover on the day. There's no escaping the lifelong blight of the big "1", and forever being looked at askance for having come to nothing more than this tap-dancing media monkey you see before you.

And I'll tell you the worst of it: even when you do get a first the nightmares still haunt you. Every time I get into a stressful situation with what I pathetically call "work", I experience terrible anxiety dreams where it's six weeks to go until finals and I haven't done a blessed thing ... and I wake up all drenched in sweat.

So take heart, Faiz old bean, from the knowledge that even with the class of degree you dreamed of, you would have ended up with the same boring job and the same terrible nightmares for the rest of your life. That is the flaw in the whole ridiculous system: even success doesn't cure you. So you're better off beating yourself up about all the sex you didn't have because you were too busy worrying about exams than bringing stupid legal actions about the exams themselves.

CHILDREN KILLED IN DUTERTE'S DRUG WAR

Richard Lloyd Parry, Manila

December 17 2016

Francis was an irrepressible little boy, a laughing, jiggling joker who was always the first to wake up in the tiny room he shared with his family. His mother, Elizabeth Mañosca, made him sleep next to the door so that he could bounce out in the morning, leaving his parents undisturbed. She never imagined that she was placing him in the line of fire of the deadly struggle convulsing the Philippines.

It happened last Sunday, when Elizabeth was deep asleep. She became dimly conscious of a knock on the door in the night and of her husband's raised voice. Then two shots rang out. Jolted awake, she confronted an unimaginable scene. There were two bullet holes in the flimsy plywood wall next to which Francis slept; her husband and son were dying.

"I was in shock," says Elizabeth, who is nine months pregnant and nursing a one-year-old girl. "Even though he was on the floor, I was shaking my husband and saying, 'Go after them! They got our boy.'"

Today father and son lie side by side in open coffins in the Barangay Santo slum of Manila. The hole in six-year-old Francis's forehead is crudely plugged with mortician's putty. The police showed little interest in identifying the killer but Elizabeth has few doubts about what happened. Her husband Domingo, 44, was a bicycle taxi driver with no obvious enemies. But he was also a user and part-time dealer of crystal methamphetamine, the drug known as shabu, a suicidal occupation in today's Philippines.

Since the coming to power of Rodrigo Duterte, the provincial mayor who was decisively elected president in May, more than 6,000 people have been killed across the country in similar bloody scenes. Some were professional dealers; many more, like Domingo Mañosca, were small-scale "drug personalities", as they are known in the Philippines. But plenty, like Francis, were innocent bystanders.

About a third of the killings have been carried out by police officers, who invariably report that they fired in self-defence having been shot at first. The rest, like this one, are carried out by vigilantes, widely believed to be acting in co-ordination with the police. They are shot as they sleep, or dumped at roadsides with hands bound and heads swaddled in masking tape, bearing signs of torture. Sometimes the killers leave messages scrawled on cardboard promising a similar fate to other pushers.

Between Mr Duterte's inauguration on June 30 and this week, 6,095 killings have been tallied, an average of 37 a day. No criminal charges have yet been brought. The number of deaths already surpasses that in the devastating Typhoon Haiyan, which destroyed the town of Tacloban in 2013, and the 3,000 political activists reckoned to have been killed by the dictator, Ferdinand Marcos, under martial law in the 1970s.

"We can't keep up," says Chito Gascon, head of the Commission for Human Rights (CHR), a constitutionally mandated organisation with 60 investigators working on the extra-judicial killings. "We're on top of 470 cases but 90 per cent are beyond our capacity."

Most remarkable of all, the bloodshed has been carried out on the direct orders of President Duterte, for whom the literal extermination of the drug trade is the fulfilment of his central election promise. Having sometimes denied it in the past, this week he admitted that as mayor of Davao he participated in the work of the city's death squads, who killed more than 1,000 people under his administration.

"In Davao I used to do it personally," he told an audience in the presidential palace on Monday. "Just to show to them [police] that if I can do it, why can't you? I [would] go around in Davao [on] a big bike, and I would just patrol the streets and [look] for trouble. I was really looking for an encounter to kill."

The president claims that drugs are destroying the country. In his state of the union address he claimed that the Philippines had 3.7 million drug addicts. In September he said: "Hitler massacred three million Jews. Now, there are three million drug addicts. I'd be happy to slaughter them." His figures are undermined by the official statistics. The Dangerous Drugs Board counts only 1.8 million users. Far from being addicts, a third of these have used drugs only once in 13 months; fewer than half of them have ever used shabu.

Similarly, the government's claims that 75 per cent of "heinous" crime is drug-related is contradicted by its own statisticians, who put the figure at 15 per cent. But so strong is his determination that Mr Duterte has promised a presidential pardon to any police officer convicted in connection with the "war on drugs".

With such a guarantee, the authorities are displaying an

almost contemptuous carelessness. A 28-year-old fruit seller named Elfren Morillo, who took a bullet through the chest, survived by pretending to be dead. He reports that he and four friends were shot at close range by police officers who planted drugs and guns on their bodies.

Harra Kazou, a 26-year-old mother, was told that her partner had been shot along with his father-in-law after he tried to grab an officer's gun while under arrest inside a police station; the autopsy showed that he had a broken arm and other signs of torture. She is now under the protection of the CHR, which has run out of room to shelter frightened witnesses.

The officers accused of killing Ms Kazou's partner are, at least, under formal investigation. But increasingly, human rights campaigners such as Mr Gascon place their hopes for justice in the future, when another president, or the International Criminal Court, may act on evidence being gathered now. "If we fail, it's going to be a long winter," he says. "But we amass the evidence for when spring comes — if it ever comes."

Polls show that despite his bloody methods, Mr Duterte's drug war is popular among Filipinos. His overall approval rating is 63 per cent, according to one poll yesterday.

Anecdotal evidence suggests, not surprisingly, that drug activity on the streets has diminished but whether the problem is being eliminated is unclear. There have been no busts of drug kingpins. Most of those killed are poor men who use them to numb the hardships of poverty. Beyond the tally of victims is an uncountable number of family members and dependants, many of them women and children.

Elizabeth Mañosca is suddenly widowed, without work or assets, with a one-year-old baby and a new one due any moment. "I am afraid about the future," she says, "but more than that I am angry about my boy. He was so full of life — he was a lovely child."

ZSA ZSA GÁBOR

Obituary

DECEMBER 19 2016

PROVIDED THAT YOU were not married to Zsa Zsa Gábor — and many people were — she could be a lot of fun. Long before reality television she was proof that you could become famous for being famous. She may not have had much talent as an actress, but she did for being a celebrity. One wanted Zsa Zsa Gábor to play Zsa Zsa Gábor, right down to the pink mink and the diamonds and the Hungarian inflections. That, "dahlink", was the role of a lifetime.

It was the husbands, all nine of them, for which Gábor was best known. For each she had a pithy quip that disabused anyone who might have thought her motives were not purely mercenary. "I'm a marvellous housekeeper," she loved to say. "Every time I leave a man, I keep his house."

"I never hated a man enough to give him back his diamonds," was another gem. At her Los Angeles home, 1001 Bel Air Road, in a house built by Howard Hughes and owned by Elvis Presley, she kept a cushion embroidered with her favourite epigram: "Never complain, never explain." Presumably somewhere else there was one with the line about the fool and his money.

Of course, Gábor did only what most women had had to do down the ages, obtaining security by trading what it was that men liked about her. She grasped what that was from an early age. "Daddy used to hold poker games with his friends," she told Wendy Leigh, who ghosted her memoir *One Lifetime is Not Enough*. "He would make me parade around the table and let each of them pat my ass."

Her father, Vilmos, was a diamond dealer in Budapest, then in the Austro-Hungarian Empire, where she was born in 1917. The chief influence on her, however, was her ferociously ambitious mother, Jolie, who lived to be 100. She was determined that her three glamorous daughters, Magda, Sári

— as Zsa Zsa was christened — and Eva would make their fortunes. The sisters would rack up 17 divorces between them.

Zsa Zsa was sent to a Swiss boarding school and made her stage debut in Vienna at 16, supposedly having been discovered by the singer Richard Tauber. She and Eva claimed to have been crowned Miss Hungary, but as Cindy Adams, who wrote Jolie Gábor's autobiography, cautioned: "There was never any truth to anything." For example, Jolie and her daughters were Jewish, but ostentatiously wore diamond crosses.

In about 1937, when she was 20, Zsa Zsa met a 50-year-old Turkish diplomat and intellectual, Burhan Belge. She said that he had joked that he would make her part of his harem if she were a little older. Accordingly, when a few months had passed, she turned up on his doorstep in Ankara with her terrier Mishka, which her father wanted out of the house. The marriage, such as it was, foundered within six months. Gábor claimed that this was because she had had an affair with Kemal Atatürk, the founder of modern Turkey. More plausibly, by then she had a diplomatic passport that, with war looming and the Nazis threatening Jews, allowed her to enter the US. Her sisters and mother joined her.

By now she had swelled into a chic if bosomy blonde, a Dresden shepherdess with an iron will. When she arrived in Hollywood in 1941, she had only an introduction to Basil Rathbone, the screen's Sherlock Holmes. Within a few months she was engaged to Conrad Hilton, the multimillionaire founder of the hotel chain. They had a daughter, Francesca, her only child, but the marriage was rocky for the five years that it lasted. "It was a little like holding a roman candle," Hilton recalled. "Beautiful, exciting, but you were never sure when it would go out."

Gábor described their relationship as a fiasco. "He thought that I was after his money," she protested. She did admit to a fling with her stepson Nicky, who would marry Elizabeth Taylor.

Next up, in 1949, was George Sanders, suave star of the *Saint* films and *Rebecca*. ("I'm madly in love with you," she said when they first met. "How well I understand you, my dear," he replied.) In his *Memoirs of a Professional Cad*, Sanders made light of his five-year marriage to Gábor, but in fact it was disfigured by his violent jealousy.

This was demonstrated by her flagrant affair with the splendidly endowed playboy Porfirio Rubirosa, who may have been Gábor's only real love. She said Sanders was once so aggrieved that he dangled her out of a window by her dress; fortunately it was made by Balenciaga so did not fray. The evidence that Sanders did love her was perhaps his later, very brief, marriage to her sister Magda shortly before he committed suicide.

Zsa Zsa claimed that he was also jealous of her success as an actress, although in truth there was little of that. Her sister Eva did make a career on the screen, for instance as the voice of the Duchess in Disney's *The Aristocats*. Apart from starring roles in the Toulouse-Lautrec biopic *Moulin Rouge* (1952) and *Queen of Outer Space* (1958), Zsa Zsa was confined to small parts in films including *Touch of Evil* with Orson Welles. Later there were cameos on television in shows such as *Batman*, and in the sequel to the film spoof *The Naked Gun*.

Her fourth husband was Herbert Hutner, an investment banker. They were engaged in 1962 on their third date, her decision to accept perhaps influenced by the $3 million ring he had sent her after the second ("Daddy told me never to settle for less than ten carats"). Hutner lasted four years, for much of which Gábor was still dallying with Rubirosa, who was killed in 1965 speeding through Paris in his Ferrari. Husband No 5, in 1966, was Joshua Cosden, an oil heir. "I had gone into the marriage not really knowing him," said Gábor, when she came out the other side, after a year. "I left none the wiser."

"I know nothing about sex," she also said, "because I was always married." Neither of those claims was true, and she spent the decade until her next wedding entertaining Frank Sinatra, Richard Burton and Sean Connery, among others. These apparently included Richard Nixon. "A great mind. A big brain," she recalled, hinting that that was not the biggest thing about "Tricky Dicky".

In 1975, ensconced in Bel Air with her nine shih tzus — Pasha Effendi, Genghis Khan and Macho Man among them — she married her neighbour, Jack Ryan. The designer of the Ken and Barbie dolls had a penchant for swingers' parties and was followed in matrimony after a year by the lawyer who handled their divorce, Michael O'Hara. Gábor's eighth husband, Felipe de Alba, a property developer, lasted only a day after their wedding in international waters in 1983. There was some doubt whether she was still married to O'Hara and, in any event, "he wouldn't have made a nice pet".

Presumably on occasion she was upset by some of these failures. Yet unlike, say, Pamela Harriman, Winston Churchill's daughter-in-law, who also made a career of snaring rich men, she was not a thwarted romantic. Nor was self-pity her style, any more than it was Scarlett O'Hara's. "A girl must marry for love — and keep on marrying until she finds it," Gábor held. She found her match in 1986 in Frédéric Prinz von Anhalt. Not the name he was born with, Prinz von Anhalt changed his surname after being adopted as an adult by Kaiser Wilhelm's daughter-in-law. Previously he had run a sauna. Perhaps Gábor fell for the bogus title, or just for someone with as much chutzpah as her. Having hired a Rolls-Royce to convince her he was rich, and then showed his class by giving her champagne to drink, he soon moved into her $10 million mansion.

His new bride was rising 70 and, as her behaviour became more erratic, she began to need someone to see to her care. In 1989 she was jailed for three days after slapping a policeman who had stopped her for driving with an expired licence. Four years later a jury ordered her to pay Elke Sommer $2 million in libel damages after a long feud in which Gábor alleged that the German star was bankrupt.

In 2002 Gábor was left partially paralysed when a car driven by her hairdresser crashed. Having to use a wheelchair was said to have depressed her, as did the discovery that her daughter had fraudulently obtained a $2 million loan secured against her house. A lawsuit was dropped at the last moment. Francesca Hilton died in 2015.

"The secret to a long marriage is infidelity," Prinz von Anhalt told the *Daily Express* in 2008, gallantly confiding to its readers that he had enjoyed a ten-year affair with Anna Nicole Smith, the former *Playboy* centrefold. Whatever the spark was — he and Gábor liked to watch the film *Babe*, about a talking pig — they remained married for three decades until her death.

Her old age was marred by ill health, which stripped from her the last vestiges of glamour. She had several strokes, broke a hip and had to have a leg amputated — because she was paralysed she only discovered this a year later. She was also rumoured to have lost millions in Bernie Madoff's Ponzi scheme.

By the end, perhaps Zsa Zsa Gábor had accepted that one lifetime was enough for anyone, at least to learn the important things in life. "The only place a man wants depth in a woman," she concluded, "is in her décolletage."

Zsa Zsa Gábor, celebrity, was born on February 6, 1917. She died of a heart attack on December 18, 2016, aged 99

CASH BELONGS IN THE PAST SO LET'S ABOLISH IT

Ed Conway

DECEMBER 23 2016

EVERY SO OFTEN newspaper columnists recycle their old ideas. Since this is the time of year for reflection and frank admissions, we should fess up. While I try to keep that kind of thing to a minimum, I admit that there is one idea I've written about more than once in the past.

We should abolish cash: every coin in circulation, every note in every bank and cash machine around the country. I love this idea for three reasons. First, however radical it may sound, it makes a lot of economic sense: no cash means no hoarding if interest rates drop below zero, which means the economy can recover faster in the wake of a financial crisis. Second, doing so would represent a hammer blow to the black market and the corrupt criminals and cronies who benefit from the anonymity of paper money.

But the best thing about this idea is that it's always relevant. After all, while the odd dictator and bankrupt nation — the Soviet Union, North Korea, Burma, for instance — has cancelled banknotes once or twice, this isn't the kind of thing we expect from a sane government. Or so I thought until last month, when India embarked on one of the most controversial experiments in monetary history. On the same day as the US presidential election (a good day, if ever there was one, to bury bad news), the prime minister, Narendra Modi, popped up on TV to announce the cancellation of all 500 and 1,000 rupee banknotes in circulation.

To put that into perspective, those two notes, the highest denomination ones in the country, account for about 86 per cent of the country's entire stock of physical money.

Now, this wasn't an all-out monetary bonfire. The decommissioned banknotes will eventually be replaced with a new run of notes, including a 2,000 rupee version. No one loses money provided they exchange their notes at their local bank.

This was, the prime minister explained, all about clamping down on the corruption and criminality that has plagued the country for decades. India's reliance on anonymous, untraceable cash, which accounts for 98 per cent of transactions — compared with less than half in the UK — does indeed mean that those who seek to launder and hide their ill-gotten gains can do so more easily. This is a country where houses are sometimes paid for with suitcases of money.

Demonetisation, as it is being called, will supposedly smoke out those who keep their money in the black market, which accounts for between 20 per cent and 60 per cent of gross domestic product, depending on whose figures you trust.

On the face of it, this all sounds very compelling. High denomination banknotes are catnip for criminals — one of the reasons why comparatively few £50 and €500 notes circulate even after having been issued. And in the days after the announcement, economists lined up to congratulate Mr Modi on his decision. If only, they added, western leaders could be so bold.

Then, as so often happens in India, the whole thing descended into a frightful muddle: queues outside banks and money-changing facilities, money being stripped out of mattresses and a sudden collapse in economic activity. Part of the chaos was due to the fact that the Reserve Bank of India isn't able to print the new notes fast enough to replace the ones coming out of circulation. The deadline for consumers to hand in their old notes is a week today, but it will take many more months for the new notes to hit the streets.

The deeper problem is that so few Indians use the banking system, so they cannot exchange their money. Less than half the population deposited money in a bank account in the most recent year; in most countries the proportion is closer to 90 per cent. For this reason alone, it is hard to think of a country less suited to the abolition of cash than India.

The real victims of demonetisation are not wealthy ne'er-do-wells, who long ago shifted their money out of cash and into other currencies and assets: gold, Treasury bonds, apartments in London and New York. No, the real victims are, as so often, the poor. Rural wage growth has now collapsed; wider economic growth and investment has dropped sharply. And no surprise. For in economic terms, Mr Modi's policy is, as one Indian economist put it, a little like withdrawing 85 per cent of the blood from a patient's body and only replacing it slowly, a few drops at a time.

The upshot is that, for the time being, schemes like this will probably remain the preserve of crackpot economies. As if to underline this, a few weeks ago the Venezuelan president, Nicolas Maduro, cancelled a swathe of banknotes in his own benighted country.

This is a shame, for there is much to be said for demonetisation — in the right circumstances. In developed economies with complex financial systems, where most transactions are processed electronically, via credit cards, contactless payments and bank-to-bank transfers, cash is increasingly irrelevant. What was once a critical means of exchange is increasingly the resort of the paranoid, the criminal, the tax evader.

India is an example of how not to do it, but handled right, handled gradually and sensitively, with safeguards to ensure savings are protected and all of society can carry on spending, demonetisation could work in the UK. Let's start gently: abolish the £50 note and take it from there.

WILD SWIMMING IS A RARE SPLASH OF FREEDOM

Edward Lucas

DECEMBER 26 2016

URBAN CIVILISATION has many advantages. But it also chafes. So most mornings I shed my clean, comfy and well-regulated life, along with my clothes, for a dose of discomfort, dirt and mild danger.

It takes the form of a brisk swim amid waterfowl and weeds in the Serpentine, the man-made lake that spans Hyde Park and Kensington Gardens. To the outsider the conditions might seem spartan. The water temperature is about 4C. The facilities comprise a cramped, unisex changing room and a cold outdoor shower. Wetsuits are frowned upon.

This may sound like the morning routine at a harshly run

boarding school. But for club members, it is an earthly paradise.

Part of the reason is a simple physiological response. All exercise lifts the spirits and immersion in cold water has extra benefits. As the body senses danger it sends neurotransmitters racing round the bloodstream, increasing alertness and producing waves of euphoria. Ice baths are now the treatment of choice for sports stars such as Mo Farah, Andy Murray and the England rugby union team.

The aesthetics are good too. At this time of year, a glint of sunlight bounces off the mist and sparkles on the ripples. Swimming backstroke, you see sky, swans and the last tints of autumn hanging on the trees.

The worries of the day ahead melt away with each stroke. You focus on breathing, the angle of your stroke, the kick of your feet, the distance travelled. If you are lucky, you may see a carp flit under you or a bat overhead. JM Barrie's Peter Pan seems a plausible presence. The ducks, geese and swans look at you incuriously, far closer than you would ever see them on land.

But there are deeper pleasures too. The Serpentine is unsupervised. The only strict rules are about not swimming under the ice, or during thunderstorms. Other regulations — about where you can swim and when you must be out of the water — are obeyed, but not enforced. In short, you can drown if you want to.

Such trust and freedom are rare privileges these days. Modern life shields us from the risk of potential unpleasantness, at the price of strictly enforced rules. But when you join the Serpentine swimmers, you sign up for the risks, including "serious injury, heart attack, infection, drowning or accident". A separate, well-lawyered clause absolves the Department for Environment, Food and Rural Affairs of any liability for infection with salmonellosis, shigellosis, amoebic dysentery, poliomyelitis, hepatitis, streptococci pseudomonas or staphylococci. It adds leadenly: "These are only some of the possibilities; there are others, including Weil's disease and botulism."

As it happens, my fellow club members — who range from the superfit to the podgy — all seem exceptionally healthy. We may imbibe the odd accidental mouthful, but nobody can recall any serious illness caused by swimming in the Serpentine's admittedly murky waters. A bit of duck poo in the water (or in the worst case sticking to your swimsuit) adds to the feeling of authenticity.

Newcomers do get friendly advice about not swimming too far away from the enclosed area in the coldest weather. First-aiders abound, with a particular emphasis on how to deal with hypothermia (don't wrap the victim in an insulating foil blanket: it will keep the warmth out and the cold in). The real point is that you are allowed to judge the risks yourself and that almost everyone does so sensibly.

That gives "wild swimming", as its devotees call it, a counter-cultural tinge. After a few months of the Serpentine, my local indoor municipal swimming pool seemed unbearably regimented. The chlorinated water was cloyingly warm and tasted like medicine. The eagle-eyed lifeguard and the strict rules against running, jumping and diving squeezed most of the fun out. Scowling fitness freaks made it abundantly clear that I did not belong in the fast lane, while the rest of the pool was too crowded to enjoy.

"Serpies", as we are called, are a self-policing community.

Co-operating with other people in a small space (the changing room is half the size of a squash court) fuels considerate behaviour. You keep your possessions on one peg, change neatly and discreetly, make space for others and avoid loud cliquey conversations.

We need more of this sort of thing. The law — thanks to a landmark judgment in 2005 — is on our side. In that case, the swimmers in Hampstead Ponds won the right to swim unsupervised early in the morning (The Corporation of London wanted to ban swimming unless a lifeguard was present). The Health and Safety Executive says, quite reasonably: "If people choose to swim in places like ponds or lakes then it is normally reasonable to expect them to take responsibility for their own safety." Moreover, almost every attempt to sue landowners for accidents arising out of swimming has failed.

Whereas swimming is in overall decline in Britain, the open-water variety is hugely popular. A splendid inland bathing beach has opened at the Rutland Water reservoir. The Lake District is a swimmer's dream; aficionados have favoured spots on the rivers Dart, Stour, Nene and Trent. The Lower Ddwli Falls in the Brecon Beacons is one of 20 idyllic bathing spots on the Fechan and Mellte rivers.

But all too often officious caution prevails among guardians of our welfare. As the author Chris Ayriss argues in his book *Hung out to Dry*, Britain lags way behind other countries in its approach to aquatic freedom. We have barely a dozen officially designated inland swimming locations. Germany has 1,900 and France 1,300. Yet figures for drowning are almost the same. Though whirlpool baths (especially when drunk) are far riskier, outdoor swimming is unfairly stigmatised as dangerous, an approach epitomised by the Royal Life Saving Society's killjoy slogan: "Don't get in, you might not get out."

We should be encouraging the opposite: Get in, you don't know what you are missing. You exercise not only your muscles, but the freedom and responsibility that our forebears took for granted. Use them or lose them.

CHILDREN OF THE INTERNET ARE HAPPY TO LIVE A LIE

Oliver Moody

DECEMBER 27 2016

FAKE NEWS HAS an awful lot in common with online pornography. Both are Technicolor illusions that owe their appeal to looking truer than the truth. Both are threats to the supremacy of established media organisations. And both, it seems, will soon have been subject to failed attempts at regulation by people who think they know it when they see it.

In Germany, a large part of Angela Merkel's party wants to make the spreading of fake news a crime. The British government says it is "considering the implications" of the phenomenon and may not be far behind. Last month the internet unhinged itself with reports that Facebook was testing its credibility scores for articles, until that too turned out to be fake news.

Everyone agrees that somebody, somewhere, ought to do something to shelter the public from this polluted deluge of information. The account of "post-truth" that has been told over and over again this year is that lying politicians and a lying press have abused people's trust so badly and so repeatedly that it is hardly surprising if they should seek out other versions of events.

But what if this story is wrong? What if intervening to protect people from baseless clickbait would be more than an incursion into freedom of speech — what if it might actually make things worse? A study from Stanford University suggests that the problem runs much deeper than is generally thought. The fault lies not so much in Moscow or Palo Alto as within our own minds.

The researchers found that 80 per cent of middle-school pupils could not tell an online news story apart from a piece of native advertising that had been sponsored by a bank. A third of high-schoolers endorsed a fake news tweet about Donald Trump's polling data over a genuine tweet from Fox News. University students did little better. "Overall," the academics wrote, "young people's ability to reason about the information on the internet can be summed up in one word: bleak."

The findings matter to everyone. These teenagers are the children of the internet. They have also grown up with a comparatively clean species of public life. Their political consciousness has been defined by the presidency of Barack Obama. For them, the words Watergate, Monica Lewinsky and

45 minutes are historical phrases. It is not that these young people have been jaded by decades of spin and mendacity. It is simply that they cannot — or, worse, will not — discern fact from fiction, or reporting from advertising. They do not have the mental wherewithal to find their way around the modern world.

This is unusual. For most of history the human nose for nonsense has been about as keen as it had to be. The impulse to make a bad thing sound good is probably almost as old as language, and since the emergence of the first democracy 2,600 years ago the public has been locked in a verbal arms race with the people who wanted to be their masters.

The ancient Athenians dedicated an entire science to the dissection of rhetoric. The Romans raised propaganda to an art form, with Cicero's brother publishing a treatise on pamphleteering and the emperor Augustus cladding his soundbites in marble and the hexameters of star poets. The American Revolution and the Great Reform Acts in Britain were followed by huge improvements in the education systems of both countries.

We used to keep up, more or less, with the diet of misinformation we were fed. And now we don't. The post-truth age is not an age in which politicians and journalists have suddenly begun to lie with abandon. It is one in which it no longer matters if they get caught.

What has changed? It is hard to think of an answer that does not start with the boundless and trackless ocean of stuff on the internet, and on social networks in particular. But there are older cultural forces at play, too. Over the past half-century the argument from authority has died a slow death. The simple fact that things are printed in *The Times* or uttered by a secretary of state is no longer regarded as any sort of indication that they are true.

This is not necessarily a bad thing. It was never an irrefutable argument anyway. But into its place has crept something much worse: a shrugging indifference that would be called nihilism if only it had the intellectual energy. If there is no universal authority and everything you read is flawed, you may as well just read things you agree with.

It is not truth that has died in the post-truth world: it is our appetite for truth. The only proper response is to get it back. So teach young people source criticism. Teach them statistics. Teach them about cognitive bias. Teach them the virtues and the pitfalls of expertise. Teach them to cover newspaper editorials in red pen marks. Teach them to fill their ears with things they don't want to hear. Teach them, above all, to mistrust the little voice that says something must be right — because it probably isn't.

In the end we must all be as responsible for our own critical thinking as we are for our votes. No one else can save you. Not Angela Merkel and not Mark Zuckerberg. Not some factory of penny-a-click magical realism in Macedonia. Not even David Aaronovitch. It's just you, on your own, against a fathomless tide of scarcely differentiated truths and lies, clichés and insight, omission and distortion and clarity. Best of luck.

HOW I CONQUERED MY MORBID FEAR OF FLYING

Melanie Phillips

DECEMBER 27 2016

EVEN WITHOUT STRIKE action or weather delays, getting through an airport can be a miserable impediment to an appropriate holiday mood. The endless queues, the screaming children and the tedious security checks constitute an ordeal to be dreaded.

For many years I would think wistfully about how much I would like to experience the airport ordeal. For I was for several decades paralysed by fear of flying.

It's hard adequately to describe the devastating, overwhelming symptoms of this fear. It's a conflation of claustrophobia, vertigo and agoraphobia in one triple whammy of hyperventilating, heart-fluttering, cold-sweating terror.

For many years I simply never got on a plane. I went everywhere by car, rail or boat. Eventually the restrictions became too irksome. Holidays in Brittany began to lose their appeal. The family wanted to go to California. There was a business trip to Spain I couldn't dodge. So I forced myself to start flying.

It was hell. Every sound the plane made, every change in the engine note (and I was sensitive to the slightest alteration of timbre), every vibration and of course every bump was a source of fresh terror.

What exactly are you frightened of, people would ask. Take-off? Landing? Turbulence? All of them.

Actually, in some ways it was worse at cruising altitude with no turbulence. That was when, with the plane appearing to glide along with no effort, the sheer unnaturalness of it and the feeling that inside this metal shell I was simply suspended in nothingness would become overwhelming. I would talk compulsively to the poor soul sitting next to me. Sometimes I would involuntarily clutch their arm in terror. Much worse than the resulting embarrassment was finding that this passenger might be sitting with eyes clenched shut and lips moving in prayer.

In those unguarded days before 9/11, crews would take frightened fliers into the cockpit. Unfortunately, this made it even worse. The view from the wide windows was simply horrifying, just a white or blue void into which we were steadily plunging.

Patiently, I was told how safe flying was. The odds of a plane crash are one for every 1.2 million flights, with the odds of dying put at one in 11 million. By contrast, your chances of dying in a car or traffic accident are one in 5,000. Even on flights that crash, 95.7 per cent of passengers survive.

So did that help? No. Factual evidence cannot address a phobia that is, by definition, irrational. About 30 per cent of the population, including some very well-known folk, are said to have a fear of flying. That didn't help either. The fact that so many people were terrified of this activity must surely prove that there was something wrong with it after all.

There are clinics that treat this particular phobia. I wouldn't go near them in case they might persuade me that flying was safe. For similar reasons I wouldn't take any medication to get me through the flight. This was because I believed my fear was well founded. It had to be; otherwise why would I be frightened? So it followed from this that if I was persuaded otherwise or had my fears subdued by drugs, I would be putting myself in danger by flying. Sounds crazy? It was an aspect of the phobia.

Today, though, I am a frequent, and relatively tranquil, flier. So how did I crack it?

A number of things helped. I used a flight relaxation tape, which played all the sounds associated with flying and required you to relax every muscle when particular sounds provoked most alarm. The concentration required to do this on the plane helped to distract from the terror.

A book published by one of the suspect clinics turned out to be excellent. It not only taught me about aerodynamics but got right inside the phobia. You think that what's outside the plane window is nothingness, it said, but it's not nothingness; it's air, and air is a substance with properties, like water, and it has currents, just like the sea.

Obvious to some, maybe; but for me it helped to deal with that terrible feeling at 35,000ft that you have lost all connection with the world and are adrift in a terrifying emptiness.

British Airways crews were not only kind, but their high professionalism was immensely reassuring. So much of the fear of flying is about the lack of control and absence of trust. I trusted BA pilots because of their wonderful British voices on the intercom, calm and clear with slightly flattened classless vowels.

They would chattily run through things such as altitude, weather and arrival time and then they'd say, "And you might also like to know that at Lord's, England are now 106 for three". A plane flown by such a pilot just couldn't fall out of the sky. The problem was that, while BA got me to fly, I thought planes would fall out of the sky if they weren't flown by BA.

I suppose the real reason I eventually overcame this phobia was that I finally accepted that the problem wasn't with the planes; it was with me. I realised it was wrapped up with other anxieties. Only then was I able to get the risk thing into perspective.

It also got better the more I flew. Indeed, there were aspects I started to enjoy, such as being insulated against the world for a few hours, out of reach of the tyranny of the phone or the relentless emails. Somehow, though, I don't think I'll be volunteering for a seat on Richard Branson's Virgin Galactic SpaceShipTwo.

YEAR OF REVOLUTION

Leading Article

December 30 2016

New year has conventionally been a time of hope, a moment to count blessings and make promises soon to be broken. The arrival of 2017, however, will be greeted not with a sense of release but of trepidation. Do the shocks, setbacks and slaughter of this dying year signal a new cycle of upheaval, an age of anger and anxiety? If so, one might reasonably ask someone in authority to show us the way to the underground bunker.

There have, of course, been other years of spectacular change. 1968 turned out to be a reckoning with the postwar generation. The botched Suez operation and the squashing of the Hungarian revolution in 1956 flagged up Britain's lack of imperial clout and the western reluctance to confront Soviet power; it was a year in which we had to accept our limitations.

To find the appropriate historical analogy for 2016, to capture its ambiguities and chilling uncertainties, one has to go farther back, to 1848, the Spring of Nations. It was a time when technological change was shaking up the lives of workers, when government was seen to be remote, when nationalists rejected the rule of empires. Revolt was in the air. It was the year when Karl Marx and Friedrich Engels wrote the Communist Manifesto and when a politically inexperienced outsider, Zachary Taylor, became a shortlived president of the United States.

The tumult of 1848 did not last, even if it did sow the seeds of future change. By contrast 2016 is likely to be part of a rolling transformation of political institutions, and of geopolitical shifts. The many cracks opened up in 2016 will widen in 2017. The triggering of Article 50 in March will, despite Theresa May's advance notice, have a shock effect on the remaining EU members. They will almost certainly initiate attempts to make the union seem more credible and robust than it really is. The Brexit referendum exposed the large number of people who feel that they are no longer needed and sent them in search of tribal certainties and a more pronounced sense of nationhood.

Many EU governments are in denial that similar strains exist in their own societies. How then will the Dutch and the French answer these concerns in their parliamentary and presidential elections in the coming months? The European establishment still believes that the populist wave is an episode of temporary insanity, that with appropriate nods to the unemployed young or by handing out free Interrail cards, the union can return to the norm, that the pendulum will swing back to the old constitutional order and old party allegiances. They are wrong; in 2016 the geography of the centre ground changed fundamentally.

This was the year in which two deep-rooted grievances converged and found expression in a quiet electoral revolution. The first was local: decades of English resentment over the failings and presumptions of the EU, real and imagined, were amplified into a broad rejection of government by elites in favour of a dream of direct control of borders, immigration and legislation. The second was global. The rapid expansion of world trade since the Cold War has brought prosperity, but not to all. It is perceived as having chiefly enriched those "citizens of the world" whom Mrs May gratuitously derided in her Tory conference speech, leaving tens of millions on both sides of the Atlantic feeling ill-served by representative democracy.

The conventional explanation for this anti-globalisation insurgency holds that inequality is on the rise across the developed world. Inequality is in fact falling, at least in Britain and America. The insurgency is also fuelled by anger: a feeling that, eight years on, there has been no proper reckoning for the 2008 crash that wrecked so many blue-collar and middle-class livelihoods.

In Europe, the ancien régime has not surrendered. It pins its hopes on the German elections next autumn. The steadying hand of Angela Merkel, the country's subtly mixed electoral system and many safeguards, they calculate, will take the steam out of the insurgents. The anti-immigrant Alternative for Deutschland may notch up as much as 15 per cent of the vote but will stay out of government, a minority party among many. Similarly, many in the EU count on the British parliament removing the sting of Brexit. They are placing bets too on the Trump administration taking in the expertise and careful instincts of consensual Republicans.

This amounts to little more than a game of blind man's bluff. It ignores the engine of change in Europe: the throb of anxiety about immigration and the assimilation of newcomers. The tragedy of Aleppo and Syria more widely will propel more refugees towards Europe. The chronic misgovernment of sub-Saharan Africa will dispatch many more thousands towards the people-smugglers of disintegrating Libya.

None of these problems was solved in 2016. A breakdown in the migration deal between Turkey and the EU would ensure that the migrant exodus would again reach the dizzying heights of 2015. This will keep the revolutionary fires burning. As long as there is no coherent way of defending the EU's external borders, its members will operate as if in a state of emergency.

The EU promised prosperity and security to its citizens; it offered less of both to Europeans in 2016. The combination of a banking and a political crisis in Italy could well translate into an existential crisis for the single currency. Meanwhile, the unresolved wars in Ukraine and Syria, both of which have given free rein to the military adventurism of Vladimir Putin, are likely to make the EU less safe. Alexis de Tocqueville, the 19th-century chronicler of revolution and democracy, presaged some of today's complacency: "It is an amazing thing, the exclusive feel of security in which all those tenants of the highest and middle storeys of the social edifice were living when the revolution broke out."

Britain will have to find new ways of anchoring its safety and its wealth. The relationship with the new US administration will need to be more transactional, less sentimental; one in which we agree to a division of labour, a common approach or, if the president decides to make a de facto ally out of Mr Putin, one where we are ready to criticise and speak out openly for the values of liberal democracy.

2016 wrongfooted pundits, pollsters and betting parlours yet it would be wrong to write it off as a chaotic interlude, or a uniquely polarising historical moment. It has ushered in a period of transformation in Britain, Europe, the US and perhaps even in the Middle East. Britons are being forced to look into a mirror, discover new strengths, revive a spirit of outward-looking enterprise. It will be a bracing rather than comfortable new year, but none the worse for it.

THE NHS IS IN NEED OF EMERGENCY TREATMENT

Janice Turner

JANUARY 7 2017

WHAT IS AN emergency? It is a question I've wrestled with lately, as my mother's illness coincided with a tough new NHS edict that only those with "life-threatening" conditions should turn to A&E. Ours was a very ordinary medical odyssey yet it made me fear that our crisis-stricken primary care system is a self-inflicted mess.

On Boxing Day my 93-year-old Yorkshire mother, who is visiting London, falls ill. It is a bank holiday so I call Seldoc, the out-of-hours service. A doctor is sent, a chest infection diagnosed, and antibiotics prescribed that disagree with her spectacularly. So two days later I call 111 and a random phone doctor tells her to stop taking them.

A day later she is no worse, has no fever, is breathing fine, eating a little. But I'm worried: she's weak and very old. Is she getting better? Does she need different pills? I've no idea. I call my GP surgery: could a doctor visit? The big-hearted receptionist laughs. They won't even register her as a temporary patient — so much for NHS tourism — and even if she was their patient they never do home visits. Take her to a walk-in clinic, she says. (But it's freezing and she can barely walk.) Or call an ambulance.

Now here lies the dilemma. Is my mother an emergency? My instinct is that she just needs a doctor to check her chest, write a prescription, then more bed-rest. Every ambulance call costs the NHS £300: it seems a stupid waste. So I ring 111 again, which — after a call handler takes me once more through 50 irrelevant questions — suggests I wait until 6.30pm when Seldoc kicks in. It is 10.30am. How crazy that the out-of-hours service is better than normal care!

So, because I am fortunate, I call a private GP. And, eventually, at about 10.30pm a suave Harley Street type pitches up and charges me £160 to say my mother isn't too bad but I should take her to A&E. Now? Couldn't we wait until morning? "Well, you could ...", he says, covering his elegant arse from malpractice suits.

And so we bundle her up and drive to A&E and at 4am, after a sleepless night of tests, she is sent home frailer than before ...

Why would anyone go to A&E unless they are truly ill? What a fiesta of Hieronymus Bosch tableaux. An obese woman bucks and screams on a trolley; a father chides his vomiting disabled son; an old, bald woman with dementia paces the corridor. And yet the patient ahead of us at triage says: "It's my shoulder, it's hurt for a few weeks, but it's worse today." Wouldn't you find a hot-water bottle, take ibuprofen — anything but spend a night here?

In 2013, the then NHS England medical director Sir Bruce Keogh declared that the work of an emergency department was "unbounded", covering problems of "all severities". Come one, come all. It was a licence for those with poorly shoulders, sore throats, even (reportedly) broken fingernails to turn up at A&E. And for surgeries like mine to dump its more costly, time-consuming duties on another health budget: home visits are at a GP's discretion. Now, overwhelmed with patients, the NHS struggles to reverse the Keogh doctrine amid budget cuts and an Amazon Prime I-want-it-now culture.

Anyway, three days later my ma got dressed, came downstairs, instructed me to book her return home, drank coffee with her grandson — and collapsed. She was unconscious for 15 minutes: I thought she was dying in my arms. Now she really was an emergency.

For 12 hours I sat with her playing A&E snakes and ladders, repeating her story to ten people, slowly moving up from nurse to registrar. I had time to reflect that it is nuts how ambulance crews must stay with patients until they're booked in, even if that means hanging around for four hours. No bloody wonder emergency call times are so long! In extremis, I learnt, a nurse may be put in charge so that crews can leave, but then there may not be enough spare trolleys for every ambulance.

I watched the drunks. “Hello, Manuel,” said a weary nurse to a burly, staggering man flanked by police officers. Could Manuel be held in a side ward? The nurse protested, then gave in. Three in ten A&E admissions are alcohol-related and they are messy, troublesome and often violent. The police are reluctant to arrest the drunk and disorderly in case they get ill in custody, so take them straight to A&E. Drinkers treat 999 like an Uber app, careless with their safety, knowing they’ll be scooped from the gutter. Why not create drunk tanks, overseen by nurses and alcohol counsellors, where they can dry out and pay a hefty medical bill to be released?

After 12 hours the registrar said that my mother had merely fainted and could be discharged. He prescribed antibiotics, the very drugs to which she’d had the bad reaction. She had scaled the A&E ladders only to be thrown down a snake. If she collapsed again tomorrow she would be back at the start. So I insisted she be admitted for observation overnight.

My ma was livid with me: her generation are deferential to doctors. And true, I’m no medic, administrator or health minister. But even I can spot an illogical system held together with dedication and gaffer tape. Why can’t GP surgeries — as doctors have suggested — be put in A&E to filter off the poorly-shoulder brigade? Why can’t Seldoc perform home visits for vulnerable patients at all times, if GP surgeries won’t oblige? Most of us know what “emergency” means: it’s the muddled NHS that can’t decide.

THE HEDGIE WITH A 99.9% SUCCESS RATE

Harry Wilson

JANUARY 10 2017

AS DARKNESS FELL on the Sydney skyline on New Year's Eve, a 43-year-old Czech billionaire stood barefoot in a yellow polo top and black shorts, an arm extended out towards a party in progress just below his terrace.

With a crop of blond hair and a fresh rash of stubble, Karel Janecek does not look like a typical billionaire hedge fund manager in the post on his Twitter account. Indeed, little about the demeanour of the maths-genius-turned-financial-programmer would hint at the central role he has played in financial markets for more than a decade, in which RSJ, the firm he founded 23 years ago in Plzen, the home of pilsner beer, has become one of the biggest players.

Even in the Square Mile, RSJ is barely known, despite being one of the most influential firms in London financial markets. On a daily basis RSJ makes markets in thousands of financial products and is one of the leading, if not the biggest, traders of short sterling and long gilt futures contracts, meaning it has a crucial role in determining the price of products at the heart of the British financial system.

Even more extraordinary is just how quickly RSJ has gained such dominance. Within two years of placing its first derivatives trade on Liffe, now called ICE Futures Europe, in 2002 the firm became the biggest player on the exchange and 15 years on remains the one to beat, turning Mr Janecek into the Czech Republic's first self-made billionaire.

Mr Janecek, who owns about 40 per cent of the company according to official documents, has made so much money from RSJ that he retired a couple of years ago to focus on pet projects, such as rooting out corruption in the Czech government and promoting his idea for "democracy 2.1", which involves using computerised voting to make the electoral system more efficient.

Explaining his ambitions to students three years ago, he said: "People who are constrained by living expenses cannot do everything and I wanted to have full freedom to be able to decide what I wanted to do ... and with the success, with the money, finally came the thought: 'What is the most important thing to do next?'"

Three years ago Bloomberg reported that the Prague-based business traded products worth a notional $106 trillion on an annual basis. To put that figure in context, each week this firm, employing about 30 traders, buys and sells contracts worth roughly the same as the annual output of Italy.

Despite its size, and there is a good case for arguing that RSJ is larger than American rivals such as Virtu, Citadel and Jump Trading, it is nearly six years since anything has been written about the firm in the mainstream press.

RSJ's size has given it a direct hand in helping to shape the regulation of the markets it trades on. When in 2007 the then NYSE-Liffe proposed a new formula for allotting orders, RSJ lobbied against the move. The firm claimed to be responsible for one in ten trades on the exchange, giving it a considerable voice in its running.

On Eurex, the Deutsche Börse-owned derivatives exchange, Bronislav Kandrik, chief trader at RSJ and one of its ten shareholders, is a member of its council that meets to discuss how it is run. RSJ is thought to be one of the biggest traders on the Frankfurt-based exchange.

In a barren year for hedge funds, RSJ's in-house proprietary algorithmic investment fund, the heart of its sophisticated high-frequency trading systems, made a return of more than 90 per cent.

Whatever shocked the markets last year, RSJ's money machine ploughed on regardless. Six days after the Brexit vote, RSJ Prop reported a net asset value per share of €791, up 5.5 per cent month on month, according to a filing with the Mauritius Stock Exchange, where the fund is listed. Donald Trump's shock election victory had no impact and RSJ reported a net asset value of €1,096 per share at the end of November, a rise of 7 per cent on October.

In the three years since RSJ Prop shares were listed, the fund's NAV has risen by 2,632 per cent. A spokesman for RSJ said that the three-year figure might overstate the performance because of changes in the number of underlying shares in the fund as investors withdrew money.

Even taking these withdrawals into account, the returns are astounding. To put RSJ's performance in context, the average managed futures hedge fund lost its investors 1.5 per cent of their money last year, while macro funds eked out an average return of 1.2 per cent. Even Renaissance Technologies' Medallion fund, regarded by many as the best algorithmic trader in the world, was on course to achieve a return of just over 20 per cent for 2016.

The size of the fund is not known and the spokesman for RSJ said that the firm did not provide information about its assets under management. However, with a minimum investment of $100,000 and a sophisticated understanding of financial markets a prerequisite to joining, this is a fund that excludes all but the wealthiest and savviest of investors.

Indeed, RSJ Prop's performance is not monitored by any of the leading hedge fund index trackers, meaning it is unlikely that the fund attracts many investors outside the firm's immediate circle of present and former staff.

Although it has generally flown below the radar of most market-watchers, RSJ's success and influence have attracted criticism. Four years ago Bart Chilton, then a commissioner of the US Commodity Futures Trading Commission, the regulator that led the Libor-rigging investigation, warned how little the authorities knew about RSJ. "We couldn't get their books and records if we thought they did something untoward ... I mean, they are from Czechoslovakia [sic], they're going to flip us the bird. They couldn't care less what we want," Mr Chilton said.

His concerns apply as much in the UK. Mr Janecek's website

boasts that RSJ, from which he has largely withdrawn from day-to-day business, is "the biggest trader on the London derivatives market". However, the firm operates in the UK through its Czech financial passport, meaning that none of its staff have to be verified by the Bank of England or the Financial Conduct Authority.

This means in effect that a Prague-based firm, supervised by the Czech National Bank, is responsible for a signficant part of the market-making in the world's three largest derivatives markets: Chicago, Frankfurt and London. This has upset small traders, who say that they are being squeezed out by RSJ and other algorithmic traders.

Andrew Bailey, the chief executive of the FCA, warned last year that algorithmic traders were "very important" and that the regulator would crack down on those who put their system to "inappropriate use". However, Megan Butler, the FCA's director of supervision, admitted that no inspection had taken place of the computer code used by traders such as RSJ. Even if the FCA asked for such information, its staff would have no direct jurisdiction.

The extent of RSJ's presence in Britain is its computers nestled as close as possible to the servers that run the world's largest derivatives markets, a practice called co-location.

While some high-frequency traders have hired staff in the UK, and other big markets in which they operate, RSJ's sole physical connection with London consists of expensive computers sitting in Basildon, the home of ICE Futures Europe's data centre. Inside these servers are what RSJ describes as its "homemade" algorithms, built on models honed over 15 years that enable it to best even the world's most sophisticated investors.

How RSJ achieves such incredible returns is a closely guarded secret. In common with other algorithmic traders, the firm jealously guards its trading models, but in pages now no longer on its website it explained the principle of how its mathematicians use advanced statistics and the law of large numbers to beat the market.

RSJ explained that its investment strategy came down to the same principle as betting on the toss of a coin. However, rather than odds of 50-50, RSJ's "long-term observation" had achieved the financial market equivalent of discovering a 50.5 per cent bias in favour of tails.

Toss the coin again and again and this small advantage in their favour builds into an almost certain money-making scheme. As the firm put it: "With each subsequent game, the probability of you making a profit will get higher. If you toss the coin 100 times, this probability will be approximately 54 per cent. If you toss the coin 1,000 times, this probability will rise to approximately 62 per cent.

"If you toss the coin 100,000 times, this probability will be approximately 99.9 per cent. There is, nevertheless, always risk. We may have got it wrong, the probability of the coin landing tails-up is lower than 50 per cent and we have lost our bet."

In RSJ's case, replace the toss of a coin with millions upon millions of "buy" and "sell" orders and the essence of its strategy is displayed.

And it looks like the coin toss is very much in RSJ's favour.

ARE YOU TOUGH ENOUGH FOR 'RADICAL CANDOUR' AT WORK?

Helen Rumbelow

JANUARY 16 2017

TODAY I WILL be "radically candid". Today will be different because I will tell people what I think of them at work. Then when they tell me what they think of me I will say: "Thank you." Today, in short, I will become a sado-masochistic German.

I start by asking a colleague on the features desk what I could do better. He said: "Stop asking me stuff to provide material for your articles." I thanked him. I then offered to critique his performance. He put his head in his arms in a sort of foetal or brace position. I wasn't sure whether to continue, so I called Kim Scott.

Scott is the founder of "Radical Candor", the latest business trend from Silicon Valley. To illustrate it in action she tells this story. She was new to her job at Google when she gave a presentation to the company's most senior staff. This was important to her because Scott had spent years trying to start or join businesses that were "bullshit-free" zones and she thought she had finally come home.

Yet was she ready for it? After a successful presentation she was taken aside by Sheryl Sandberg (then Scott's immediate boss, now the Facebook executive). Scott thought she was about to take a victory lap with Sandberg, but no. Sandberg told her she had said "um" too much. Scott brushed it off, a minor detail. Sandberg persisted: what if Google were to get Scott a voice coach? Scott said she was too busy for that. Finally, Sandberg said: "You know, Kim, I can tell I'm not really getting through to you. When you say 'um' every third word, it makes you sound stupid."

The words hung in the air as Scott felt their sting. Of course, if Scott sounded stupid, this makes Sandberg sound rude — and which is worse? Yet Scott says that was the "kindest thing she could possibly have done for me". Sandberg cared enough to speak directly. Scott reflects on an incident on the street when she was struggling to get her dog to sit at the kerb. A stranger walked past and managed it with a harsh "SIT!" in the dog's face. As he walked off he told Scott, "It's not mean, it's clear."

So Scott's idea of "Radical Candor" was born. A useful little mantra for those struggling to be radically candid in practice, me included, is: "It's not mean, it's clear." Put the thought that this relates to a dog out of your mind. Scott laughs when I mention her dog. "Yeah, the point I learnt was the dog didn't understand nuance. It wasn't helpful to the dog to say: 'Would you mind sitting please?' "

To say that Scott's approach is generating a buzz in tech companies is to put it mildly. Scott is an influential figure. She went from Google to Apple, developing the "managing at Apple" course. She has coached the chief executives of Twitter and Dropbox. Her new book, *Radical Candor*, has a glowing endorsement from Sandberg on the cover. There are tech companies all over London using the technique and I talk to some of them, including one where they hold a weekly meeting to share all the harsh-but-fair feedback they have received. I can also attest, if Sandberg is interested, that Scott does not say "um" once when I talk to her.

In fact, she is pretty good at selling the technique. It is often mistaken as people being "brutally honest" with one another, but Scott resents that. Telling people where they fail may be tough, but it is performed in the spirit of generosity: "It's not OK to be a jerk." That's why it is important to say thank you afterwards or, as I like to be old-fashioned, "Thank you, sir, can I have another?"

There's a neat little axis that sums this up. If you challenge people but don't care, you're "obnoxiously aggressive". For British readers this may bring to mind a boss like Gordon Ramsay. If you're too nice, you're not doing anyone any favours, which is a "ruinous empathy". Perhaps a Hugh Fearnley-Whittingstall. However, a non-evil frankness, let's say Mary Berry: that's the sweet spot.

What about crying? I ask Scott if that means you are doing it wrong. Not at all, she says. Don't let the fear or reality of workplace sobbing put you off as long as the intention of the candour was good. "If somebody's fly is down or they have spinach in their teeth — sometimes these simple examples are helpful — if you care about them you'll point it out. If you're so worried that they won't like you if you tell them, then you're not doing the best you can for them."

This was the spirit of one of the founding fathers of Silicon Valley, Andrew Grove, who was chief executive of Intel when, Scott says, "Intel was on top of the world". Grove cultivated an atmosphere of what has been described as "ruthless intelligence". He didn't mind being berated by a junior if he had made a mistake. Loved it, in fact. "He was very well known for telling people what he thought and very open to other people saying what they thought," says Scott. "In many ways Grove was the godfather of Radical Candor."

At the end of the conversation I push Scott to be radically candid with me. Go on, I say, how was my interview technique? We have a useful little discussion about interruption, but she softens it by saying she likes being interrupted. All these years and I have never asked an interviewee how I did. Why not? I feel as though this is a breakthrough. I feel high on criticism.

But then I try to corner one of my bosses into some radical candour. Go on, I say, hit me. We say lots of radically candid things about other people who are out of earshot. I recognise this as my comfort zone, so I stop. Please, I say, be as rude about me as you like. We go on like this for a while, me begging to be insulted and him withholding. It's like a particularly kinky scene from a David Lynch film.

I need Scott's help. Are we, I ask her, just unable to override our British factory settings? One BuzzFeed journalist observed that *Radical Candor* "sounds to your average Brit like a waking nightmare". There is a time and a place for radical candour and that is the Christmas party at 3am. If we say what we really think we fear that the entire fabric of our civilisation will be destroyed.

Scott isn't having any of it. Sure, we find it hard to override our manners. A lot of Americans find it hard too, because they want so much to be liked. "But I think you're better at it than we are in this country," she says. "I found when I was managing an international team at Google, the Brits on the team were more candid than the New Yorkers. Which is not the reputation but, partly as a result of the education in the UK, which stresses oral argument, you don't shy away from it."

I wonder if she is here referring to our House of Commons, which surely falls into the obnoxiously aggressive quadrant. Scott hopes Radical Candor has a role in 2017 to improve politics beyond office politics. By which I think she means Trump etc, but she won't be drawn. "We've seen, in your country and mine, communications styles that are obnoxious: they sell, but they're terrible for civil discourse. I believe this can get us to a better place."

And the British really can do this. I speak to Kieran O'Neill, who founded his first company aged 15, sold it aged 19 for $1.25 million, and is at 29 years old more experienced than most. Sure, he says, "candour and Britishness are not natural bedfellows", but for him it is no coincidence that the tech firms are leading the way. "Software engineers tend to be a lot more direct. It's a cultural thing. I don't want to generalise too much but, yeah, value of truth in that community supersedes niceness."

For O'Neill, candour takes a lot of staff training but it is worth it. His latest venture, Thread, an online stylist service for men, even has an open email system so any staff member can access emails sent by anyone. "During job interviews we ask: 'What's one thing about the interview you didn't like?' Some people just find it awful, but we look for people who are more direct, able to have a mature conversation about it. One out of ten times people still say 'nothing', which is a pretty bad answer."

Next I speak to Rob O'Donovan, the co-founder of Charlie HR, a human resources tech start-up. He also says that it helps that most of the adopters are young. "We're lucky in that. Ten years working in a corporate environment sucks it out of you. I have friends who always say work is shit. I say: 'Have you told your line manager?' They'll say," and here O'Donovan howls, "'Nooo.'"

He continues: "It's a communication style more than anything else. People who are smart and self aware don't want someone else to waste their time thinking about how they can compassionately construct a sentence that their work wasn't as good as it usually is. People get used to hearing it straight and saying, 'Yeah, fine.'"

Scott says we have to practise this to improve. So I email a senior columnist at *The Times* and ask him what I could do better. I get back a three-point bulletin that covers everything from what I did at lunch to being bolder on a work project. It's pretty candid. Last week I would have found a way to resent him. Now I reply, "Thank you", and mean it. So I can only end this by saying: what did you — really — think?

OUR WEEK: EVERYONE

Hugo Rifkind

JANUARY 21 2017

Monday

Donald Trump
I have great love for Europe. Great people, great little place. Which is why I started this week with an interview with a pair of European newspapers. That intern *The Times* of London sent? Smart!

Steve Bannon
We've got to have tanks, I'm telling the chief. And missiles. With big frigging bows on them. That's the kind of procession we're after.

"I could drive the tank," says Donald. "The best tank."

"And soldiers!" I say. "Doing that march where their feet go really high? Only, not in their regular uniforms? Perhaps in black ones? At least the shirts?"

"No," says Jared Kushner. "None of this. Especially not the last bit."

"Or brown," I say. "I'm not fussy."

Vladimir Putin

In Kremlin. Am congratulating FSB chief on persuading Asset Trump to declare Nato obsolete.

"Again," say FSB chief. "Am swearing. Not asset."

"No, but really," haff said.

Donald Trump

"So Donald," says Kellyanne, who does my press. "There's a problem about the Nato thing."

Forget global stability, I tell her. Let's talk about my inauguration concert. It's going to get the best reviews. Only I'm wondering which A-listers have said yes.

"Still only Kanye West," says Kellyanne.

"No," I say. "Not Kanye. Stand him down. Great guy. The best. But he's too ... What's the word? I normally have the best words. He's just too ..."

"I get it," says Kellyanne.

Hillary Clinton

Donald Trump calls. I don't know how he got my number. Probably the Russians.

He wants me to know that, even though his approval ratings are already terrible, mine would be worse.

"Your liberals," he says. "So bitter. What more do they want? I just did an interview where I said Iraq was the greatest mistake this country ever made!"

"Maybe," I suggest, "they feel they can think of another one?"

"Vietnam?" he says.

"I'm hanging up now," I say.

Tuesday

Donald Trump

We're navigating the Senate confirmation hearings of my cabinet. Also, we're still sorting my inaugural concert. It's a hassle. Bigly. Can't wait until I'm actually president and can have a rest!

Ivanka Trump

"Listen," I say to Donald Jr. "Have you seen Dad's speech? He says he's writing it himself. And I'm not sure that's a good idea."

"It'll be the best speech!" says Donald Jr. "So strong! The losers and haters will love it! And if they don't? Sad!"

"I feel you've been speaking to him," I say.

Nigel Farage

No, let me finish. None of this would be happening without the Bad Boys of Brexit. Which is why I'm flying to Washington with Arron Banks, and whoever that other guy is.

"Woah," says Arron, checking his phone before we take off. "Trump has just attacked John Lewis. And I thought he was an anglophile?"

"No, no," says the other guy. "This is a black John Lewis."

"I don't know that one," I say. "Is it in Brixton?"

Donald Trump

"There's a problem," says Mike Pence, my future vice-president, "with this naked rodeo clown from Texas."

"Ditch him," I say. "I think we only want singers."

"No, no," says Pence. "He's supposed to be the agriculture secretary."

Vladimir Putin

"But Comrade," am saying to FSB man, bewildered. "He's attacking the UN now. Check again."

Theresa May

Back in London, I'm running through my big Brexit speech with Philip Hammond. And he says there's only one thing about it he doesn't understand.

"Which is why," he says, "you're delivering it dressed as Rod Stewart?"

"Do you think I'm ..." I begin.

"Please don't," says Philip.

Wednesday

Boris Johnson
I've been called into Downing Street to see Fiona and Nick, who are Theresa's scary henchmen.

"Cripes!" I say. "Obviously I wasn't really suggesting that Johnny Frenchman was a Nazi and about to administer a punishment beating! I mean, who would do that?"

Fiona glances at Nick, who is holding a cricket bat.

"Lock the door," she says.

Barack Obama
In the White House. Joe Biden is stuffing prawns inside all the curtain rails. They won't find them for months, he says. Maybe never. Then he asks if it's time for him to do that interview telling everybody I actually am a Muslim.

"No Joe," I say, firmly. "Because I truly believe our country can heal."

"Inshallah," agrees Joe.

Vladimir Putin
Enough smearing of Russia. Haff again denied existence of Russian programme of kompromat, designed to embarrass foreign politicians. It's not like we haff kept on file photo of Theresa May's outfit from Tuesday, for example.

Kellyanne Conway
The singer in the Bruce Springsteen impersonator band we've booked for tomorrow's concert calls me to say they don't want to do it.

"Right," I say, "but do you actually mean that? Or are you just impersonating Bruce Springsteen?"

"Both," he says.

Thursday

The former president of Gambia
I am refusing to step down, despite the end of my term. Screw your election.

Michelle Obama
"Honey?" I say, "have you heard about the Gambia thing?"

Jeremy Corbyn
Labour MPs are going to oppose the government by supporting it on triggering Article 50. Yes, it does make sense.

Donald Trump
"This is the Lincoln Memorial," I explain to Melania, on the way to the concert. "We own it now. Really super. Might change the face."

Melania Trump
Had always believed American pop music more professional than Slovenian pop music. But no.

Jon Voight
I don't speak to Angelina much any more. Can't explain it.

Jeremy Corbyn
What I mean was, Labour MPs will support Article 50 if they want to. But not if they don't. Although I'll tell them to. Although I might not, either. Stop harassing me.

Nigel Farage
No, let me finish. We're at the Bad Boys of Brexit party in Washington! Although it's rather quiet.

"Do you think he'll come?" says Arron, who is looking anxious.

"Of course he'll come," I say. "What sort of person would go to a massive ball in their own honour when they could be here, drinking warm beer and eating fish canapés with us?"

"Maybe I didn't spend enough money," says Arron.

Piers Morgan

I'm on *Question Time*. That's literally the only reason I'm not in Washington, because I was totally invited. We're really good friends. Maybe I didn't mention.

Jeremy Corbyn

Actually I'm not sure anybody is really listening.

Friday

Donald Trump

The big day. We started with breakfast. The best breakfast. That weird Brit Nigel Farage wanted to come and make it. "Let me finish!" he said. "They call me Mr Breakfast!" Limey freak. What the hell's a kipper? He comes near me again, he's getting shot. Then we met with the Obamas.

Barack Obama

"Donald," I say, solemnly. "I have left you a letter in my desk. As is traditional. I hope you find it interesting. It's my Kenyan birth certificate."

"What?" says Trump.

"Just kidding," I say. Then I tell him I wish him all the best, and there's no hard feelings about all that Kenyan, Muslim stuff, and that maybe our nation really can heal.

"So much winning," says Trump. "So much."

"Inshallah," I say.

"What?" says Trump.

Hillary Clinton
I'm so glad it's raining.

Kellyanne Conway
The president-elect says it's not raining and I think we should take his word for it.

The Supreme Court chief justice
"So you'll put your hand on the Lincoln Bible?" I say.

"Have you washed it?" says Trump. Then he says he'll be swearing on his own Bible, too.

"Why?" I say.

"It's smaller," he says.

Donald Trump
American carnage! America first and also last but mainly first. We stand at the birth of a lewd millennium. We're going to discover space! The forgotten people will not be forgotten except for the people I've forgotten. Now arrives the hour of action. Maybe two hours, some days. I will fight for you with every breath in my body and every hair on my head. I'm going to build tunnels and a wall, but not tunnels under the wall. Winning like never before.

Steve Bannon
No, we haven't already discovered space. That was a hoax. Read the internet.

Jared Kushner
I'm still a good person, right?

Melania Trump
Have I left the iron on?

Donald Trump
And then we're whisked away by the Secret Service. Who are not, by the way, the secretest. I'd be way more secret than that.

"Dad," says Barron. "That was all really boring."

"Tell me about it!" I say. "Just sitting there. I haven't tweeted in, like, ten whole hours."

"Here's an idea," says Ivanka. "Maybe we could do it every day?"

TOURIST EXODUS LEAVES GIGOLOS HUNGRY FOR LOVE

Jerome Starkey, Banjul

February 7 2017

Business was bad for the gigolos. The restaurants were shuttered, the hotels deserted and the nightclubs, usually full to bursting with middle-aged female sex tourists, had been silenced by the threat of war.

When a political crisis in the Gambia forced thousands of tourists to flee last month, the young men locally known as bumsters were among the hardest hit. They are the men with gymnasts' physiques and an affable patter who loiter on beaches and outside bars to meet middle-aged western women looking for more than just a suntan.

"It's because of poverty," said Amadou Sarr, 33, as he sat outside a bureau de change, one of the few businesses still open on the main tourist strip in Senegambia, a cluster of resorts near the capital Banjul. "You know, you find a white lady, you help her, she helps you. It's because we are poor and we believe they can change our lives for the better."

With wages for menial workers about £20 to £40 a month and unemployment among the under-30s running at 38 per cent, many young Gambian men see the hordes of European tourists, half of them British, as their ticket out of poverty.

The most successful bumsters have followed their lovers back to Europe, according to Mr Sarr. Others have received cars or homes or regular cash stipends as a result of their liaisons, invariably with older women.

"You don't ask for money," Mr Sarr explained. "You tell them, I look after you, you look after me."

It was rarely as transactional as conventional prostitution. "In new relationships she gives you food or money and later, in the future, when she sees you are good she can change your life. She can give you a new life," Mr Sarr said. "I am 33 and I want a woman who is maximum 61, or 65, you know, who make each other happy."

Was he physically attracted to women twice his age? "In the Gambia age is just a number," he replied. His last girlfriend was 51, from Nottingham, and they were deeply in love.

"There are some bumsters who put one lady on the plane and meet another off it. They are not good bumsters. They give us a bad name," he said. "I am looking for someone who wants to get me a house here and I will sit here and wait for you and be honest."

In the bureau de change behind him, one of more than a dozen shops on the street offering cash remittance services, the man behind the counter said that most business came from tourists sending money to Gambian friends. "Romantic friends, friends with benefits, you name it. Mostly it's tourist friends who are sending money here."

A well-to-do British woman, who asked not to be named and refused to give her age, said that she had found love with a Gambian man when she first came on holiday two years ago but insisted that she was not a sex tourist.

"Some women do literally just come here to have sex with a black man," she said. "The sort of women who do that are not the sort of women who are going to get a man in England."

Mr Sarr was more sympathetic: "Maybe they don't want to be lonely."

He said that business had collapsed when the tourists left but he had a new idea.

"Put my name and my number in *The Times*," he suggested. "Any woman who wants a good man, they can contact Amadou Sarr."

BIG BRANDS FUND TERROR

Alexi Mostrous

FEBRUARY 9 2017

SOME OF THE world's biggest brands are unwittingly funding Islamic extremists, white supremacists and pornographers by advertising on their websites, *The Times* can reveal.

Advertisements for hundreds of large companies, universities and charities, including Mercedes-Benz, Waitrose and Marie Curie, appear on hate sites and YouTube videos created by supporters of terrorist groups such as Islamic State and Combat 18, a violent pro-Nazi faction.

The practice is likely to generate tens of thousands of pounds a month for extremists. An advert appearing alongside a YouTube video, for example, typically earns whoever posts the video $7.60 for every 1,000 views. Some of the most popular extremist videos have more than one million hits.

Big advertising agencies, which typically place commercials on behalf of clients, have been accused of pushing brands into online advertising to boost their own profits.

Companies are concerned that they are paying huge mark-ups for digital promotion and receiving "crappy advertising" in return. Leaked documents from one "top-six" agency show that about 40 per cent of its advert-buying income in 2015 came from hidden kickbacks as well as from "other income". One source said this mainly derived from mark-ups applied to digital commercials.

Analysis by *The Times* of online extremist content reveals that blacklists designed to prevent digital adverts from appearing next to it are not fit for purpose.

On YouTube, an advert for the new Mercedes E-Class saloon runs next to a pro-Isis video that has been viewed more than 115,000 times. The commercial appears a few seconds after the start of the video, which plays a song praising jihad over a picture of an Isis flag and an anti-aircraft gun. A commercial for the F-Pace SUV from the British carmaker Jaguar runs next to the video.

The luxury holiday operator Sandals Resorts is advertised next to a video promoting al-Shabaab, the East African jihadist group affiliated to al-Qaeda. Last night a Sandals spokeswoman said that it made every effort to stop its adverts appearing next to inappropriate content. It said that YouTube had "not properly categorised the video" as sensitive.

Adverts for Honda, Thomson Reuters, Halifax, the Victoria & Albert museum, Liverpool university, Argos, Churchill Retirement and Waitrose also appear on extremist videos posted on YouTube by supporters of groups that include Combat 18.

After *The Times* informed Google, which owns the social media platform, it took down some of the videos. It is understood that in some cases advertising revenues had gone to the rights holders of songs used on the videos rather than to the video owner.

A Google spokesperson said: "When it comes to content on YouTube, we remove flagged videos that break our rules and have a zero-tolerance policy for content that incites violence or hatred.

"Some content on YouTube may be controversial and offensive, which is why we only allow advertising against videos which fall within our advertising guidelines.

"Our partners can also choose not to appear against content they consider inappropriate, and we have a responsibility to work with the industry to help them make informed choices."

Several brands have accused agencies of not acting in their best interests. Marc Pritchard, chief brand officer at P&G, the world's biggest advertiser, warned last week: "We have a media supply chain which is murky at best and fraudulent at worst. We need to clean it up."

Many of the companies said that they were unaware of and "deeply concerned" by their presence on the sites. They blamed programmatic advertising, a system using complex computer technology to buy digital adverts in the milliseconds that a webpage takes to load. Many agencies have their own programmatic divisions, which often apply mark-ups to digital commercials without the brands' knowledge.

One Combat 18 video on YouTube, showing an armed man standing in front of a burning swastika, hosts an advert for the hospice charity Marie Curie. An authorised Nissan dealer's adverts appear on the official YouTube pages of far-right parties including the BNP and the English Defence League, while Sony is promoted on an anti-semitic video entitled: "The cunning of the Jews".

The retailer Argos is one of a number of brands advertised on sexually explicit YouTube videos. The V&A and Waitrose advertise on the website of the far-right party Britain First. Commercials for HSBC, Eurotunnel and JD Sports appear on "alt-right" and Islamist websites, including one promoting a "Holocaust Amnesia Day".

Adverts for John Lewis, Dropbox and Disney are embedded in sunnah-online.com. The website hosts lectures by Abu Ameenah Bilal Philips, a preacher banned from Britain who has argued that a husband cannot be charged with rape, and Esa al-Hindi, a terrorist sentenced to life imprisonment. Lloyds Bank is advertised on eramuslim.com, a site banned last month by the Indonesian government for allegedly promoting hate speech.

Last night MPs called on Google to explain why hundreds of extremists were making money from advertising on YouTube. Users that intend to make money from advertising must be approved by Google, which is supposed to ensure that videos do not breach the site's terms and conditions.

"This is deeply disturbing," Chuka Umunna, a member of the home affairs select committee, said. "There is no doubt the social media companies could be doing far more to prevent the spread of extremist content."

Programmatic advertising enables agencies to track potential customers around the web and serve them adverts on whichever website they are browsing. Some agencies have been accused of making huge undeclared profits as a result.

"Programmatic advertising is a big concern for us and the whole advertising industry," Hicham Felter, a spokesman for ISBA, the trade body representing Britain's biggest advertisers, said. "There is a greater risk of ads appearing in violent, pornographic, extremist and other 'unsafe' brand environments because of the volume and speed at which programmatic trading is carried out." He added: "The suspicion is that the surge in programmatic trading is being fuelled by the profit media agencies can make rather than because it delivers better results for their clients."

The six top advertising agencies each denied any wrongdoing, conflict of interest or sharp practice and said that their relationships with clients were transparent.

BEING OFFENDED IS OFTEN THE BEST MEDICINE

David Aaronovitch

FEBRUARY 16 2017

IN THE SECTION of its website headed "Attending a Performance", between the bit on latecomers (they aren't allowed in) and age restrictions (strictly nobody under the age of six), the Royal Court theatre in London has added a new paragraph headed "TRIGGER WARNINGS". The theatre tells patrons that it is aware that various plays contain moments that "can be particularly distressing for some individuals" and that "if there are certain themes that you know would cause you extreme distress" then call or email, and someone — a theatre trauma counsellor perhaps — will be able to advise you if that play is triggerish.

Imagine explaining the plot of *Oedipus Rex* to an inexperienced and delicate would-be playgoer. "He does what to his mother? And *both* eyes?" The Society of London Theatres went to some lengths to suggest that the Royal Court's action was nothing new. Had not the Lyric theatre once warned playgoers of a production containing strobe lighting, smoke and nudity? This seems an odd combination of different hazards. Strobes might provoke an epileptic attack and smoke could be a genuine risk for those with breathing problems. But what is the danger of nudity? (To the audience, I mean. I can imagine some of the pitfalls for the actors. Splinters, ridicule, etc.)

The *Times*'s report on the Royal Court went on to reveal the existence of companies offering writers the service of "sensitivity readers". These helpmeets will give your manuscript the once-over to make sure that unintended offence is not committed. The author can publish safely knowing that no "Eskimo" has slipped through the Inuit cordon.

This last month there have been occasionally riotous attempts by some students in the US to stop the needy "alt-right" provocateur Milo Yiannopoulos from speaking at universities, an act roughly equivalent to throwing Brer Rabbit over and over into the briar patch. And mostly based on the argument that his presence will create an unsafe space for people on campus. Hardly a day goes past without a demand from somewhere on the political spectrum for this or that website or image to be taken down by the service providers for fear of the effect they will have on someone else.

It is horribly obvious from the emails and tweets I get and the articles I read that so-called snowflakery is a gift to genuine bigots. It is now routine for any complaint of racism, antisemitism or violent misogyny, however well-founded, to be greeted with the "liberal snowflake" jibe. I find myself in near-constant disagreement with Diane Abbott but her revelations this week about the grim racist and sexist abuse she's suffered over the years, largely in silence, is a reminder that stoicism is not always rewarded. Readers, just because someone is called a racist doesn't mean that they aren't.

Even so, up to now I have worried principally about the effect of banning people and words on the people who are banned (which could be any of us) and on the societies where the bans take place. But there is a substantial argument that trigger warnings, sensitivity training, safe spaces, no platforms are all based on an assumption of fragility: an assumption that can do harm to those supposedly being protected. In other words, the students who are told to fret about their campuses being a maze of hidden triggers, or who wish to be excused the appearance of unpleasant or challenging views, are likely to be weakened as a result.

Take the triggered playgoer. Let's suppose there is some upset in the past that can be reignited by a drama on stage. There is no therapeutic regime I can think of that would advise dealing with that upset by avoiding all possible suggestion of it. Usually the best way to conquer a phobia is habituation. If normal life contains discourse that is upsetting, then it's best to deal with it.

Sir Simon Wessely, the outgoing president of the Royal College of Psychiatrists, appeared on BBC Radio 4's *The Life Scientific* this week. He reminded listeners of what the establishment, including psychiatrists, believed would happen to British civilians when the bombing of cities began in the Second World War. They'd panic, go mad and run for the hills. But in the event, as Sir Simon said, people "proved more resilient than planners had predicted, largely because [the authorities] had underestimated their adaptability and resourcefulness".

Indeed this is one of the main conclusions of his

distinguished career in psychological disorders, best summed up as "people are tougher than we think". Sir Simon pointed to the experiences of those caught up in the 7/7 London bombings. Many of those directly affected received a "debriefing" with a trained counsellor. But when Sir Simon and others came to examine the outcomes they discovered that the counselling had often made people worse. Nowadays the policy, he said, is to wait and see if people are still distressed 10 to 12 weeks after a shock, at which point they can be offered help that is usually valuable.

Listening to Sir Simon I recalled reading the neurologist Suzanne O'Sullivan's book *It's All in Your Head*, about her career dealing with physical illnesses that had no discernible physical origin. She was careful not to suggest that people with such conditions were malingering or exaggerating. But she did speculate that too great an interest in one's body and health might be linked to psychosomatic illness. Crudely, if you think about it, it happens. If you're told you're fragile, then fragile is what you'll be.

This took me back to the problem of what has become known as "false memory syndrome" or "recovered memory". I'm prepared to bet that when the final story is told about the Great VIP Paedophile Panic of 2012 to 2016 we will discover that suggestive hypnotherapy lay at the heart of it. You look for insult, you look for offence, you look for abuse, you look for illness — all things that can and do exist — and you'll find what you're seeking. Run away and you run away from yourself.

The answer is, of course, to be sensible. To realise that Milo is Milo's problem and that it's only when you try to ban him that he becomes everyone's problem. Trigger warnings at the theatre? If you're Abraham Lincoln maybe. Otherwise, we're almost certainly healthier for doing without them.

OUR MAGICAL WEMBLEY MOMENTS

George Caulkin

FEBRUARY 25 2017

MIST HUNG LOW over Wembley, shrouding the arch, glistening like tears. Feet shuffled across the turf, testing its spring, a bark of laughter cracking the silence, but the stadium, by and large, was empty. Three rows of men, separated by age and eras, joined by history, lined up along the far touchline, murmuring together, swapping phone numbers, gazing deep into the stands. Quiet settled and the camera clicked.

Gareth Southgate was present, squirming at his central place in the photograph — "There are some legends here and I'm not sure I should be at the front," he said — but prominence is unavoidable for the England manager. Wembley is a home now, but it is also where something melded for him, ambition and achievement, "a sense of belonging". Around him, other stories, other memories.

The League Cup was established in 1960–61, but this year marks the 50th anniversary of Wembley staging the final. It was a competition born into antipathy; during its formative moments, *The Times* thundered against a "useless" tournament but it has grown into its robes. When Manchester United play Southampton tomorrow, nobody will sneer. A universal response: wish we were there.

Perhaps our judgment had merit when finals were settled over two legs, when the big clubs stayed away, when European football was not offered to the winners and a glut of extra fixtures prompted us to write that "a further spread of mediocrity will be the dose". Maybe too many games still stifle our development, but mediocrity does not glimmer like this.

To commemorate a half-century of resilience and growth, of fantasy and fulfilment (and to make our reparations), *The Times* and EFL invited a player from each winning Wembley side to return to the ground for a unique team picture, wrapped in their colours. Amid the well-worn anecdotes, the surprising admissions, a consensus emerged; nobody would swap it.

Southgate lifted the cup with Aston Villa in 1996. It was a transformative season for the centre half, who would play every minute of England's run to the semi-finals of the European Championship finals that summer. Winning brought acceptance. "I always looked at big players and what they had won," he said. "It was never going to be about what I earned. It was about caps and medals. Ultimately, I felt that was how my career would be judged. I was definitely driven by a desire to win something. I had just got into the England squad, so to be a cup-winner made me feel more deserving of my place. That was an important moment, to get over the line in a big game at Wembley. The following weekend we lost in the FA Cup semi-final and I started my first England match on the middle Wednesday. It was an incredible passage of time."

When Southgate retired as a player ten years later, his feelings had shifted. There had been another League Cup with Middlesbrough — held at Cardiff's Millennium Stadium while Wembley was rebuilt — the club's only leading trophy.

"I'm a bit more balanced now," he said. "Sometimes you've got to be at certain clubs to win certain things. Lesser players can be at bigger clubs and win more than better players.

"You recognise that football is about memories. In the end, really, you think about the people you played with and played for. You meet again and pick up the thread. The great occasions in your life are shared with other people and sharing that day with Middlesbrough, a club that had never won before, makes you realise you're involved in something far bigger. It was more than a football game. That's meaningful."

The League Cup provided that meaning, just as it did for Luton Town in 1988. Regarded by many as its finest final, the underdogs took the lead against Arsenal, then conceded two goals before Andy Dibble repelled Nigel Winterburn's penalty, Gus Caesar famously dallied in defence, Danny Wilson equalised and Brian Stein sealed a 3–2 victory in the 90th minute.

"Arsenal were massive favourites and nobody gave us a chance, but we believed," Mick Harford, the former Luton striker, said. "We were a very good cup team. We wanted something to show for it and, to be part of a Luton team winning their first major honour, a small-town club, was huge, magnificent."

Yet jubilation is democratic. Manchester United claimed their first League Cup in 1992, Brian McClair scoring the only goal against Nottingham Forest. Twelve months later, they would win the title for the first time in 26 aching years. There had been other staging posts, other trophies, but as plain old Alex Ferguson surveyed his dressing room, something stirred.

"We had won the FA Cup after a replay a couple of years before, we had won the European Cup Winners' Cup and it was continuing a run," McClair said. "That was the manager's emphasis — it was really important. We put more silverware on the table at a time when we had a chance of finally winning the league and, although Leeds United pipped us, winning breeds winning. We could feel it coming.

"It was a huge event, a massive thing. It lifted things; win, keep winning. The manager would always say 'you must celebrate wins' and we did. We had a good night and a good journey back on the train to Manchester the next day, with families and friends. That was always a cracking trip — when you had won."

United can feel too monolithic for intimacy — the money, the worldwide reach — but strip it back and every club is a collection of pulses, fellowship, hope. McClair is chipped from granite, but he feels it. "It's so special to be here," he said. "You look around and go, 'Yeah ... we were part of that history.' Wembley, as a kid, was a dream: England v Scotland, finals. I think about it now: Manchester United, League Cup winners. Goalscorer: McClair."

Garry Birtles scored twice in his final and, even now, it irks him. This was the Forest side of 1979, the year that Brian Clough's miracle men won the first of their European Cups.

"I had two goals disallowed, which I'm not at all bitter about, as you can tell," he said. "Not many people have scored a hat-trick at Wembley."

Birtles was fortunate that he could focus on the ball, let alone kick it. He said: "We got to our hotel the night before and the gaffer said, 'Right, drop your cases off and get back down here.' There was a room set aside, a buffet stacked up, loads of food on the table. 'Whatever you want to drink, lads.' There was cider, lager, wine. There might have been champagne but I preferred a pint or a glass of wine. Still do.

"Cloughie and Peter Taylor started relating stories about when they started off in management at Hartlepool United. We had a lot to drink. Archie Gemmill stood up at one point to leave the room and the gaffer said, 'Where do you think you're going?' 'Up for a bath, gaffer, like always before a game.' 'Sit down, you go when the rest of us go.' When we eventually went upstairs, I tripped and ended up on all fours.

"We went 1–0 down to Southampton the next day. We were probably hungover. We got a rollicking in the dressing-room at half-time. There had been heavy snow and the pitch was awful, a mud bath, but we won it. Then I dropped my medal. It was bouncing along the floor in the royal box. An absolute nightmare. Coming from non-League, it was just unbelievable, unreal. In 1976 I was laying floors. In 1979 I was playing at Wembley."

Luton preferred to celebrate afterwards. "We went to the Savoy in London," Harford said, still imposing, stringing out a slow Wearside drawl. What happened? "We got very drunk, as you could probably imagine."

Some revelry is more harmful; when Arsenal beat Sheffield Wednesday in 1993, Tony Adams hoisted Steve Morrow on to his shoulders; Morrow slipped, broke his arm and was rushed to hospital. Paul Merson tried and failed to suppress a giggle. "Stevie went flying," he said. "That's what I remember most. I felt for him. He didn't play all that often and to get the winning goal and for that to happen ..."

Merson had plundered an equaliser and then teed up Morrow. "One of those games when everything went right," he said. "I even crossed with my left foot for Stevie's goal. I probably kicked the ball with my left foot ten times in my career.

"We won the FA Cup a couple of months later but I was useless in that final. Shocking. I have better memories of this one. I am a big believer in the competition; it blows my mind when managers don't play their strongest teams. Everybody would want to be here. When I was growing up, I used to play a game called 'Wembley' in the park with my mates. To stand here, to walk here … I get a shiver down the spine.

"I grew up watching players walk to the royal box and to have made that same journey is something that is difficult to get my head around. It was something I always dreamt of.

"You score a century at Lord's or a try at Twickenham: that's the ultimate in those sports. Scoring a goal at Wembley? It has got to be every footballer's ultimate. I've always thought of this as a massive competition."

It was a little different, in every sense, when Mark Lazarus achieved a similar feat with Queens Park Rangers in 1967. The match was held at Wembley for the first time, a single tie, played in front of nearly 98,000 people and QPR, then of the third tier, were confronted by West Bromwich Albion. "Being at Wembley gave it more status, but I think our game really set the tournament alight," Lazarus said.

It was a surreal beginning. "The atmosphere before the match was astonishing. Four fans from Westbourne Park had made a coffin with 'WBA' written on it, put it on their shoulders and started walking towards Wembley. By the time they got to Wembley Way, there was a parade of about 4,000 people following it. It was funny to see that. A great day, lovely sunshine, all the family here, a packed house.

"We were 2–0 down at half-time but won 3–2; the whole thing was just a fairytale. We won the third-division title that year and were a good side but I think us being there made it bigger."

Lazarus is 78 now. "The memories are still with me," he said. "We've lost a few players from that team and that worries you a bit. It goes so quickly. But I remember scoring and jumping over a little fence that separated the running track from the crowd and going over and shaking hands. I reckon I could still do that."

Birmingham City were another team of improbables. In 2011 they were flailing to stay in the Premier League, a challenge that would elude them, but they went down swinging, beating Arsenal in the final.

"It was in the latter stages of my career and it was unexpected," Lee Bowyer said. "On paper, we should never have won that match but we had a togetherness. We wanted it more.

"Alex McLeish [the manager] instilled that. It was like Braveheart before matches; his team-talks were unreal, broad Scottish, inspirational. I swear to you, we would walk on to the pitch thinking, 'Well, we're not going to lose this.' It had been so long since Birmingham had won anything. It was a hard season, but managers like David O'Leary and Graeme Souness always told me, 'It's not what you earn from the game, it's what you've got to show for it' and that stuck in my head."

For Kenny Sansom, football was not like that. The game was more functional, more practical. "Whenever I went out on to a pitch, I wanted to do my job," he said. "That was all I thought about before kick-off: I do my job. It's about a team, but it has to be about individuals first; if I did my job, I could help Tony Adams do his. He could help Steve Bould. I didn't really think about winning trophies that much."

It would change when the full back captained Arsenal to a 2–1 victory over Liverpool in 1987. Something broke. "I cried my eyes out when I was walking off the pitch," Sansom said. "Yeah, I was very emotional. Walking up the stairs to get the trophy, I was terrified. It was nerve-racking. Somebody had given me a hat. And then you turn to your fans and they just go berserk. You think about them, you think about your family.

"A few days later I got a lovely letter saying, 'Well done, Ken.

Our first trophy for eight years. Brilliant.' I was chuffed with that. Then I got a few more: 'Why did you wear that hat?' And then another one, 'Why do you have that stupid moustache?' But you take it in good humour. It was just great, lovely to be captain. The next year we lost to Luton, a massive, massive disappointment. But, in the end, that is what makes football so appealing."

Sansom's life has been complex, scarred by alcohol, but he looked healthy that day. Poignancy simmered. Matt Elliott, there to represent Leicester City, spoke of the "outstanding individual highlight of my career". Pat Jennings described himself as "one of the lucky ones". Denis Smith, a winner with Stoke City in 1972, recalled a "sea of red and white. Tears come into your eyes straight away. It's very emotional."

What would Newcastle United fans, without a domestic trophy since 1955, give to weep like that, just once, to have something tangible for those hard yards of support? As Southgate said, for all the cold, grey controversies about priorities and weakened teams, "when it comes to League Cup final day, everybody is watching and saying, 'Bloody hell, I wish I was playing.' Winning trophies is special."

It is frequent for some and for others a novelty but, for big clubs and small, these are occasions to reflect, to consider what and who we are, the nature of support, to commune with those close to us and reconnect. To flood Covent Garden and Trafalgar Square. To dream. For players, winning is a craving; to do it at Wembley, with the world bearing witness, represents affirmation, a reward for sacrifice and dedication. This weekend, nothing compares.

The League Cup: an apology. You are anything but useless. You are beautiful and beguiling, even when you gleam for ever out of reach.

"I am sat here looking around at the superstars of our game," Wilson, victorious with Luton and Sheffield Wednesday, says. "It does feel special." He glances across at Harford. "We managed to break into that little circle; maybe only for a small while, but we did it. We should feel proud of what we did."

SPINAL COLUMN: I KEEP SEEING THE GHOST OF MELANIE PAST

Melanie Reid

FEBRUARY 25 2017

THERE ARE TIMES when I'm on my own, in a potentially tricky situation, when I see the ghost of Melanie Past. It's usually an occasion, as last week, when I have been bold and ventured out on my own. When, inching my way across rough tarmac in my wheelchair, praying no one offers, pityingly, to help me, out of the corner of my eye I see her. She's hurrying, as usual — two minutes ago, she threw her car in a space; in another three, she's got her appointment, and her big long legs are striding out, floating over kerbs and potholes. In fact, she's multitasking, on the phone, making decisions. She dominates the clock. She makes the hours.

She doesn't notice me as she passes. I may be invisible. I wish I was. I watch her go and then, jaw tight with determination, put my head back down and forge on. As if on an obstacle course, I scan for the position of the drains and the height of the kerbs, plotting my path.

This is my habitat now, low, close to the road. I see the jagged edges of tarmac patches, how the grit is first worn into and then washed out from the potholes by car tyres, like a mortar and pestle. My world in a grain of sand. My heaven in a wild flower. I smile mirthlessly.

When next I look up, she's long gone, my phantom. I can see the entrance door closing. Was it her? It's going to take me another five minutes to get there. Remember the childhood poem about Ozymandias, king of kings? At moments like this, the words return like an earworm, mocking me. "Two vast and trunkless legs of stone ... Round the decay of that colossal Wreck, boundless and bare/ The lone and level sands stretch far away."

Does it ever get any easier, that knowledge of what we once

were? Us awkward squad, us colossal wrecks, limping and inching and creeping behind the hubris of our past. I'm not sure "easier" is a word I'll ever use again. But in a way, that's why I keep taking on challenges, because it represents some kind of symbolic progress towards where I would like to be once again.

For that reason I insist on going to hospital appointments on my own now, despite the scariness, the gamble of finding a parking space, the rough access, the heightened anxiety. The margins of safety, when you're a tetraplegic on your own, are tiny. Partly, for sure, I do it because I get so weary of having a minder. Anyone. Dave. Friends. I am tired of wasting other people's time; I crave my own company, the luxury of spontaneous decisions, the ability to linger, explore, be fleetingly independent. The brief conceit of owning time again.

But deep down, I guess it's because I still chase the phantom. Melanie Past is ever ahead, tempting me; and I may be the wreck of her, but I'm still trying to follow her. Andrew Marr, in his recent TV programme on stroke rehabilitation, made me feel better, because he's doing it, too. His slow flare of delight at tiny new movements — the new flex in his left ankle, the flicker in his left forefinger. The tough, unself-pitying message that says, keep going, keep questing, hope is not dead. Keep staggering across the desert towards what might be an oasis. But might well be a mirage. Do it anyway. My left hand, defying expectations, makes the same infinitesimal improvements as his. Where once it could grip and lift only a piece of paper, now it can just about do the same with a newspaper. I don't believe in God, but by God I do believe in neuroplasticity.

A lot of people, when they write to me — and I'm sure the many thousands more who contact Marr — say the same thing: "You're inspirational." From that, with sincere gratitude, I take the compliment. But I think they're wrong. Courage can be dumb. Faith is like fake news: it's dangerous. I could well be a rotten inspiration for newly disabled people, who would be better off accepting their fate and just enjoying what they have. My body would certainly be a lot kinder to inhabit if I had killed off the ghost of Melanie Past.

That way, I'd stop seeing the bloody woman wherever I go.

Melanie Reid is tetraplegic after breaking her neck and back in a riding accident in April 2010

SPRING

SCRAPS, STORMS AND TRENCH HAND — ALL IN A 23FT BOAT

Damian Whitworth

MARCH 2 2017

IN 1789 A ROYAL NAVY SHIP was sailing from Tahiti to the West Indies when members of the recalcitrant crew seized control of the vessel from her commander, Lieutenant William Bligh. In an episode that would become known as the mutiny on the *Bounty*, Bligh and a group of loyal sailors were forced into a 23ft launch and cast adrift in the vastness of the South Pacific with five days' worth of food and water. Their epic 4,000-mile, seven-week journey to safety in Timor is regarded as one of the great maritime survival stories.

In 2016 nine men, all strangers, set out in a replica boat to re-create that voyage. Their captain was Anthony Middleton, a former special forces soldier who puts recruits through their paces in the series *SAS: Who Dares Wins*. Some of the men were experienced sailors, but the others, including a handy man, a junior doctor, a brand ambassador and at least one colossal pain in the arse, were hardly seasoned survivalists.

Five days into the expedition they hit a big storm while sailing, at night through an area littered with reefs. In the first episode of *Mutiny*, the Channel 4 series about the voyage, embedded camera operators capture the reactions of men who signed up for what sounded like a jolly adventure and are now confronting the reality of life-threatening conditions.

"I am hanging on for dear life," says one terrified man as wave after huge wave crashes over the tiny boat. "F***ing scary," says another as he huddles with a haunted look at the bottom of the boat, holding the hand of a crewmate.

Mutiny takes reality TV into uncharted waters and makes *The Island* with Bear Grylls look like a Scout camp. "Oh beyond, beyond Bear Grylls," says Middleton. "And I am a big fan of Bear Grylls. This is set apart from any reality TV; nothing like it out there."

It is hard to overstate how miserable the experience looks. Nine men are crammed into a small, open sailing boat, navigating, 18th-century style, with map, compass and sextant, eating 18th-century rations (ship's biscuit and dried beef) and enjoying 18th-century privacy and toilet facilities (they squat over the side of the boat).

A tarpaulin proves ineffective in lashing rain and their clothing, although modern, is mostly wool and cotton in an attempt to be more authentic. "Horrendous," says Middleton. "Like cardboard." The crew are seen quickly becoming soaked to the skin and they stay that way. After a few days one man has such a bad case of trench hand, or frostbite, that he cannot hold a rope or an oar.

"People need to see the real suffering, the real pain, the real hardship: the storms and the rotting of the flesh," says Middleton. But we will also see "the real joys. It was an amazing opportunity to sail the same waters as Bligh. You will definitely get an idea of what Bligh and his men went through."

One of Bligh's men was stoned to death by hostile natives and others died soon after the voyage ended. The modern crew set out to island-hop like Bligh from Tonga, to Fiji, Vanuatu and islands off Australia before reaching Timor. As a concession to modern health and safety they wore life jackets and a safety boat tracked them from a few miles away.

"If somebody got attacked by a shark, obviously we had the means to call in the safety boat, but I made it clear from the very beginning that I would make that final decision and didn't want any of them to think they had that option," says Middleton. "I know how far people can push themselves. People will question when it gets to episode five whether we did go over the line."

I meet Middleton, 36, in a pub in Wapping, east London, where Bligh lived. Today Middleton has the neatly trimmed beard of a Hollywood pirate, but by the end of the voyage he looked "like Tom Hanks in *Cast Away*". He has lavish tattoos and the biceps you'd expect of a former marine who led teams of 40 men on the ground in Afghanistan with the Special Boat Service.

You'd bet on him to island-hop his way across the Pacific, but what about the rest of them? "I wanted to see if the modern-day man could stand up to such hardships. I genuinely believed as a leader, as a captain, that I could take any man on the street and get them through this voyage and complete one of the hardest maritime survival feats known to man."

He was not without doubts though. "I thought to myself: can the modern-day man do this? People feel encaged in this health-and-safety world where you can't climb a ladder without wearing safety boots. I think people want to test themselves both physically and psychologically. They want to see where their limits lie. These men obviously volunteered to do this because they wanted to push themselves."

And were they up to it? "All of them made the mistake of thinking that it was just going to be a sailing journey. The moment I stepped off that safety boat into the 23ft open boat I was in survival mode. I didn't think of it as an adventure. I thought of it straightaway as survival. And they didn't."

He won't say how many of the men, if any, completed the voyage, but "it certainly presented its challenges and after a couple of weeks I was thinking: 'What have I got myself into?' "

At sea the men had to sleep sitting or curled on the deck and become accustomed to consuming little more than 400 calories a day of ship's biscuit and dried beef and less than a litre of water each. When they anchored at islands they went ashore to hunt and forage. Middleton put on 10kg in preparation and lost 21kg during the voyage.

Two of the group were experienced sailors but were used to having GPS, weather reports that could warn them of storms and a cabin to dry off in. "They may be hardened sailors but I guarantee you they have never been exposed to anything like that in their lives."

Physical hardship was not, though, the biggest challenge for Middleton or the crew. "I am used to my body feeling pain, to being sleep-deprived. I am used to being malnourished, I know what dehydration feels like. It was the psychological side that really pushed me as a leader and that came from the longevity of the voyage. Constantly my main priority was the welfare of the men and making sure they were psychologically OK, that they weren't sinking into depression. People got extremely low. People lost their minds on that boat," he says and gives a grim little laugh.

Was he among them? "I had bad days. I couldn't afford to lose my mind. If I was a crew member I could have, but they were looking to me to lead. If you see a weakness, see your leader crumble, then I guarantee that will have a knock-on effect and before you know it the whole team will be down."

There were good moments too, including watching a pod of dolphins following the boat and returning triumphant from successful hunting trips. "People went from extreme depression and hypothermia to next day the sun coming up and they are just in a completely different space."

His greatest fear? "Losing the command and control of the men, losing their respect." Was there a mutiny? "Not in episode one," he says, knowing that's all I've seen. Did anyone come to blows then? "Not to blows. I wouldn't allow physical violence."

Chris, a self-styled "adventurer" from Liverpool, has clearly been chosen by the production company to drive everybody else crazy and create conflict. He has been to prison for an undisclosed offence and says he has turned his life round. He dreams of sailing round the world. The problem on this voyage is that he refuses to do what is asked of him, whether it is an instruction from Middleton to collect firewood or a plea from his crewmates not to risk his life and the expedition by diving off perilous rocks. "If you say to me, 'Don't do it, stop it', I'm gonna fockin' do it," he says with the grinning pride and logic of a particularly infuriating teenager.

Of course, he cuts his leg jumping off the rocks, gets an infection and has other members of the group screaming at him within the first two days of what could be a two-month trip. "When you chuck people in at the deep end they either tread water or they drown," says Middleton. "Chris started drowning straightaway. I found out very quickly that he wasn't a team player and also that he had a problem with discipline and authority. I had to focus a lot of time on Chris. It was like looking after a child."

Middleton has had his own experience of prison. On an alcohol-fuelled night a few months after leaving the Special Boat Service in 2012 he assaulted two police officers. He served four months of a 14-month sentence.

He emerged with a plan and the determination to plot a career in television. "When I came out of prison I made a conscious decision. If I can train my mind to be an elite military man I can train my mind to be an elite civilian.

"I found myself in a shameful situation and I didn't belong there. One minute I am an elite special forces operator, team leader, the next minute I am in a prison cell sitting next to robbers and murderers. It was a massive wake-up call for me."

Tracing Bligh's route was in some ways tougher than fighting in Afghanistan. "This challenge was longer and, to be honest with you, this challenge psychologically has been the hardest test as a leader. Not the biggest test psychologically and physically combined. That would be in the special forces: you are being shot at for two or three hours, the rev count is in the red all the time. Here, it's the longevity: two to two-and-a-half months at sea. Making sure I got these guys home safely was such an immense stress that I was just engulfed psychologically with their feelings, their mental state, their physical state. I was torn from pillar to post."

Middleton has four children with his wife, Emilie, and a son by a previous relationship. Emilie is used to him being away, but in the military he was in contact regularly by email and phone. "This was the longest time I have been without talking to my wife at all. I was more emotionally connected on this journey than I was in Afghanistan because I had time to think about my wife and family and I could let some emotion show because I wasn't going out fighting wars."

He returned on the due date for his fourth child with Emilie, and their son was born a few days later. They named him Bligh.

"It seemed very fitting. To me it was such an amazing journey. I loved doing it. I'd do it again tomorrow, but that's just me."

WE ALL NEED TO LEARN HOW TO TALK ABOUT DEATH

Alice Thomson

MARCH 8 2017

I HAD FORGOTTEN his pink denim suit and floral kipper ties, but as we sat in Mortlake crematorium in west London it all came back. My godfather, Willie Goodhart, was an inspirational barrister and founder member of the SDP who wrote the party manifesto. He was deeply self-effacing about his intellect but proud of his flamboyant wardrobe. Our families had been bound together for more than a century and I suddenly remembered his love of singing *Mud, Mud, Glorious Mud* as he sat on an orange corduroy beanbag; being given my first diet bitter lemon by his wife, Celia, in her kaftan; and his smiling up at me in the Lords when he was the Liberal Democrat shadow lord chancellor and I was this paper's junior political correspondent.

His humanist funeral on a freezing January day, with a blessing by Rabbi Julia Neuberger, was extraordinarily joyful. At the end everyone sang *Happy Birthday* to his 13-year-old granddaughter.

Death embarrasses us too often now in Britain. We have lessons on sex education, careers advice and pre-natal classes. We swap tips on how to extend our lives but we rarely mention the end except when we discuss social care failures, inheritance tax or the morals around assisted suicide. "Fathers are expected to be present at the birth, but no one told me about the importance of being there at my father's death and I missed it," one friend explained.

When I interviewed Samantha Cameron recently she talked powerfully about the death of her son Ivan and how it overshadows everything else in her life. Many successful people I've interviewed seem to lose parents at an early age yet they almost all prefer not to dwell on it, acknowledging briefly perhaps that it may have acted as a spur to fulfil their lives. Studies have shown that children who lose parents, and adults who are orphaned young, often develop an instinctive drive to survive and thrive. But it is very rare for people to talk frankly about bereavement. A new book by the psychotherapist Julia Samuel, *Grief Works*, aims to change this using her case histories to illustrate the overwhelming pain of losing a parent, partner, sibling, friend or child. Just reading one of the case studies about Mimi, whose son Aiden was stillborn, is devastating: "Her eyes were dark pools of sadness with no life," she writes.

We need to understand how we can help. People often worry that they will be tactless so they become paralysed with fear. Meanwhile, those suffering find that death has irrevocably changed their lives.

Ms Samuel explains that sharing pain is the only way to make a difference yet most of us aren't sufficiently aware of the impact a traumatic bereavement has, the ripples it leaves or how long they persist. Nor do we understand how to explain death to a grieving child. It's 50 years since CS Lewis wrote *A Grief Observed* and Elisabeth Kübler-Ross explained the five stages of grief in *On Death and Dying* yet we appear less able now to confront mortality.

The ancient Egyptians planned their exit from childhood. The Victorians grieved properly, holding wakes and wearing mourning with glass lockets representing tears so people could empathise. They felt closer to death. One of my great-great-grandmothers lost eight of her siblings before she was 23. But clinging to elaborate public mourning practices during the First World War was impossible, and people were expected to pack up their troubles in their old kit bag. Death during the past century was moved discreetly from the home to the hospital and sanitised, so that grief is often now treated with antidepressants.

Ms Samuel shows that we need more emotional help but there could also be better practical advice. Four fifths of people say they never discuss their own death, half of couples have no idea of their partner's end-of-life wishes and more than two thirds of adults haven't written a will, according to the National Council for Palliative Care and the Dying Matters campaign. Even a quarter of GPs admit that they avoid discussing death with their patients.

This means that already-fragile families are often left reeling by the administration a death incurs. It's as hard to organise a funeral as a wedding and although for some it can provide a distraction, it can become a terrifying ordeal. Only 25 per cent of bereaved people across Britain feel supported after a death, while 32 per cent don't feel that their employer treated them compassionately. Willie Goodhart's eldest daughter, Frances, a clinical psychologist, said that the undertakers were her unsung heroes. "They were supportive, sympathetic and respectful, and they have to do this every day," she explained.

Cash-strapped councils, however, increasingly take advantage of families' vulnerability to hike up the prices. The cost of a burial has doubled in the past five years in some areas and now averages £4,136. Even if there is a will, a third of families end up arguing over a dead member's estate. Others have found that it is simple things that floor them, such as not being able to access the deceased's computer.

There is an art to death. If possible, the dying should make plans, write and discuss their wills, suggest funeral ideas, explain whether they want to be buried or cremated and leave their passwords. Employers should be sympathetic, as should companies dealing with delayed payments when bank accounts are frozen.

The younger generation is also providing a way forward. Their tributes on Facebook show that sharing grief is one of the best ways to help one another. As WB Yeats wrote, "Let's talk and grieve, For that's the sweetest music for sad souls."

WHAT'S A NICE ASIAN BOY DOING IN A PLACE LIKE THIS?

Sathnam Sanghera

MARCH 18 2017

IN NEUROLOGY, MEDICAL professionals sometimes talk about the "clasp-knife response", a term that describes how, during an examination, certain joints will not budge at all but then suddenly give way. Some writers have, in turn, used the phrase to describe patterns of emotional response to serious medical diagnoses, although, at risk of trivialising its use, I can't help but feel that it also encapsulates my feelings about learning to ski at the age of 40.

One minute I am, in a state of cheerful cluelessness, rather looking forward to the whole thing; the next I am dreading it more than an avalanche. Though to describe myself as clueless would be to understate things. Growing up in Wolverhampton, and knowing no one who skied, my references come almost entirely from the ZX Spectrum game *Horace Goes Skiing* and TV chat show interviews with Eddie "the Eagle" Edwards. I know so little about winter sports that when I am sent to the World Economic Conference in Davos as a news reporter in my twenties, I go in my office brogues, somehow not realising that there will be snow in a ski resort, and spend all my time falling over. The first time I try on my borrowed ski clothes (thank you, Mountain Warehouse), I put everything on at once, more than five layers, not realising that each set of thermals is for a different day.

What am I thinking? Not much. If I imagine anything at all, it is sporting a nice anorak in a snowy scene reminiscent of the video for Wham's *Last Christmas*. But then I can't help but notice that the ski jacket features "technology that makes you searchable in the event of an avalanche", which is not as reassuring as the manufacturer seems to think it is. When I ask for beginners' advice on Facebook, the responses, while encompassing the random ("Never eat the yellow snow") and the racial ("You are evolutionarily designed for the Punjab plains: it's hot, dry and flat. Skiing is not"), mainly dwell on pain and injury. As a result I google so much safety advice that algorithms begin emailing me articles about celebrity ski deaths (Michael Kennedy, aged 39, in Aspen, Colorado; Sonny Bono, aged 62, Heavenly, Nevada; Natasha Richardson, aged 45, Mont Tremblant, Quebec).

I have a preparatory lesson indoors at Chel-Ski in London, and while being taught how to put on skis and the basics of how to stop by forming skis into a pizza slice-shaped wedge, I can't help but notice that ski boots resemble plaster casts. In Geneva airport I can't help but notice the number of people returning from ski trips in actual plaster casts. In the drive up to Megève I note that the taxi driver says he has never skied himself, despite being a local, because he "can't afford to hurt himself".

It's enough. The knife has clasped, my goal going from having a bit of a laugh to not being in a wheelchair by day four. On the junior slope, among the hundreds of toddlers and children who are my companions for the week, my preternaturally upbeat and charming ski teacher, Guillaume, does his best to calm my nerves. He tells me that as well as teaching children and the very rich (some of his time is spent waiting around in chalets just in case millionaires decide they want a ski lesson), he recently taught an 82-year-old Russian man to ski. He informs me that he has a relaxed and holistic approach to teaching that he calls "emoski" and is informed by yoga, martial arts and "sophrology", a healthcare philosophy consisting of physical and mental exercises that create a prepared mind and focused body. He describes skiing as "dancing with the mountain with your magic foot" and has a line in semi-comprehensible but nevertheless soothing motivational sayings, such as: "I never have an injured person, because I respect the rhythm of the person."

And: "Every new action on the snow makes you new." And:

"You can wear a helmet. It is law in America. But you might as well make the most of being free here."

And: "Skiing is an extension of the natural. It is an occasion to get into a new state of constuteness [sic]."

And finally, if not inevitably: "Let's not report this injury because there will be too much paperwork."

For I am only a few hours into skiing before I cut my left thumb open. It's entirely my fault — Guillaume has warned how sharp skis can be: "The ski is like a huge knife." But I am too warm and have removed my gloves. Indeed, of all the many surprises about skiing, such as the fact that lots of ski resorts use artificial snow, that you can ski uphill as well as downhill, that mountains are subject to droughts, that it is more painful and difficult to get up after you have fallen than to fall down, that people actually make snowmen and have snowball fights on slopes, that people go skiing in March, that skiing holidays are essentially self-cancelling, in that the better you get at skiing, the quicker you come down the mountain and the longer you spend not skiing, the single most unexpected thing is that you are too warm most of the time. Or to be more accurate: your head is too cold, while your feet feel prepared for a moon landing as your torso roasts.

I remove some clothes for relief and, before I know it, I am on my back for the 16th time in 90 minutes, this time the snow around my hand resembling raspberry ripple. It's not serious, but there is quite a bit of blood, I can't hold a knife for a fortnight and, as I am taken for unofficial first aid, I see someone with a more serious injury being ferried down the slope. Guillaume attempts reassurance, remarking, "There can't be more than two people stretchered off this mountain on any day; it is nothing." Which strikes me as something you wouldn't have to say about a beach holiday. Or my preferred activity: staying at home and reading.

To be frank, if I had travelled alone I would have given up. But because I'm here with my girlfriend, who has skied a little before and we are at that stage of a relationship when I am still pretending to be a better, braver person than I actually am, I continue in one-handed, bloodied agony, progressing in the space of a day from being unable to put on my skis without falling down to being unable to move forwards 3ft without falling down, all the while being overtaken by supersonic toddlers.

The second day is even more of a killer, in part because the hotel is so lovely. Research informs me that Megève was apparently developed in the Twenties as a "response to Switzerland's irritatingly swanky St Moritz" and that while "Courchevel took over as France's top resort, Megève's smart hotels still attract the old money". But I'd like to pay it the ultimate compliment by saying it is even prettier than the town in the video for Wham's *Last Christmas.* We stay in two different hotels owned and run by the Sibuet family, which are swanky beyond belief, with roaring fires at every turn, animal skins draped on funky furniture, pedigree dogs belonging to the rich guests available to pet in corridors, exquisite food (having oysters on a mountain is, I think, the most decadent thing I have ever done) and staff with brilliant teeth for whom nothing is a problem, whether it is lighting fires in your room, bandaging your hands or fitting and warming your ski boots. The only problem is that we have to leave the comfort and luxury to go bloody skiing.

The challenge of day two is intensified by my injury and the fact that Guillaume is not around in the morning to carry our skis, to tell us where to go and to pick us up as we fall down every 30 or 40 seconds or so. It pretty much takes us three hours to get dressed, leave the hotel and get on to the junior slope, our journey being slowed down at various points by the sudden realisation that we probably need to arrange winter-sports travel insurance and that we probably need to hire helmets. When we finally arrive and put on our skis I promptly fall down again, this time getting stuck beneath the plastic orange feet of a blow-up cartoon character put up for the children, a line of surly French parents glaring down at me witheringly, and my beloved partner plugging on ahead, failing to respond to my pathetic pleas for help.

In the end, a seven-year-old gets me back on my feet and, when I finally catch up, there is an argument. We are still bickering when Guillaume turns up at the mountaintop café as arranged at 13.13, and he begins explaining why he likes to meet at such specific times.

"Because time is something that can be strange while skiing: one minute can be hour; one hour one minute, and it has an impact on consciousness. We are connecting to a different reality, and time is an abstraction."

Near by a small child complains that his sausage sandwich has not come, as he requested, in focaccia, and in that moment I hate everything about skiing. The way the public-school types around us seem to consider it compulsory to spray everyone with snow as they pull up to the restaurant. The incomprehensible terminology for the lifts, the funiculars, gondolas, chairlifts and T-bars, which is perhaps even more impossible than getting on and off the damned things. The ski food — what is *raclette* after all, if not just a glorified pizza topping, or skiing in food form, involving, as it does, a great deal of faff and potential injury as you assemble it yourself on your own table. I hate that a light lunch can cost €180. That just after you have spent a fortune, there is always one more thing to pay for, whether it is a ski pass or helmet hire. That after my legs have been twisted in ways they have never twisted, and after I have been forced to use muscles I didn't realise I even had, I am aching in ways that didn't seem imaginable.

Eventually, Guillaume picks up on the tension. "This first time is very intensive. It is like a washing machine of emotion," he soothes. "You feel so many things. We have fear, pain; we don't know where we go; couples and families always argue ... We think we can deal with emotions but they are stronger than us." He says that the previous day, a woman in her forties had cried for an entire day of tuition, and offers more motivational statements, which include: "In skis, as in life, we have no default, the body make it best, to do what we want ... Sometimes we are too rude with ourselves, you get a bit upper level than you realise."

And: "It's like we are planting a seed: we can never hang it to make it grow. You can never, what do you say in English, force? When something start to grow, you cannot hang it to make it grow faster. You have to give it water, give it your best energy."

And: "The breathing is the key for everything. If you blow through your emotion, you have the energy to use it, to make sure you are not catched by the angriness or the danger."

"Angriness" is mainly what I feel. I complain about the cost of the coffee. And the Nineties techno that would embarrass even 2 Unlimited, but is somehow deemed passable on the slopes. But Guillaume does a clever thing at this point: sensing that we are demoralised by being outskied by toddlers, and going up and down the "magic carpet lift" with schoolchildren, he takes us on to a proper slope, which features long easy green runs and less easy blue runs, plunging us in at the deep end. Or rather, throws us down a steep slope.

Slowly but surely, still falling over every few minutes, we make our way down a 2km slope in a blizzard. Looking back at the phone footage we are still absolutely pathetic at skiing: I doubt we exceed two or three miles an hour at any stage. We do almost the whole thing with the aid of the pizza-wedged snowplough move, the sure sign of a beginner, with people zooming furiously around us as we destroy their masturbatory enjoyment.

But there are moments of parallel skiing, occasionally we manage to look up from our skis, and I suddenly get the point.

On the way home I read an interview in the in-flight magazine for Swiss airlines with two ski stars who talk about the thrill of enjoying a "well-prepared piste", how when they are skiing they "can shut out everything else", the excitement of "the sheer speed" of skiing, and I know what they mean. The feeling of gliding down a slope, in snow or bright sunshine, the fresh air against your face, is amazing. I'd equate it to managing your first 10k run without stopping, or perhaps to driving a Ferrari for the first time, and towards the end of the second day I have the feeling I had as a kid when it was snowing, and I was playing outside, and my mum called me in, and I didn't want to go home.

Not that the feeling lasts, or that it sticks for very many people at all. According to a survey published by the National Ski Areas Association, 83 per cent of first-time skiers and snowboarders never become enthusiasts.

But in the days that follow I manage to see the positives. The scenery is sensational. *Vin chaud* is delicious: like alcoholic Lemsip. It's cool how you can refill your mineral water bottles on ski slopes from streams running with water of better quality than Evian. But God, the pain. And the interminable falling over. It just never ends. All that essentially changes between days one and four is that the causes for my falls become more ambitious: by the end I am falling over while trying to make videos on my phone and eating, rather than slipping over because I can't fasten my skis. And there is no getting over the fact that the single best moment of the holiday is the ten minutes it takes to get out of ski boots on the final day, having physically survived the whole thing.

Which brings me back to the question of race and why brown people don't ski in huge numbers. I actually think class is the more pertinent issue: I know more Indians who ski nowadays than people from inner-city Wolverhampton. But it comes up quite a bit. Before I go, a friend jokes that we Asians are genetically incapable of coordinating our legs in a V while moving ("I mean, when in the Indus Valley has such a movement ever been required? We're trudgers, carriers and squatters"). Another remarks: "You will be the only brown person on the slopes as I'm not going this year. It's quite the responsibility." The photographer spots graffiti on a ski lift pronouncing, "No brothers in the powder", which could be a threat or a simple statement of fact. My girlfriend gets asked by someone who works on the slopes whether she is my minder, presumably because the only other brown people around are princes from the Middle East, who have western minders.

Online, there are long Quora posts putting the lack of

ethnic enthusiasm for skiing down to everything from a loathing of cold weather to the cost and tradition, while my colleague David Aaronovitch has put the Jewish aversion to winter sports down to the fact that his people "are particularly uninterested in endangering ourselves for fun", that Catholics, in comparison, "have a steady belief in their entitlement — given some properly observed formalities — to the afterlife", and that they "might be said to have few natural predators".

Theology, however, can't really explain the Indian lack of interest; if anything, our belief in reincarnation should mean that we are throwing ourselves down mountains in the Himalayas in our millions. For what it's worth, I'd put it down to the extraordinary faff that skiing involves. If my Punjabi family are anything to go by, Indians are incapable of doing anything without a large degree of fuss at the best of times. As a kid, even a picnic in the park had to be planned with the kind of precision and detail that Steven Spielberg usually reserves for a film shoot: hours to make the food; hours to pack the necessary dal, parathas and samosas into carrier bags, and additional hours for calling around in case anyone else wanted to join. But given that skiing inherently involves so much preparation, from the purchase of clothing, to the fitting of clothing, to the daily replacement of clothing, the booking of ski passes, the fitting of ski boots, the arranging of travel insurance and first aid, and so tediously on, it is just an impossible prospect for many Indians. Most Punjabi families would not even make it to the slope on a conventional ski holiday.

I realise, however, that for some enthusiasts the occasional moments of bliss are worth the effort, just as for some people classic-car ownership, with its breakdowns and discomfort, is worth it for occasional afternoons of pleasurable motoring. I also realise that for some people, especially the English upper classes, the faff is the point: for not only does skiing give them the perfect excuse to indulge the English predilection for talking about the weather, it also gives them a way of not engaging with their families in any meaningful way while on holiday. Basically, it's a very expensive form of emotional repression. If you're one of the people who need this, fair enough. Have fun on your next trip. Break a leg.

GIVING BIRTH IS A LETHAL GAMBLE IN VENEZUELA

Lucinda Elliott, Caracas

MARCH 21 2017

THERE ARE PLENTY of reasons to avoid getting pregnant if you live in Venezuela.

So impoverished has the country become that maternity units cannot afford to feed expectant mothers from Friday afternoon until Monday lunchtime. Antibiotics, blood pressure treatments and painkillers are a rarity. Medical staff have to re-use surgical gloves. Perhaps unsurprisingly, maternal mortality is soaring, up 43 per cent in three years.

Angeyeimar, a 30-year-old primary school teacher from Caracas, is expecting her second baby, a boy, in April and arrived for a routine appointment at a private clinic, having been turned away twice before. The first time there was no running water, the second no electricity.

"It's all a bit of a waste of time at this stage," she said. "It wasn't like this with the first-born."

Angeyeimar should be one of the lucky ones. Like many middle-class families, she took advantage of the private healthcare perks offered by her employer. About 37 per cent of Venezuela's 31 million people are covered by private medical insurance, according to a quality-of-life survey last year.

The deep recession has, however, taken its toll on private obstetrics. As the cost of private care soars, premiums rise and quality declines, Venezuelans are throwing themselves at the state system, which is already on its knees.

Angeyeimar had her first son eight years ago in another private clinic and recalls that the care was "exceptional". Since the socialist movement — known as Chavismo, or the cult of Hugo Chávez, the late president — swept the nation at the turn of the century local manufacturing has collapsed and currency controls have made imports scarce. For pregnant women, drugs to control blood pressure, to prevent seizures and to relieve pain, such as Demerol, are scarcely available, either in a private clinic or a state maternity unit.

For Ana, a 29-year-old first-time mother, the shortages were clear early in her pregnancy. She paid 30,000 bolivars (£8 using the unofficial black market exchange rate) for a private ultrasound scan. "They don't print the picture because there's never any paper," she said.

Ana has not seen any nappies for sale in her upmarket Caracas neighbourhood of Altamira since she became pregnant five months ago. A 32-pack of disposable nappies is being sold for 40,000 bolivars (£10) via the popular Instagram account Todoparachamos ("everything for little ones"), the equivalent of the monthly minimum wage.

Supermarkets and pharmacies no longer stock nappies because of government restrictions on imports so online shops that source baby products from abroad — predominantly provided by the wealthy after trips to Miami and Panama City — are replacing traditional vendors. The alternative is to barter with illegal street sellers.

Women spend much of their pregnancy scouring their neighbourhoods to try to stock up on milk formula, vitamins and medicines.

Securing a delivery room bed in a private hospital will cost 700,000 bolivars (£150). Ana's insurer no longer provides 70 per cent of the cost of a pregnancy and, unable to afford the fee, the vast majority of expectant mothers are turning to the state. However, admitting yourself to a public hospital in Venezuela comes with previously unthinkable risks.

In Maternidad Concepción Palacios — the biggest public maternity hospital in Caracas and the first of its kind in Latin America — a long-serving epidemiologist who declined to be named told *The Times* that the unit lacked medical equipment and trained anaesthetists. She said that the list of risks to the life of a pregnant woman and her baby once inside the hospital was "endless" but included dirty operating tables, used surgical gowns and gloves.

Health statistics, the doctor added, have become "a nasty business" in Venezuela: "There's been no real data for eight years. Everyone mistrusts the system." The government has failed to publish a great deal of medical data since shortages worsened.

Scrolling through an Excel spreadsheet that is shared annually with the health ministry, however, shows that the hospital recorded 14 maternal deaths in 2016, a level last seen a decade ago and up from six in 2014.

According to data compiled by the charity Médicos por la Salud (Doctors for Health), Venezuela's maternal mortality rate has soared from 68 to 101 deaths per 100,000 pregnant women since President Maduro assumed office in 2013. That represents a 43 per cent rise in three years and the biggest increase during any presidential term since 1940. Mr Maduro is yet to complete his five-year term.

Figures obtained by Human Rights Watch from Venezuela's Ministry of Health suggest that the rate could be even higher: 130.7 maternal deaths for every 100,000 births between January and May 2016, which is well above Syria, El Salvador and Cuba.

Julio Castro Méndez, a renowned doctor and professor at the Central University of Venezuela, said: "If as an investigator I had to choose one statistic that reflects the state of our national healthcare system, it would be the rate of maternal mortality."

At Maternidad, where mothers are not fed from 4pm on a Friday to Monday lunchtime, family members are relied upon to bring in meals.

"They're expected to breastfeed already malnourished newborns while practically fasting," said a senior neonatal doctor dressed in lavender scrubs. She said that in her 16 years at the hospital she had never imagined that the system could fail mothers the way it has.

For Angeyeimar, her time to decide where to give birth is running out. "If I can't get the money together then I'll have to go to the public hospital in Santa Monica," she said.

In better news, her husband, Carlos, just managed to get hold of a jumbo pack of 250 newborn nappies from a cousin on his way back from Miami. "We've got the first two months covered," she said.

CHUCK BERRY WAS A POLITICAL REVOLUTIONARY

Daniel Finkelstein

MARCH 22 2017

CHARLES EDWARD Anderson Berry was a person of great political importance. Which is a pretty odd statement to make, given that he hardly ever said or did a political thing.

Let me start with this. "He sort of had this persona of wanting to be Hawaiian, the way his hair was, his shirts. He would say he was part Hawaiian, and in a way he could look Hawaiian. I think that something with his being Hawaiian was knowing that he could be more successful if maybe he wasn't black."

This observation, by the record executive Marshall Chess, is not the only time one of Chuck Berry's friends commented on what his biographer Bruce Pegg has called the musician's "racial ambivalence". Johnnie Johnson, his musical collaborator over many decades, once remarked that Berry "wanted to be everything ... but an Afro-American I guess". When the band were stopped by the New York police, Johnson noted that the singer's driving licence identified him as "Indian".

Chuck Berry was the grandson of a slave. He grew up in Missouri in an area so segregated that the first time he saw a white person was at the age of three. It was a firefighter, and he thought it was merely the heat and fear of the fire that had whitened the man's skin. When, as an established star, he performed in the south, he found it so hard to find somewhere to stay that he took to sleeping in his own car.

So he can hardly be blamed for playing down his racial origins. He did it for commercial reasons — to reach bigger audiences — and for safety. He will have been only too aware of how in 1956 Nat King Cole had been beaten up on stage, in front of the audience in the middle of his show, by members of the Alabama white citizens council.

Understandable though it was, Berry's reaction wasn't everyone's. His great hits, the zenith of his career, came during the turbulent days of the civil rights movement and urban revolt. As black people and liberals all over the world took up the cause of racial equality and resistance, Berry was silent.

Indeed, he died at the age of 90 having written an autobiography and starred in many documentaries, leaving behind (as far as I can tell, and I've looked pretty hard) not a single properly political statement or song. He once said he was pleased to see the first black president elected, played at a concert to encourage the Democrats to stage their convention in his home town, and gave $1,000 to a Democratic leaders victory fund. And that's it.

So why argue that he was an important political figure? It's because of the significance of rock'n'roll to cultural life and Berry's significance to rock'n'roll.

Few deny the writer of *Johnny B Goode*, of *Memphis, Tennessee,* and of *Roll Over Beethoven* the right to be called one of the great pioneers of rock music. It wasn't just the power and wit of his early records, it was his ability to reach new audiences.

Berry's first hit, *Maybellene* (the title inspired by a bottle of mascara), crossed over not just from the R&B charts into the pop charts, but from black to white audiences. Before *Maybellene*, most black music became a hit only when recorded as a white cover version. Berry's record was one of the first to outsell its white cover versions.

And then in the south, Berry desegregated his audiences. Not by political statements or any act of conscious resistance. Just by playing. The promoters would allow in black and white fans so long as they were separated by a rope down the centre aisle. And each time, as the rock frenzy grew, the rope would come down and everyone would be dancing together.

Berry wasn't much interested in the political implications of this. He was interested in its financial implications. More record buyers, more money. As the guitar hero Bo Diddley once said: "Chuck Berry is a businessman. I admire him for being a businessman. The name of the game is dollar bills." His local paper headlined a piece on his film *Chuck Berry Hail! Hail! Rock 'n' Roll* with the words: "Hail! Hail! The Bankroll."

Yet it was because of this, not despite it, that Berry was a liberator. He wanted to sell to everyone. Rock'n'roll is the fullest expression of consumer culture. Its impact was deep. It reached out to people whatever their race, whatever their class, whatever their gender or sexual orientation. It made posh accents seem ridiculous and inherited social distinctions seem bizarre. It was — it is — entirely democratic.

It breaks down national borders too. John Lennon and Paul McCartney lived in a port town, where African-American records came off the boats. Keith Richards first noticed Mick Jagger because Jagger was carrying a rare Chuck Berry record that had to be ordered from Chicago. Then the Beatles and the Rolling Stones went to America and sold back American music to them.

Rock's power isn't that it was the counter culture, but that it became the culture. The only barrier it didn't initially break down was age. There are people whose politics and social attitudes have as their main point of reference some time before 1958, when Berry cut *Johnny B Goode*, and those whose reference point is after that.

The generation gap written about in the Sixties didn't repeat itself, as everyone thought it would. Instead it was a single gap, separating the era before rock from the era after it. The people who feared that rock would sweep away customs and barriers and change cultural attitudes were right to fear it.

Sir Tom Stoppard's play *Rock'n'Roll* tells the (true) story of the attempts by the communist Czechoslovakian government in the mid-Seventies to suppress a rock group called the Plastic People of the Universe. They were not avowedly political but the Husak government could see that nevertheless they were.

They couldn't allow the Plastics just to do their thing. They appreciated that unless they imprisoned them and made them cut their hair, there would be no stopping the revolution. Their culminating act of oppression (in Stoppard's drama) is to smash the western record collection of the play's central character.

Even if Chuck Berry didn't see himself as political, the Czechs could see that he was wrong.

ON WESTMINSTER BRIDGE

Leading Article

MARCH 23 2017

THE PALACE OF Westminster, the very heart of British democracy, has come under attack. Not in a sophisticated cyberintervention, but from the crudest of weapons: a car driven at speed, steered by a man with a knife. The trail of dead and injured stretching down Westminster Bridge to the gates of parliament is a sign of how the wars of the world have encroached on our way of life.

Since the dark days of the bombing campaigns of the IRA,

Britain has been largely spared a major terrorist assault. The 7/7 attacks in London, the 2013 murder of Fusilier Lee Rigby in Woolwich, the murder of the member of parliament Jo Cox: all these events were deeply shocking, a bracing reminder that we are not immune from the overspill of an apparently global pool of anger. Yet for the most part we have been content to rely on the efficiency of our intelligence services to fend off danger, and to envelop ourselves in a sense of British exceptionalism. That complacency has now surely run its course.

It is too easy to talk today about erecting new bollards in Parliament Square or throwing an even tighter security cordon around the whole of Whitehall. Increased vigilance is necessary but not sufficient. It was fitting that in Washington yesterday a meeting of 68 foreign ministers debated the practicalities of taking the fight against terror to the ragged armies of the Islamic State and other jihadist groups. To protect our own traditions of tolerance and liberal values, we have to be ready not only to fight in concert against terror but also to address its causes.

Even though little is known about the background to the Westminster attack, it bears the hallmarks of the kind of "lone wolf" operation that has been ordered up by the many propaganda channels of Isis. On Bastille Day last year a lorry driver mowed down and killed 86 people on Nice promenade. A few months later in Berlin a stolen vehicle was used to crash into a Christmas market, killing 12 people and injuring 56 others. Yesterday's bulldozing of innocents was on a smaller scale but its intent was clear: to strike out at a national symbol; to show contempt for democratic tradition.

There were already plenty of reasons for concern. Britain's official terror level was declared to be "severe" — that is, an attack was deemed "highly likely". Britain is a target not just because it is an active participant in the wars against Isis in Syria and Iraq, nor because it is a close ally of the United States. Its readiness to defend the principles of an open society is in itself offensive to jihadists and their sympathisers.

The modern expression of this grievance is asymmetric warfare. For all the work of the security services, we cannot predict where or when these agents of terror will strike next. French schoolchildren felt perhaps more secure on Westminster Bridge yesterday than in Paris, a city that has been rocked by its own bloody terror events. At 2.35pm yesterday they received a terrifying reminder that this kind of warfare is global.

There were other reminders. After intelligence reports that jihadists are planning to smuggle bombs inside laptops on to passenger aircraft, the US and Britain have imposed a ban on electronic devices in cabins on flights to and from some Middle Eastern countries. This was met with outrage by business travellers and yet now seems a sensible precaution. The anniversary of the Brussels airport attacks, meanwhile, marked by moving ceremonies, brought home the ubiquity of the threat.

President Trump seeks to address these insecurities by going on the offensive against Islamic State. If properly funded and supported by the US political as well as military establishments, this is at least the beginning of a strategy. Isis must be shown that it cannot occupy lawless space and use it as a base for wreaking international havoc. It must be squeezed, and if this causes its adherents to seek out softer targets then they too must be met with coherent counterterrorism measures.

This war has to be intelligence-led, a compelling argument for the president to make peace with his intelligence community, and for preserving intelligence sharing between the US and its closest allies. It is too soon to assume any direct connection between Isis and the innocents mown down on Westminster Bridge, but it is past time for the free world to agree a strategy that vanquishes barbarism with sophistication and resolve.

Overcoming the Isis strongholds of Mosul in Iraq and Raqqa in Syria has been declared the Trump administration's military priority. The logic is impeccable: these are the nerve centres of the self-proclaimed caliphate. Impatient for quick

Above: *Jeremy Corbyn cast himself as the scourge of the establishment in his first big speech of the general election campaign at Church House in Westminster. Richard Pohle photographed the Labour leader in April as he left the venue after the speech in a throng of supporters and cameramen: an early sign of the surprising popularity his party would gather during the short campaign*

Top: *Tony Bellew assails David Haye in the tenth round of their heavyweight fight at the O_2 Arena in March, captured by Marc Aspland. Haye was knocked through the ropes in the next round.*

Above: *Richard Pohle photographed Dan Mothersole stoking the furnace of the tugboat* Portwey *during its 90th anniversary on the Thames*

Above: *Ladies Day at Royal Ascot always means an abundance of exotic headgear. These were some of the more restrained examples, pictured by Richard Pohle in June*

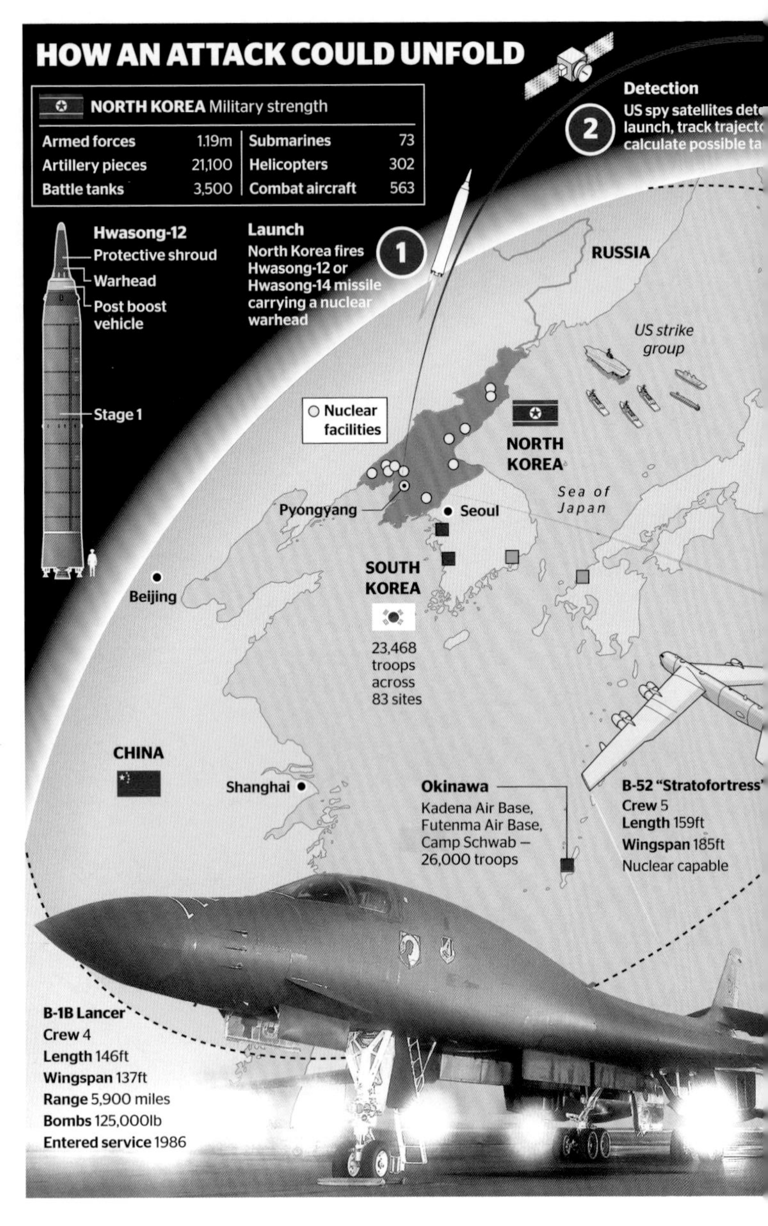

North Korea tested a hydrogen bomb and fired ballistic missiles capable of

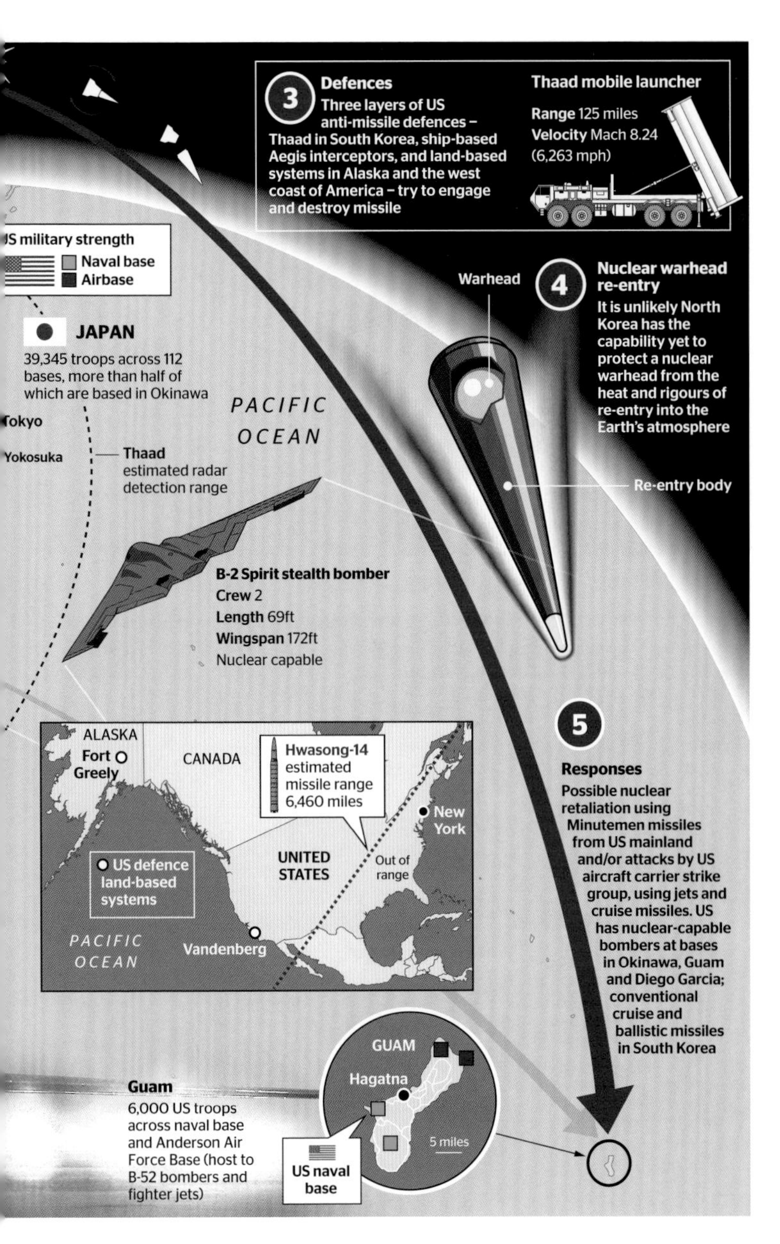

hitting US territory. President Trump responded with a threat of "fire and fury"

The Times *political cartoonist Peter Brookes was appointed CBE but that did not stop him making fun of the establishment.* ***Top:*** *Theresa May says goodbye to the EU.* ***Above:*** *the Grenfell Tower fire inspired a more serious message*

***Top:** Two gifts to cartoonists, the North Korean and US leaders, continue to provoke disbelief months after this depiction in April. **Above:** Brookes had some fun with the troubled publication of the Labour Party manifesto in May*

***Above:** Armed troops were deployed on the streets of London in May in response to the terrorist attack at Manchester Arena. Richard Pohle photographed them in Westminster, where Khalid Masood had killed five people in an attack two months earlier*

Top: *The cracks are showing in the government's economic policy according to Morten Morland's cartoon after the Grenfell Tower fire.* **Above:** *Morland seemed to find some sympathy for Donald Trump's beleaguered aides*

***Top:** Theresa May's change of direction on social care did not play well with voters during the election campaign. **Above:** Morland linked the terrorist attack in Barcelona with the solar eclipse in August to create a haunting illustration*

***Top:** James Glossop photographed this eye-catching great grey owl at the Scottish Owl Centre in Bathgate, West Lothian, in April. **Above:** Theresa May suggests another species of bird at the Conservative Party manifesto launch in Halifax the following month, captured by Richard Pohle*

Above: *The centenary of the battle of Passchendaele was marked at the end of July at the Menin Gate in Ypres. Richard Pohle photographed this serviceman in front of some of the more than 54,000 names inscribed on the monument remembering Commonwealth casualties who have no known grave*

Top: *Jack Hill photographed this group of internal refugees in the Siixawle camp, Sool province, Somaliland. A devastating drought had robbed the families of their livelihoods and homes.* ***Above:*** *The Ship Inn cricket team has to time its matches at Elie Beach, Fife, to avoid the incoming tide. Bradley Ormesher caught this game in August*

***Top:** A firefighter, photographed by Jack Hill, keeps up the search for bodies in Grenfell Tower the day after fire devastated the block in June. **Above:** Tony Blair appears to be alone with his thoughts in this image by Richard Pohle from the dedication in March of a memorial in Horse Guards Parade to Britons who served in Afghanistan and Iraq*

Above: *Usain Bolt strains every sinew during the 100m heats at the World Athletics Championships in London in August. Marc Aspland caught the determination on the sprinter's face during one of his last solo races. Bolt was left only with a bronze after Justin Gatlin and Christian Coleman cast a shadow over his farewell appearance*

results, President Trump has in effect announced that the gloves are off.

There are, nonetheless, pitfalls in using overwhelming force against Isis-occupied cities. The risks are threefold. First, Sunni states may come to believe that their co-religionists are being killed without proper discrimination between terrorists and innocents. This could weaken the currently high level of solidarity behind the Trump administration's military push.

Second, Isis on the back foot threatens to become as dangerous as Isis at its brazen worst. Its digital reach allows it to trigger sleeper cells across the world. Experts argue that its use of lone wolf killers is a sign of weakness. Yet, as Nice, Berlin and perhaps Westminster have shown, their impact can be devastating. Third, every western airstrike that takes civilian lives, however carefully that risk is minimised, serves as a recruiting sergeant for fundamentalism.

The war against Isis is the same war that British intelligence and police officers fight every day to prevent attacks such as the one that sent MPs running for cover yesterday. It must be fought with subtlety. Its pace should not be dictated by US domestic politics or showmanship and its ingredients are legion. In the Middle East, Isis fighters must be prevented from moving from Mosul to Raqqa and their leaders tracked to their strongholds. From Europe to Asia, their support networks must be disabled: these are as important in the end as the exact moment that Mosul falls.

In London, as in every city across Europe bloodied by maniacs in the past 16 months, life will go on. Yet public wariness will intensify and with it the government's duty to keep the public safe. There is no such thing as absolute security in an open society, nor is there a silver bullet on either side in this asymmetric war. There is only the relentless work of the police and security services, side by side with the softer arms of government, to anticipate plots the better to defeat them; and the stoicism of a citizenry that will never let hate win.

IT'S TIME TO RECLAIM OUR RIGHTS FROM BIG TECH

Iain Martin

MARCH 30 2017

MY 12-YEAR-OLD SON is good at puzzles and ejoys the Codeword in this newspaper. I have no facility for unravelling puzzles — other than deciphering the meaning of Theresa May's speeches — but my dad does. With my son in London and his grandparents in Scotland, via FaceTime they finish the day seeing each other and talking about words, clues and assorted amusing events. And they complete the puzzle.

Many families surely have similar stories of how the internet revolution has strengthened bonds across the generations through cyberspace. Perhaps it is because there have been such obvious practical benefits to our lives that we in the West have so far made such a mess of unscrambling the puzzle of how to rein in the companies behind the revolution. For the burglary of content and accumulation of power undertaken by the tech giants since the start of the century amounts to nothing less than one of the biggest heists in human history.

The cleverest part of the scam is the illusion that what we get from tech comes free of charge. No — we are the product. Our data and our choices are collected and sold as thousands of data points. That is why Google is valued at $578 billion. It is not magic. Google and Facebook are simply the biggest ever advertising businesses and you are for sale. Meanwhile, Amazon is turning itself into the West's one-stop marketplace.

The Silicon Valley arrogance that this produces makes journalists and estate agents look humble. Indeed, the annoyance of those in government at having to deal with the tech companies after last week's terror attacks is rooted in years of being patronised by people who refuse to take responsibility. "They think they're gods and we're little people," is how one minister puts it.

Of course, journalists and publishers have an interest to declare here. Too many of us in the media once naively embraced the illusion that everything should be free at the click of a mouse.

If you are tempted to dismiss such complaints as the griping of hacks angry at having their lunch eaten, be assured that the tech giants want your industry on the menu next. Almost every profession or trade, from accountancy, law, finance and retail, through to driving, building and bricklaying, faces epic disruption by big tech.

The conventional free-market response to this conundrum — and I am generally as pro-market as they come — is a shrug followed by a "so what?" Innovation creates casualties and the new players will rise and fall. We all benefit in the end.

Well, up to a point. One of the central lessons of the financial crisis is that we should be wary of cross-border industries that become far too big, because they cost us dear when they get it wrong.

The message of the period before the 2008 crash was that banking was globalised and superior, floating above silly old national governments and taxpayers. But when their bubble burst, what do you know? The bill was not global and landed on national governments and the taxpayers who fund them.

Similar vulnerabilities to future crises are building up in tech, whether it's the prospect of our exposure to armed drones that are able to fly long distances, or artificial intelligence mutating, or jihadi hackers finding a way of halting the modern food supply system that operates on a 24 to 48-hour cycle.

If — when — tech's bright, shiny future goes wrong, there will certainly be recriminations directed at one of the, by then, newly infamous entrepreneurs, but it will be too late. The taxpayer will look in the first instance to government to co-ordinate an emergency response, to strengthen national defences and to make tech giants live by the same set of rules that the rest of us are expected to follow.

So why wait for the emergency before we act? In the United

States of the late 19th and early 20th century there were similar fears about the cynical concentration of power. A generation of leaders, including President Theodore Roosevelt, set about "trust-busting" to break up the oil and financial cartels. Not all of it was a success. But in seeking to cut monopolies down to size, Roosevelt defended vigorously the important idea of the public good. Quite simply, large corporations should live under the rule of law and follow fair rules, like all good citizens.

What would a similar effort in Britain look like now? No one is better placed to be more robust on this than Theresa May. She seems hard-headed about security and power.

What is needed is a simple and uncluttered approach over several years, working through each component of the problem: making sure the online mega-corps are taxed on a level playing field; establishing that we own our own digital data; where necessary updating competition law; and going to town on the security of the digital infrastructure on which modern life depends.

It is difficult to work out whether the tech giants see the danger. They certainly spend vast sums on lobbyists in London, Washington and Brussels, which suggests that they can feel fear. On the other hand they hide behind the notion that all is fine because we the consumers ticked the terms and conditions box (without reading it). They should ask the bankers how that turned out. The T&C defence did not save the UK's financial industry in the case of the payment protection insurance racket and £26 billion so far has been paid out on that scandal alone.

Something similarly robust on an even bigger scale will need to be done to big tech, and soon.

OUR ADDICTS TURN BLUE, THEN THEY DIE: THE TOWN AT THE CENTRE OF NEW US DRUGS EPIDEMIC

Rhys Blakely, Huntington, West Virginia

April 1 2017

People were turning blue, their muscles contracting, their pupils shrinking to pinheads. The voice of a police officer crackled over the radio. He sounded confused. Seven people had collapsed on a single street. "They're just ... dying," he said.

It was a Monday afternoon in Huntington, West Virginia, a small coal town in the foothills of the Appalachians where most of the mines have shut. This community is at the sharp end of a nationwide heroin and opioid epidemic. A bad batch of drugs had just hit the streets.

One victim collapsed in a Burger King car park. Minutes later three more were found — as blue as their denim jeans, said the man who found them — passed out in a flat. The police radio kept crackling. "I've just got another one ... And we just got another one ... I've got two additional overdoses."

A man in his fifties was found, not breathing, in the bath. Another was slumped behind the wheel of his car, in traffic. One woman tried to resuscitate a friend but could see her own fingers turning blue. Even as she pumped her friend's chest, she herself was overdosing.

In all, 28 people overdosed in four hours, in a town of fewer than 50,000 people. Two died and 26 were revived with an antidote. The incident made national headlines but local children took it in their stride. "It was a normal day, but worse," said Jenelle Anders-Lee, 15, who lives just up the street from where the first overdoses were reported. "It's kind of sad for a teenager to be saying that, isn't it?" she conceded.

The US is in the grip of a drug problem unlike any that has gone before — a product of economic hopelessness, aggressive marketing campaigns by pharmaceutical companies and a new wave of deadly, synthetic painkillers concocted in China and Mexico.

Few places have been harder hit than Huntington. About one in five people here lives in poverty. At least one in ten is believed to be an addict. Only pawnbrokers and fast-food restaurants seem to be thriving. An Amazon distribution centre, perched on a hill, is the one sign of economic vibrancy. People walk the streets glassy-eyed. A pejorative was coined to describe them: pillbillies.

In the 1970s, when Richard Nixon announced a "war against heroin addiction", overdoses accounted for about 1.5 out of every 100,000 deaths in the US. During the crack cocaine epidemic of the 1980s, it rose to two per 100,000.

Today overdoses account for ten out of 100,000 deaths nationwide. In West Virginia in 2015 the figure was 41.5. In Huntington it is twice that.

Firefighters spend far more time administering Narcan — an opiate antidote injection — than putting out fires. There are at least five calls a day. Jan Rader, the fire chief, said that 70 per cent of them involve children being at the scene. Watching someone being dragged back from the edge of death can be a jarring experience. They will often wake up belligerent, angry that their high has been disrupted.

"Sometimes the kids are just playing video games, like it's no big deal," Ms Rader said. "It's very scary that this is their normal."

She worries about the mental health of her firefighters. She has been in the force for 23 years. She was a decade into the job before she had seen "a significant number" of dead people.

Today a young firefighter in Huntington can see 20 dead young people in a year — and perhaps twice as many. "These are people they know. This is a small town. In the past five years the job has changed entirely," Ms Rader said.

One commentator wrote that in communities across the US, pain pills and heroin have "joined shuttered factories and Donald Trump as a symbol of white working-class desperation".

A rising mortality rate among poor, white, middle-aged Americans has drawn comparisons with the sickly final days of the Soviet Union.

In Huntington about one in five children born in the local Cabell Huntington Hospital suffers withdrawal symptoms because their mothers have used opiates. These babies have tremors and unnaturally high-pitched cries. The local police talk about compassion fatigue, and worry that it will become post-traumatic stress disorder. Tales of small children being prostituted to feed their parents' habits are not uncommon.

The drugs are so dangerous that workers in funeral homes in some communities have been advised to keep opioid antidote injections ready. There is the danger of encountering minute amounts of the drug on an overdose victim's corpse. There has also been a rise in the number of grieving relatives who overdose at funerals.

The path to hell, according to Will Lockwood, a former opioid addict who lives in Huntington and who has been brought back from the brink of death four times after overdosing, begins with a sensation of delicious warmth. Opioids and heroin induce numbness, both physical and emotional. Life becomes simpler. Many addicts were first prescribed medication for pain for workplace injuries before graduating to heroin. Mr Lockwood was prescribed pain pills after having his wisdom teeth out at 15. By the time he was 16 he had a $300-a-day habit.

At first the drugs induced euphoria. Over time, however, his objective shifted. He took them not to get high, but to stave off symptoms of withdrawal: nausea, sweats, diarrhoea. What you must understand, Mr Lockwood said, is that when an addict hears about a cluster of overdoses, he or she does not think that they must avoid the batch of drugs responsible. "The first thought is — how do I get some of that?"

It is sometimes argued that working-class towns such as Huntington, which voted overwhelmingly for Mr Trump, are guilty of casting themselves as victims. "The economy isn't putting a bottle in their hand. Immigrants aren't making them cheat on their wives or snort OxyContin," David Fresh, a conservative pundit, wrote.

Those who have emerged alive from the pit of addiction give more nuanced answers. Mr Lockwood points to the role played by OxyContin, which was released in 1996.

Purdue Pharma, its inventor, marketed it as a slow-release, and therefore theoretically safer, form of the powerful and highly addictive painkiller oxycodone, a synthetic form of morphine. But initially it was easy to release the whole dose at once; smash or dissolve the OxyContin pill and snort or inject it.

The marketing push was unprecedented. In the 1990s doctors were urged, by advocates funded by the drugs industry, to recognise "pain" as a fifth vital sign alongside pulse, respiration, blood pressure and temperature.

Doctors who prescribed the most pain pills were taken on all-expenses-paid retreats. Purdue gave away samples. Sales of OxyContin grew from $48 million in 1996 to more than $1 billion in 2000.

A study published in the *American Journal of Public Health* called the marketing strategy a commercial triumph and a public health tragedy. A vast appetite for opioids was created. In Kermit, West Virginia, a town of 392, one chemist distributed about nine million pills in two years.

Then in 2010 the government began a regulatory crackdown on opioid pills. Addicts were forced to look elsewhere to get high. "We sent them to heroin," Jim Johnson, the director of drug control policy in Huntington, said.

The years that followed brought sharp increases in hepatitis C and property crime.

Now the big killer is fentanyl, a synthetic opioid many times more powerful than heroin that is produced in China and Mexico. This is the drug thought to have been behind those 28 overdoses. "This is public enemy No 1," Mr Lockwood said. "It will turn you into a shell of a human being."

THIS IS THE END OF DEMOCRACY, CRY PROTESTERS AS NATION SPLITS IN TWO

Hannah Lucinda Smith, Istanbul

April 18 2017

Never has Istanbul, the metropolis that straddles Europe and Asia, felt more like a city divided. The day after a referendum that gave President Erdogan the mandate to grasp almost total power over Turkey, the joy of his supporters, who said that this was "democracy in action", contrasted with the growing acrimony of his opponents, who claimed that the vote was skewed.

Despite the insistence of Turkey's electoral board that the poll was legitimate, international election monitors said that there were irregularities in the campaign and expressed concerns that they had been denied access to some voting booths.

The Organisation for Security and Co-operation in Europe questioned why the Turkish authorities had made last-minute changes to the rules governing vote-counting.

The president rejected the criticism outright, telling the organisation to "know your place" and said that the country did not "see, hear or acknowledge" criticism that the vote did not live up to international standards. Shortly afterwards Turkey said it would extend its state of emergency by three months: the third extension since a failed coup attempt in July.

Mr Erdogan's "yes" campaign won on Sunday night with 51.49 per cent of the vote, according to the latest unofficial count, with a victory margin of 1.4 million over the "no" camp.

"They stole this," said one man, dazed and depressed and unwilling to give his name in fear of a possible crackdown on critics. "The end of democracy, and for what? A couple of percentage points?" Claims that the referendum had been manipulated helped to fuel a second night of protests. In Kadikoy, the middle-class, bohemian district of Istanbul, about

3,000 people — young and old — took to the streets in anger over the "yes" victory. Kadikoy voted 81 per cent against.

Protesters, some chanting "Thief, Erdogan", "No to the presidency" and "This is just the beginning", stuck to the narrow streets of the district because most roads are too small to accommodate a water-cannon truck. Such demonstrations have not been seen in Turkey for four years and protesters were scrutinised by hordes of undercover police and the riot squad.

"We can't accept this result," said one young woman. "We know the vote wasn't fair."

As the crowd passed through the streets, chanting "We will not bow", elderly men and women hung out of their windows, cheering and banging cutlery, pots and pans. One old lady blew kisses to the demonstrators.

As night fell, the protests spread across the city.

"I don't believe the result, and I believe the protests will grow," said a graduate, 22, in the Besiktas borough, which voted 83 per cent "no" and was also the scene of large protests on Sunday night. More have been called.

In the divided metropolis — President Erdogan's home city, where he started his political career as mayor in the 1990s — the ballot varied wildly. Erdogan supporters crammed the streets and squares all night in some areas, ecstatic at how the result had played out.

The overall vote in Istanbul was split almost down the middle, with 259,000 more people voting "yes" than "no". Turkey's next two biggest cities, Ankara, the capital, and Izmir, on the coast, voted "no".

The People's Republican Party (CHP), the main opposition party, called for the result to be annulled and said that it would bring a case against President Erdogan to the constitutional court and the European Court of Human Rights. Baris Yarkadas, a senior CHP MP, said: "What kind of a victory is this? They can't govern this country without a state of emergency. They have become a government addicted to the state of emergency.

"The result they declared didn't gain acceptance by the

public. Fifty per cent of the public opposed the new regime. No one believes that the government won this referendum fair and square. The 'no' voters proved a point to the government: they are not going to be allowed to change the regime. They have to accept this fact. We are ready for a difficult period full of struggle."

Bulent Tezcan, the CHP deputy chairman, said: "It will take its place in the dark pages of history with its open voting but secret counting. The [board] did not and cannot stage a safe election."

Meanwhile, a jubilant President Erdogan was already hinting at how he might use his new mandate yesterday. He is expected officially to resume his position at the head of the ruling AK Party at the end of this month. In his victory speech, he said that the reintroduction of the death penalty would be considered — a move that would herald the end of Turkey's relationship with the EU.

Amid the mounting calls for a recount, there are signs that Turkey could face a summer of violent protests as it did in 2013, the last time that there was a mass opposition movement against the president. That would pit the two sides of Istanbul's population of 15 million people — put crudely, the conservatives and the secularists — against each other.

DROUGHT CASTS THE SHADOW OF DEATH

Catherine Philp, Sool, Somaliland

April 21 2017

Yusuf, almost two years old, has never felt rain. Droughts have devastated his birthplace in eastern Somaliland for decades, but none that anyone can remember has been as crippling as this.

Elders remember the Dabader, or long drought, of 1974.

This one they call Lagamalito: the worst.

Exacerbated by climate change, it stretches across a swathe of east Africa, threatening famine, mass migration and an end to the traditional way of life for millions of people forced to leave their homes in search of water. Sool, the worst-affected district, has been waiting for rain since before Yusuf was born. This breakaway region of northern Somalia may have avoided the conflicts tearing through its chaotic southern neighbour but the drought here is the worst in a hundred years.

The roads that cut through the desiccated landscape are littered with the skeletal carcasses of goats and camels, once the livelihood of its semi-nomadic people. Now human lives are imperilled, the youngest most of all.

A mobile clinic run by the Somali Red Crescent and funded by the British Red Cross was bouncing along these pitted roads last week when an emergency call came in: cholera had broken out in a makeshift camp of displaced herders forced to abandon their homes and go in search of water when their shallow wells dried up and their livestock died.

The water source they had trekked two hours to find was tainted. In 24 hours ten women and children had died. Other lives hung in the balance.

Yusuf lay on a soaked grass mat on the floor of the village school, the still centre of a chaotic whirl of medical staff and vomiting, crying children.

Nuah Mohammed, the village elder, had ordered the school to be opened as a makeshift hospital for the visitors encamped near by. The village name, Goljanno, means mountain of heaven. "It doesn't feel like that any more," Mr Mohammed, whose children left years ago for London, said.

Abdul Kareem Mohammed, Yusuf's father, hovered near by, grief-stricken. He had brought his son to the school that morning, along with his pregnant wife, Zahara. She died before rehydration treatment could take effect. The couple had already lost two children shortly after birth. Yusuf was the only remaining son.

"I don't know if he will live," Mr Mohammed said, his eyes brimming. "I have lost everything else: first my livestock, then my wife. I loved my wife, she was my life. She was everything."

More than 25,000 people have contracted cholera across Greater Somalia since the start of the year, a figure set to double by the summer. The United Nations is racing to prevent a repeat of the 2011 famine that killed more than 260,000 Somalis, but funding falls far short of what is needed.

That much is apparent outside Goljanno, where cholera took only hours to tear through the huddle of dwellings fashioned from branches, cloth and tarpaulin. Similar encampments dot the bleak landscape, housing those who once considered themselves wealthy thanks to their herds of livestock. At Sihawele, 300 families have gathered from different areas along the Ethiopian border, close to the nearest well from which they can still draw water.

Amina Mohammed Abdi, 70, walked for a week to reach Sihawele with her family after they lost their 300 sheep and all but two of their 15 camels. "We were rich before, we had milk and meat to eat and sell," she said. "But the land dried out and there is no longer anything for the animals to eat or drink."

They now rely on the generosity of relatives in other areas and food distributed by aid organisations. "But that is not how we want to live," Mrs Abdi said. "We want our independence back."

The day before, Somaliland's president, Ahmed Mohamed Mohamoud Silanyo, had decreed a day of prayer for rain to end the drought. Having prayed for two years for rain themselves, the people in Sihawele now fear a downpour, worried that their fragile shelters will be washed away by the deluge.

The rains, even if they come, will not bring back their livestock nor solve the longer-term question hanging over the sustainability of the pastoral life in this rapidly withering corner of Africa. Life in these remote, arid lands was never easy, aid officials acknowledge, but population growth and increased drought have made it harder than ever.

"It is easy to see why such a way of life can quickly reach a tipping point that turns a drought into a humanitarian crisis," Alexander Matheou, the director of programmes at British Red Cross, said.

Or as Mrs Abdi, crouched inside her tiny shelter, put it: "If the rains come now, they will be too late. We have already lost everything."

Not quite everything. Five days after Yusuf's mother died, word came through that he had survived, thanks to lifesaving treatment.

He remains at the clinic, being treated for malnutrition, one less loss for his father to bear.

NEPAL IS BACK: ANCIENT TEMPLES, MOUNTAINS AND BENGAL TIGERS

Tom Chesshyre

April 22 2017

Ruby-red rhododendron trees with trunks adorned with delicate white orchids line the path to the remote village of Panchase Bhanjyang. Below, the mountainside plunges to crop terraces and clearings with water buffaloes. Smoke rises from far-off dwellings. Luminous clouds scuttle across the valley, cooling us as we pause after our five-hour hike.

We are on the edge of the Annapurna region of mountains in central Nepal. Somewhere to the north is Fishtail mountain (Nepalese name: Machapuchare, 6,993m, or 22,942ft), which resembles a half-submerged fish descended from the heavens. Somewhere to the southeast is Everest (8,848m), the granddaddy of the Himalayas. All around, snow-capped peaks lurk behind clouds.

This is a mystical, soul-lifting place.

We continue upwards, tackling a steep rocky section. My

guide, Su, pauses to examine leopard droppings. "About a month old," he says. Only once has Su spotted a leopard here, when the creature disappeared in a flash after encountering a group of British backpackers in fleeces. "Very shy," he says, striding onwards.

All is quiet. Since the morning we have passed a mere handful of hikers: French walkers with porters heading to Pokhara. And when we arrive at Panchase Bhanjyang, having covered eight miles, we are the only guests. Maya, one of the three sisters who own the Happy Heart Hotel, ushers us to a plank-like perch in front of the wood fire in her smoky kitchen so we can warm up with tin cups of lemon ginger tea.

As she tends the rudimentary stove she tells us about April 25, 2015, when an earthquake measuring 7.9 on the Richter scale struck Nepal, bringing the loss of almost 9,000 lives, destroying tens of thousands of homes, turning centuries-old temples to rubble and in a few terrifying minutes ruining the tourism on which so many parts of the nation depend. "It was big shaking," she says. "Big, big shaking. Our main house collapse."

The costly rebuilding of this property took a dozen workers three months, but the hotel itself escaped serious damage. Yet since then guest numbers have halved at its ten well-appointed, but simple rooms: £4 a night, with electricity, clean toilets in sheds and pictures of the Hindu elephant god Ganesh on the bedroom walls (he is said to bring luck). "People are too scared to come because of the earthquake," says Maya, who has a remarkably laid-back take on the disaster.

Nepal has been through a lot in the past two years, not least a pair of powerful aftershocks soon after the initial quake, which brought down many more buildings. Now, however, with reconstruction of some (but far from all) temples and the immediacy of the trauma fading, tourists like me are beginning to trickle back. I have signed up to a ten-day tour, beginning in Kathmandu, with visits to sights in the Kathmandu Valley, Chitwan National Park (to the west), and culminating in our magnificent Annapurna hike.

The country is still a long way from normal — and the effects of April 2015 are obvious on the drive from the airport to the centre of Kathmandu. Buildings with precarious-looking support beams, great piles of rubble and roads with teams digging up cracked pipes (the authorities are modernising the water system) create an impression of barely suppressed chaos.

This is heightened by the awful traffic jams. The earthquake came as the capital was struggling with a population influx from the countryside. In recent years many youngsters from rural areas have sought more glamorous lifestyles glimpsed on the internet, turning their backs on the hard grind of working the paddy fields. The result is that Kathmandu is busy, and the pollution from vehicles and building sites is dreadful. So much so that my city guide, Archana, regularly loses her voice after leading tours. She hands me a face mask to keep out dust. Despite this, my lungs ache at night after a day's sightseeing.

See the sights we do — what's left of them. In Durbar Square, in Kathmandu's medieval centre, the white walls of the old royal palace are cracked and crumbling, with crude support beams and an exclusion zone in case the crippled edifice decides to call it a day. Beyond, many of the temples are little more than construction sites behind corrugated metal walls.

"This is the temple of Vishnu," says Archana. "At least, it used to be."

Near here I get talking to an Australian couple from Sydney. "We sat up there where the pillars were last time we came," says Jill, a retired teacher. She's looking at a picture on a display board. "Now everything looks like it was hit by a bomb."

Yet there is a still a huge amount to see in Kathmandu. The Sydneysiders and I chat for a while, and they tell me how they were asked for donations by "very polite" Maoist insurgents when they went trekking in the mountains in the 1990s (Nepalese politics has had a rollercoaster ride in recent years). Then we go to see the beautiful temple of Kumari. This is home to the eponymous "living goddess", who is now aged ten and who was selected for her unusual role when aged three. When she menstruates for the first time, Archana says, a new goddess will be selected. No photos of her may be taken in the temple.

On our visit Kumari happens to come to the window of her balcony, dressed in a red and gold robe and wearing Cleopatra-style eyeliner. She regards her audience (us) somewhat disdainfully, pouts and returns to an inner room. The 20 or so tourists in the courtyard are delighted.

Afterwards, we visit "Freak Street". This is close by and is where hippies hung out in the 1960s, enjoying the Himalayan nation's plentiful marijuana, now illegal, although the waft of weed is not an unfamilar smell in Thamel, Kathmandu's tourist district and very much backpacker central.

Then we drive to see the remarkable cremation temple of Lord Shiva, known as Pashupatinath Temple, on the Bagmati River. Here a series of funeral pyres, ghats, are ablaze by the murky water's edge. Wood crackles. Thick white smoke swirls up. Many Indian tourists are taking pictures — this is a key Hindu pilgrimage site. Cows graze by the river and monkeys skip about on rocks. Palm readers, who are Hindu priests in saffron robes, sit cross-legged by a path, patiently waiting for customers. On an impulse I have my palm read by one. He clasps my right hand with his turmeric-stained hands and says that I "could be very rich", "will travel a lot" and may have "two or three children, but not with family planning". With this, the priest winks and asks for 500 rupees (£3.85).

We go to see the great white stupa of Boudhanath in the city's north, which has had part of its golden tower repaired since the 2015 quake. Shops all round the stupa sell knock-off branded shoes and climbing wear — North Face jackets are available for £15; "North Fakes", as they are known locally. Monks in maroon robes jostle past. Local couples circle the stupa for good luck. About 12 per cent of the Nepalese are Buddhist; 80 per cent are Hindu.

So concludes our final afternoon in Kathmandu, but before heading northwest for the Annapurna trek, we have three stop-offs planned, each revealing the state of Nepal's post-quake recovery.

The first is the medieval city of Bhaktapur, about eight miles south of the capital. The labyrinthine red-brick centre of this much smaller city, which was the centre of power in the country until the late 15th century, has been preserved over the years, yet its frailty meant it took a bad hit two years ago. Now just about every building is propped up by wooden beams, some of which look makeshift. Many of the central temples are still being painstakingly rebuilt. And parts of the recently reopened National Art Museum are off-limits because of cracks in the walls.

This museum is home to fantastic medieval paintings of Hindu gods, as well as portraits of Nepalese kings, beginning with the founder of the Kingdom of Nepal in 1768, the much-loved Prithvi Narayan Shah, and ending with the last king in 2008, when the monarchy was brought to an end. This decision came after the world headline-grabbing royal massacre of 2001, when Crown Prince Dipendra went on a shooting spree, murdering his father, King Birendra, and killing himself. The final portraits have a spine-chilling quality.

Tin "earthquake victim shelters" are still in Bhaktapur, as are faded blue tents supplied by China. Some families are living in buildings that are not considered safe. "They are taking a risk," says Su, who is accompanying me from here to Annapurna.

Onwards we go, driving up a mountain overlooking Bhaktapur that rises to 1,950m, and on to the hill town of Nagarkot. Along the way we pass army bases where Gurkhas who later join the British Army are trained — they can be seen running along the steep single-track road carrying rifles and heavy packs (no wonder their fitness levels are renowned). We check in at dusk to the Sunshine Hotel, get an early night after a power cut (Nepal's electricity supply is still in a parlous state), then wake at the crack of dawn to do what everyone does at Nagarkot: watch the sun rise.

At 5.45am we are on the hotel roof with binoculars gazing across a hotel that is still being rebuilt after the earthquake to see the sun slowly appear beyond the jagged ridge of the

Himalayas. Orange and peach light rises in heavenly shafts, soon forming a fiery blaze above the icy peaks. The tip of Everest can be seen in the distance by a band of cloud. We look on in awe before having breakfast, where Subbha, the waiter, tells us how his grandfather died in a collapsed building on this hillside in 2015.

Almost everyone has an earthquake story. Su is no exception. When the ground began to move he was in a street in Kathmandu, and he imagined he was simply experiencing a dizzy spell. Then, when moped riders began to topple in the street, he realised something significant was afoot. Phones were not working, telecommunications towers had come down, so he rushed as quickly as he could to his village to check that his wife and son were OK.

This took nine hours, including a 15-mile hike. His wife and son were, thankfully, fine, but their house was badly damaged. He bought a tarpaulin to act as a tent in their garden. A month later he was allocated a tin emergency shelter, in which they still live. "I need $25,000 to buy a house," he says. "Everyone in my village is in the same boat. We are all in it together."

It is a seven-hour drive from Nagarkot to Chitwan National Park. Here, we check in to the Jungle Villa Resort overlooking the Rapti River. As we do, staff at the hotel wave us over to a deck. A single-horned rhino, of which there are about 500 in the park, is wallowing in the shallows.

So begins a marvellous two days, witnessing rare sloth bears, more rhinos, gharial and mugger crocodiles, and finally — best of all — a Bengal tiger. The creature is pacing through shrubland and, when it sees us, turns and disappears almost immediately. Yet for a few seconds we have witnessed the elusive beast, of which there are about 120 in the park. Apparently there is a one in 20 chance of such a sighting (even the guides are thrilled).

It's worth adding here that when I arrive there is just one other hotel guest. Sahodar, the hotel manager, tells me that business is down about 70 per cent since 2015. In 2014 127,000 foreigners visited Chitwan National Park. Last year this figure was 56,000. It's an excellent time to go to Nepal if you want to avoid tourist crowds.

This is true on the trekking trails too. At the Happy Heart Hotel, after our eight-mile hike, I get to know the handful of Spanish, American and German guests — trekking is very sociable — and in the morning we all head off our own ways after a dawn visit to Hindu and Buddhist temples on a peak. Su and I tramp for 18 miles through beautiful rhododendron forests and villages growing garlic, cabbages and spinach, all the way down to Pokhara, with its backpacker hostels and bars.

We are exhausted and, to celebrate, we go for Everest beers and chicken curries at a bar in the middle of the strip, which was, luckily, unaffected by the quake. Hardly anyone is around. Rolling Stones and Beatles songs play out across empty bar stools as we raise our beers to our adventures. Nepal is back ... even though the mountains never went away.

LE PEN CAN BE PRESIDENT IF SHE PLAYS THE LONG GAME

Giles Whittell

April 29 2017

On monday thousands of French nationalists will march through Paris in honour of Joan of Arc and the woman they consider her spiritual heir, Marine Le Pen. In past years these marches have been defiant but bedraggled affairs; this one promises to be glitzier. There's an election in progress with Le Pen in the running and the fate of the Fifth Republic at stake. And Lionel Tivoli will be there, with a fresh face and a story to tell.

Tivoli is 28 and secretary-general of the National Front in Nice. The hardline anti-immigrant party has always done well in the city, where the Alps meet the sea and wealthier pieds noirs liked to settle when war drove them from Algeria in the 1960s. But it has done especially well since Bastille Day last year, when a Tunisian-born loner ploughed through the crowds on the Promenade des Anglais in a 19-tonne lorry.

The attack killed 86 and wounded several hundred. Squat steel posts now march down the middle of the promenade to prevent a repeat. The city has taken the opportunity to plant new palms where old ones were mangled by the lorry, and the National Front has seized the moment too. Its headline demand is for an end to the Schengen system's open borders.

Since last July its local membership has doubled. "We make the link between immigration and security for two reasons," Tivoli says, exhausted after a day spent printing posters for round two of the presidential election. "The world is at war with Daesh and they infiltrate our country because the borders are open."

On the face of it round one all but secured the presidency for Emmanuel Macron, the uber-liberal who dared to marry his teacher and conjure a political movement from thin air. But Tivoli takes a different view of recent French history and of the next eight days. He believes that Le Pen's moment has come.

He believes that the 7.2 million conservatives who voted for the Catholic, Thatcherite François Fillon in round one (despite Fillon hiring his wife on the taxpayer's dime to do precisely nothing) will lurch further to the right in the end in much greater numbers than the pollsters say.

He is optimistic but not delusional. Across the south of France, and in much of the north, the first stage of this contest left millions of voters with no appetising option. Many now look to round two with open sympathy for Le Pen as the next victim of a great establishment stitch-up — Fillon being the first — and a what-the-heck impulse to stick it to Macron. These people include an unknowable number who voted for Jean-Luc Mélenchon, firebrand of the far left. They are all likely to be grumpy for at least the next five years, and what then if Macron fails? What keeps the French political class awake at night is the thought that Tivoli has correctly predicted the result, if not of this election, then the next one.

All the polls give Macron a lead of at least 20 points over Le Pen. They tell three stories. One is of his undoubted talents. He's a "political Casanova" who can seduce anyone while revealing nothing of himself, says a Republican politician who considers him a friend.

Another is the story of President Hollande's near-total failure to reform the French economy or seduce anyone except his girlfriends; and the Socialists' implosion as a result. A third is the story of mass *dégagisme*, the chucking out of both main parties by mainstream as well as fringe voters disgusted with what they have concluded is an unshakeable, bipartisan political habit of getting nothing done.

Last Sunday 40 per cent of French voters turned their backs on the centre. That rejection ends the long first act of the Republic and carries echoes of last year's US election, with this difference: Trump was a have-a-go hooligan but Le Pen has been laying siege to power for 30 years. What is easy to miss as national attention swings to Macron is Le Pen's long-run achievement in recalibrating what is acceptable in French society and politics.

Whatever happens on May 7, Le Pen is likely to win more than twice as much of the vote as her openly racist father did against Jacques Chirac in 2002. Already the National Front is the biggest single party in two giant regions — Hauts-de-France in the north and Provence, Alpes, Côte d'Azur in the southeast — and the only reason that it does not run their regional governments is that Socialists withdrew to give Republicans a free run.

"She promises to secure the frontiers. What's wrong with that?" asks Serge behind the counter in a sports shop off the promenade. "The only aliens she'll expel are the ones on terror watchlists," says Christian, a friend. They manage to make Le Pen's offer to voters sound perfectly reasonable, and indeed her efforts to detoxify her brand (her *dédiabolisation*) have passed a major test. She is a shameless revisionist who does not believe France bears responsibility for its treatment of Jews in the Second World War, but that did not appear to hurt her in round one.

A few blocks away Valerie Collin, who owns a gift shop, and Bruno Carnazza, a retired policeman, are buying fruit and accommodating themselves to the choice of May 7. Both voted for Fillon in round one. Both have grown-up children. Both are fascinated by Brexit. Valerie is hesitant but leaning towards Le Pen for round two.

Bruno is not hesitant at all. He's had it with Islamists, including the one who killed a fellow policemen a few days earlier on the Champs-Élysées. He's had it with overstretched hospitals. He's "all fired up".

Macron has taken a commanding lead without having to grapple seriously with the concerns of people like Valerie and Bruno. The French centre-left was demoralised enough to embrace such a fluent alternative to machine politics and big enough to sweep him to 24 per cent of the vote on Sunday. But he cannot take even moderate conservatives for granted in round two.

"He's a talented guy, but he doesn't know the country," says Julien Hubert, a Republican deputy in the national assembly who has known Macron for 16 years, including two when they were students at the École Nationale d'Administration in Paris. "He minimises the difficulties of the path the country is on and problems with globalisation. His programme consists of happiness and a positive attitude. It doesn't offer anything to those left by the wayside.

"Le Pen could win 45 per cent of the vote because the elites already think everything's going to be fine, like normal. The problem is that this country is boiling, and it loves to kill the favourite."

This is a political rival's caricature, but a knowing one. Hubert will vote "blank" on May 7, but he doesn't want Macron to fail. His worry is that his old student chum, who is scrambling to field candidates for his En Marche movement in June's parliamentary elections, will be forced into an impractical coalition that succumbs to France's familiar political paralysis. And that leads to the deeper fear, shared by many, that the National Front "could win the next election".

Hubert represents a rural constituency in the hills of Provence, the sixth poorest in France. It is centred on Carpentras, population 30,000, with a grand gothic cathedral and a dark place in recent history. In 1990 its ancient Jewish cemetery was attacked by thugs. Thirty-four graves were desecrated and a recently buried man was dragged from his tomb, left to look as if he had been impaled with an umbrella. L'affaire Carpentras prompted a protest march through Paris attended by 200,000 people, President Mitterrand among them. It went unsolved for seven years, blamed without proof on the National Front, which turned it into a parable of its own persecution.

In 1997 one of the perpetrators died and another came forward. They belonged to an extreme nationalist group with links to the National Front that the party denies to this day. It's not hard to find members who offer the standard line. "I was here when they accused us of it," says Jacques Dibastian, an 82-year-old veteran of the Algerian war soaking up the sunshine on a bench in the market square. "It was just delinquents, and you get delinquents anywhere."

In fact Carpentras is a National Front fiefdom, says Philippe Aldrin, a political science professor at Sciences Po in Aix-en-Provence. It is also an illustration of how the front's long march towards the mainstream is changing France. Half an hour's drive by smooth dual carriageway from Avignon and the TGV, it should be prospering but isn't.

This is *la France profonde*, although Aldrin prefers the less pejorative and slightly more urban France *périphérique* — one of hundreds of middle-sized towns with no economic growth engine of their own, too many under-qualified young people and more immigrants seeking work than jobs vacant.

The town divides naturally in two. The better-off north side falls into Hubert's constituency although even there his majority over a socialist challenger at the last parliamentary election was wafer thin. The southside houses blue-collar locals and most of the immigrants who make up 40 per cent of the population. It has a different MP: Marion Maréchal Le Pen, Marine's niece, more strident than her aunt and much closer to her grandfather, Jean-Marie.

Since Marine's decision this week to relinquish leadership of the party to focus on the election, "MMLP" has become, for some, the new, true tribune of the hard right. For now that tension has been put on hold. A spokeswoman denies any policy differences between the women and focuses on the contest at hand.

Marine won 19,000 of France's 39,000 communes in round one to just 7,000 for Macron, she says. "Marine defends the people. She's our hope for our children. Macron is the candidate of the banks, of Merkel, of ultra-globalisation. He defends only power."

Macron is supremely confident, with a good grasp of what ails France after two years as President Hollande's economy minister. The outlines of this illness are easy to sketch: unemployment stuck at 10 per cent, public spending at 57 per cent of GDP, a tax base that cannot fund this spending because of a labour code that makes hiring too expensive, and unions so powerful that in 40 years the code has never been substantively reformed.

This macro-economic mess has been neatly illustrated throughout the campaign by a showdown outside a tumble-dryer factory in Macron's home town of Amiens.

On Wednesday it flared up. Macron was on the back foot politically having taken his staff to a meal costing €7,000 last Sunday night in what looked like a premature victory celebration for an election barely half won. He had promised to visit the Whirlpool factory at Amiens, whose American owners plan to shut it down and open a cheaper one in Poland. Instead, bizarrely, he arranged a closed-door meeting with union representatives in the centre of town.

Le Pen pounced. She showed up unannounced at the plant to ridicule the former Rothschild banker and spent 20 minutes basking in the affection of striking workers against a backdrop of burning tyres. Then she left. It was a challenge that Macron could not ignore. Within an hour he had left his meeting and was heading for the plant.

I met him there and asked why he had changed his mind. His answer was revealing: "The union asked me to come." It was not, he tried to suggest, his own idea. This was a clash in which the candidate who promises to embrace free markets and deregulation had decided he could not be seen to take sides.

For more than an hour he told angry workers everything that they did not want to hear. He would not try to tell a private company what to do. He would not make promises to save their jobs. "I don't propose nationalisation and you don't want me to suppress globalisation. The closure of our frontiers would mean the destruction of millions of jobs. In Belgium and the Netherlands there are factories like this that could have moved and haven't. Ask yourselves why."

He arrived to boos and left in silence. He had won the Whirlpool workers' attention, if not their respect. For someone mocked as eager to offer all things to everyone, it was a surprising and impressive performance. Whether he can surprise France by unleashing its caged and cautious entrepreneurialism is one of the great questions of the next five years. If he fails, Le Pen will be there to pounce again.

DUKE RETIRES RATHER THAN GROW FRAIL IN PUBLIC

Valentine Low

MAY 5 2017

THE DUKE OF EDINBURGH decided to retire from royal duties to avoid his growing frailty being exposed in public, *The Times* has learnt. Prince Philip, who turns 96 next month, will continue to carry out public engagements before stepping down at the end of the summer, Buckingham Palace announced yesterday.

He had spent several months considering his future as he increasingly felt the strain of his official duties, it is understood. He broke the news of his planned retirement to the Queen over the Easter weekend at Windsor Castle and she immediately gave him her full support.

The duke came to the decision after a busy run of engagements last year, which included the Queen's 90th birthday. The landmark royal event this year is their 70th wedding anniversary in November.

Over recent months Prince Philip has been feeling the relentless pace of engagements — he carried out 219 last year, and more than 22,000 since 1952 — and while he remains in good health, *The Times* understands that he can find himself lacking energy.

In recent outings, however, he has appeared in good spirits. Attending the service for the Order of Merit at the Chapel Royal, St James's Palace, yesterday and a reception afterwards, he was in characteristically humorous form. "I'm sorry to hear you're standing down," the mathematician Sir Michael Atiyah told him. "Well, I can't stand up much longer," he replied.

For the duke, a man who has been fit and active all his life, to draw a line under 65 years of public service was a tough decision. But he had reached a growing realisation that even someone of his stamina eventually had to slow down. As he said at his 90th birthday: "It's better to get out before you reach your sell-by date."

By stepping down at the end of the summer, he has timed his retirement to perfection. At the same time the Duke and Duchess of Cambridge are moving their operations from Norfolk to Kensington Palace so that Prince William, 34, can take up full-time royal engagements.

The announcement comes after a number of health problems for Prince Philip. In 2013 he spent 11 days in hospital for what was described as an exploratory operation on his abdomen. Although sources have suggested that it was more serious, he has had no significant problems since. He has in the past received hospital treatment for bladder infections and a blocked coronary artery.

The news was broken to the royal household by the Lord Chamberlain, Earl Peel, and the Queen's private secretary, Sir Christopher Geidt, yesterday morning. Several hundred of the 500 staff that the Queen employs gathered in the ballroom of Buckingham Palace to hear Sir Christopher, 55, tell them how, after the duke stepped down, other members of the royal family would support the Queen by carrying out engagements with her and on her behalf.

That was followed minutes later by a statement from the Palace that said: "His Royal Highness the Duke of Edinburgh has decided that he will no longer carry out public engagements from the autumn of this year. In taking this decision, the duke has the full support of the Queen."

In a "farewell tour" the duke will appear in public at events including Trooping the Colour and the Spanish state visit and he has not ruled out attending occasional functions after that. The statement added: "Thereafter, the duke will not be accepting new invitations for visits and engagements, although he may still choose to attend certain public events from time to time."

Tributes were led by Theresa May, who said that he had been a "steadfast support" to the Queen. The Labour leader,

Jeremy Corbyn, an avowed republican, praised the duke's "clear sense of public duty".

In a reference to the duke's outdoor cooking at Balmoral, David Cameron said: "The Duke of Edinburgh is an outstanding public servant. We owe him a huge debt of gratitude. I always enjoyed his company, especially his BBQs."

LANDSLIDE FOR MACRON

Charles Bremner, Adam Sage; Paris

May 8 2017

Emmanuel Macron won the French presidency last night, crushing Marine Le Pen, the far-right candidate, after a vicious contest that has ended decades of rule by established parties. Mr Macron, 39, a pro-EU, free-trade proponent who made a bold pitch for power with no electoral experience, is France's youngest new leader since Napoleon Bonaparte in 1799.

The victory marked a historic upheaval in the country's political landscape and inflicted a reversal on the nationalist, anti-globalisation cause that has made inroads in the US and Europe. Mr Macron, a former economy minister under President Hollande, won 66.06 per cent of the vote in the second-round run-off to Ms Le Pen's 33.94 per cent.

A low turnout of 74 per cent and a record 12 per cent spoilt or blank ballots reflected widespread rejection of both finalists who emerged from the first round on April 23. Although Ms Le Pen's score was the highest by the National Front in a presidential election, it fell behind forecasts and was far from the 45 per cent that her party had hoped for. She still almost doubled the vote share of her father, Jean-Marie Le Pen, who won 18 per cent against Jacques Chirac in 2002.

Mr Macron's landslide triggered relief in European capitals, which had feared the destruction of the EU if Ms Le Pen won.

Several thousand supporters celebrated with Mr Macron outside the Louvre. In a signal of his commitment to Europe, he marched alone towards the stage to the sound of Beethoven's *Ode to Joy*, the EU's anthem.

"Tonight France won. Europe and the world are expecting us to defend the spirit of enlightenment," he told the crowd. In a swipe at his doubters, he said: "Everyone told us that it was impossible, but they didn't know France." Theresa May congratulated him, saying that France was one of Britain's closest allies and "we look forward to working with the new president". Downing Street said that they discussed Brexit briefly in a phone call.

President Trump, who had earlier indicated support for Ms Le Pen, tweeted: "Congratulations to Emmanuel Macron on his big win ... I look very much forward to working with him!" Donald Tusk, the European Council president, saluted the French "for choosing liberty, equality and fraternity over the tyranny of fake news". Mr Macron also spoke to Angela Merkel on the phone. The German chancellor described the result as "a victory for a strong and united Europe".

Mr Macron, a former merchant banker, said in a television address: "A new page in our long history opens tonight. I want it to be one of hope and trust restored." In solemn tones, he said: "Let us love France. I will serve her with humility, devotion and determination."

To National Front voters and supporters of other extreme candidates, he said that he understood the "anger, anxiety and doubt that a large part of you have expressed ... I will fight with all my strength against the divisions that are undermining us". He said that he would revive France's "spirit of conquest" and defend a reborn nation. "Our civilisation is at stake," he said, pledging to restore French leadership in Europe.

Ms Le Pen, 48, said that she had phoned Mr Macron to congratulate him. She called her tally of 11.4 million votes "historic and massive" because it made the nationalist right the new opposition. A "major remake of political life" had created a new duel between "patriots and globalisation supporters", she said. She would now re-create her National Front into a broader "patriotic" party that would seek power in parliamentary elections next month.

Mr Macron said that his priority would be to impose "new morality on public life", referring to his pledges to clean up the practices of MPs who abuse expenses and employ family members. François Hollande, the Socialist president who abandoned his run for re-election after his protégé sought his job, wished him well.

The president-elect aims to win a governing majority for his fledgling En Marche movement in the elections. If he fails, he could be forced to forge a coalition or accept the formation of a government by the opposition. The conservative Republicans, formerly led by Nicolas Sarkozy, are the biggest threat to him, polls show.

Jean Pisani-Ferry, Mr Macron's chief economic adviser, told Radio 4's *Today* programme that the new president had no interest in forcing through a hard Brexit. "He is definitely a reformer," he said. "He needs to build trust, be bold and quick. I don't think anyone has an interest in a hard Brexit. There are interests in both sides and those have to be considered. There is a need for clarity and expressing beliefs. Macron knows that. He is a committed pro-European but he certainly doesn't want to punish Britain.

"There is not nervousness but there is certainly a huge sense of responsibility. This was a major shock. There has been distrust, division and despair. To build inclusiveness in France is going to be a huge challenge to begin with."

Six out of ten voters told pollsters yesterday that they did not want Mr Macron to win a governing majority. François Baroin, the new leader of the Republicans, vowed to win power in parliament. "I am going to fight at the side of our candidates for an absolute majority," he said.

Mr Macron was backed by less than a quarter of voters in the first round of the campaign. Half voted for candidates seeking withdrawal from the EU as it exists. He faces a mountainous task to reconcile a nation deeply divided over the economy and riven with tension over identity and immigration.

Mr Macron's first attempt at presidential gravity contrasted with a light-hearted celebration of his first-round victory that was deemed unseemly. The new solemnity was slightly marred when TV showed him having make-up applied, unaware that he was on air.

GIVING A VOICE TO THE LOST GIRLS OF ROCHDALE

Andrew Norfolk

MAY 10 2017

THE ROCHDALE SAGA began, for me, with the arrival of an explosive email. Its anonymous author wrote of a bungled police inquiry into the grooming and sexual exploitation of young girls by a group of men in the town. A failed 2008-09 investigation, claimed the sender, left offenders free to rape and abuse even more children. Two years on, a new criminal inquiry into the same suspects was under way. It was all being kept quiet.

My mystery correspondent said the men were of Pakistani origin, their young victims white. Greater Manchester police, terrified of the ethnicity factor, were trying "to keep the Asian element away from the public".

The email landed on the afternoon of January 5, 2011. Its timing was no coincidence. That morning, the headline on the front page of *The Times* was "Revealed: conspiracy of silence on UK sex gangs". Across five pages, the newspaper described a hidden pattern of street-grooming sexual abuse across the north and the Midlands involving vulnerable girls and organised networks of men, largely from a subsection of the Pakistani community.

It was the first of what was to become a series of articles over the next four years exposing failings by the police and child-protection authorities who knew of such crimes yet failed to protect victims and prosecute offenders. The emailer told me that that day's article had been "spot-on". As, our inquiries soon established, were his or her claims about Rochdale. We published the story six days later.

In May of the following year, after a high-profile criminal trial, nine men from Rochdale and Oldham were convicted of multiple sex offences against five local girls. They were jailed for a total of 77 years.

The furore unleashed by those January 2011 articles features briefly in *Three Girls*, a drama that will be screened on BBC One over three consecutive nights from next Tuesday (May 16, 17 and 18). It tells the story of Rochdale through the lives of three young teenagers at the heart of the case.

Had it been a work of fiction, the events it portrays might have seemed barely credible, such is the scale of the blunders by statutory agencies that are laid bare. The tragedy for so many young girls and their families is that the truth breathes through every scene.

When I first heard that the BBC had commissioned a docudrama, my initial shock that the corporation would choose to tackle such a controversial subject was swiftly replaced by wariness. I feared that innate squeamishness would result in a sanitised exercise that shied away from uncomfortable realities. More fool me. *Three Girls* pulls no punches. It tells a raw, harrowing story in a way that makes for searingly compelling drama.

Central to it is the girl who became the star prosecution witness in the 11-week trial that opened at Liverpool crown court in February 2012. Four years earlier, aged 15, she was arrested after a disturbance inside a kebab shop. A day later, she was interviewed by a bored male detective from Rochdale CID. That filmed interview, and a second eight days later, were shown to the jury on the second day of the trial.

Before and after Rochdale, I sat in courts up and down the land to hear weeks and months of evidence from the child victims of similar crimes in towns and cities including Oxford, Birmingham, Telford and Rotherham. Some witnesses had a lasting impact. Five years after I first gazed at a Liverpool courtroom video monitor and saw the girl who is called Holly in the BBC drama, the memory has not left me. At the time, *The Times* reported that "the slim teenager sat hunched forward, arms crossed protectively in front of her body". She barely looked her age and her voice was "at times only a whisper".

What so disturbingly hit home was the incongruity between the softly spoken child on the screen and the vile events she was describing. Holly was a rebellious teenager who had left home after a series of arguments with her parents. Other girls introduced her to a world of free alcohol and food in the back rooms of local fast-food outlets.

The gifts came at a price. In those police interviews, Holly told the officer of seven occasions in the preceding three weeks when 59-year-old Shabir Ahmed had persuaded or forced her to have sex with him and other Pakistani men.

She described being raped on a bare mattress in a grubby room above the takeaway, of being delivered for encounters with men in taxis, houses and flats. When she protested that she was below the age of consent, Ahmed told her that in his country "you're allowed to have sex with girls from the age of 11".

Ahmed, she said, "kept bringing people, making me have sex with them and then giving me money to keep quiet". He told her that sex was part of the deal: "I bought you vodka. You have to give me something."

Holly told the police: "I didn't think I had a choice. At first I was scared. After a while, it was like I didn't care any more about anything. It was like it wasn't me. Most of the time I was just dead drunk so that when it happened it wouldn't feel as bad." The interviewing officer made little effort to hide his incredulity that she had returned to her abuser after the first sexual assault. At one point he yawned, loudly.

A criminal inquiry was launched in August 2008 and Rochdale's safeguarding children board was informed of Holly's claims, but for the next four months no action was taken to remove her from the house where she had stayed since leaving her parents. In those four months, the court heard, she was used for sex by at least 21 more adults.

Of the 2008 investigation, jurors were merely told by the prosecution that "regrettably, the police officers who looked into the matter didn't take the investigation further at that stage". That was not entirely accurate. Ahmed was one of two men arrested and released on bail but in 2009 the case was dropped after the Crown Prosecution Service ruled there was insufficient evidence to bring charges.

A fuller truth emerged after a four-year investigation by the force's professional standards branch that found that the entire case had been left in the hands of a junior officer who had "no specific training on dealing with sexual offences". He was single-handedly trying to investigate matters that, when the case was reopened two years later, required a full-time team of more than 50 detectives.

The lack of support for the initial inquiry was partly explained by a target-driven culture in which the sexual abuse of working-class teenagers was a lower policing priority than burglary and car crime. A police community impact assessment seemed more concerned about the potential stigmatisation of "residents of south Asian heritage" than the "threat and risk of harm" posed by the men to so many young girls.

Ahmed's DNA was found on Holly's underwear. Other girls had linked him to similar offences at the same kebab shop. Yet when the file reached the CPS, a specialist rape prosecutor decided that she would make an unreliable witness. "It is a tragic case that one so young has fallen into this lifestyle and has been taken advantage of in this way. However, we would have to convince a jury that all of the acts were without her consent and I do not believe that we could do that."

The prosecutor's stance mirrored attitudes within social

services. In 2007, a year before Holly fell into Ahmed's clutches, Rochdale council had identified 50 local girls with "clear links to takeaway food businesses and to associated taxi companies". Opportunities to protect them were missed because damaged children were dismissed as wilful teenagers consenting to their abuse.

A serious case review concluded that child-protection workers seemed disinclined to ask why socially disadvantaged young white girls were spending so much time with "middle-aged Asian men". Ahmed and others were belatedly held to account for what they did to Holly and another four girls because a specialist police team and a new chief crown prosecutor, Nazir Afzal, looked at the case with fresh eyes.

For far too many years in Rochdale, barely a shaft of sunlight pierced a grey, fractured world of troubled children routinely betrayed by adults — kebab shop workers, taxi drivers, police officers, lawyers, social workers — who treated them with varying levels of contempt.

To turn such bleak misery into three hours of gripping television drama was no small challenge. In the hands of a brilliant writer, Nicole Taylor, and the production team behind the BBC's widely acclaimed drama *Five Daughters*, about the 2006 serial murders of young women in Ipswich, *Three Girls* succeeds admirably.

A strong cast helps. Maxine Peake, as the NHS sexual health worker who tries to warn the authorities that an organised grooming network is trafficking children across three counties, was born to do feisty. Her frustration seethes.

As Holly's father, Paul Kaye captures the swirl of emotions — bewilderment, anger, grief — felt by so many parents in the same situation. Seemingly overnight, a loved daughter becomes a stranger. Powerless to protect her, your world falls apart.

However, it is the girls who are the real stars of this work. The decision to tell the Rochdale story largely through their eyes brings it viscerally to life. Molly Windsor brings a haunting quality to Holly that draws your eyes to her in every scene. The viewer follows her into what seems at first, for a young teenager pushing at boundaries, a world of adult adventure. Then comes the moment it all starts to go wrong. The swiftness of her ensuing descent is brutal.

In a fleeting scene from the third episode, as the case finally reaches court, a *Times* journalist called Andrew Norfolk is challenged by a reporter from a rival newspaper. He suggests that *The Times*'s numerous articles on grooming — "innocent white victims, dark-skinned abusers" — have been a gift to racists and the far-right.

My reply is brief: "It's uncomfortable, isn't it?"

Would that in real life I were capable of such concision. *The Times* spent four years exploring the underworld of such sex crimes. The climax was our exposure of a scandal in a town 40 miles from Rochdale.

In Rotherham, South Yorkshire, the authorities sat back, sighed and twiddled their thumbs for 16 years as, an independent inquiry later found, at least 1,400 Hollys were groomed, trafficked and sold for sex by groups of predatory abusers who were "almost all" of Pakistani origin.

That story generated headlines worldwide and took child sexual exploitation to the top of the public agenda. *Three Girls* will hopefully ensure that it stays there.

QUEER CITY: GAY LONDON FROM THE ROMANS TO THE PRESENT DAY BY PETER ACKROYD

Review by Robbie Millen

May 13 2017

Rump riders. The rubsters. Bring on the dancing boys. Soft and slippery. Continually wet.

If there was a prize for the most evocative or salacious

chapter headings, then Peter Ackroyd's new book, *Queer City*, would be the undisputed victor. They capture the rudery and naughtiness, although not the erudition, of this entertaining history of the "queer" experience in London from Roman times onwards.

Ackroyd introduces us to a polymorphously perverse cast of characters from the shadowy world of past homosexuality. Historical records, for instance, show that in 1394 John Rykener, a prostitute who called himself Eleanor, was "detected in women's clothing" while "committing that detestable, unmentionable and ignominious vice" with a client.

Rykener confessed that in Oxford he had "practised the abominable vice often" with eager scholars; at the Swann Inn in Burford he had sex with two Franciscans, one Carmelite and six "foreign men"; on his return to London he admitted to intercourse with three chaplains in the lanes behind St Katharine's by the Tower. Naturally, he also enjoyed the pleasures of numerous nuns. Busy chap.

The Church has always been a bit suspect. In *The Anatomy of Melancholy* (1621) Richard Burton mentions that in 1538, when officials inspected the cloisters and dormitories of monasteries they found "gelded youths, debaucheries, catamites, boy-things, pederasts, sodomites, Gannymedes". More than 400 years later, cousin Jasper in *Brideshead Revisited* proffers some useful advice: "Beware the Anglo-Catholics. They're all sodomites with unpleasant accents."

In 1822 the Bishop of Clogher, a prominent member of the Society for the Suppression of Vice, was caught in full clerical garb with a guardsman, the latter's breeches round his ankles, in the back parlour of the Lion Tavern in Haymarket. Wisely, he fled to Paris, but henceforth was known in the popular prints as "the Arse-Bishop". This ditty circulated: "The Devil to prove the Church was a farce/ Went out to fish for a Bugger/ He bated the hook with a Frenchman's arse/ And pulled up the Bishop of Clogher."

Ackroyd has a good ear for doggerel and popular ballads. He

notes a song of 1727, *Two Kissing Girls of Spitalfields*: "She kisses all, but Jenny is her dear/ She feels her bubbies, and she bites her ear." *The Affectionate Shepherd* (1594), a poem about a man's love for "a lovely lad" is similarly relaxed about the love that dares not speak its name: "Of that fair boy that my heart entangled/ Cursing the time, the place, the sense, the sin/ I came, I saw, I viewed, I slipped in."

Ackroyd, who has written bestselling biographies of Dickens and Shakespeare, as well as London, is strongest on how homosexuals were seen in literature. Chaucer, says Ackroyd, gives us one of the earliest sketches of a queeny, unmanly Englishman. The narrator of *The Canterbury Tales* says of the Pardoner — who has long blond hair, clean-shaven cheeks and a voice as high as a nanny goat — that "I believe he was a gelding or a mare".

The Pardoner is recognisable as Mr Fribble, created by David Garrick for a 1747 farce. Mr Fribble wibbles away in this affected manner: "But my dear creature, who put on your cap to-day? They have made a fright of you ... Where's my cambric handkerchief, and my salts? I shall certainly have my hysterics!" The lady-averse Waterloo Sedley in *Vanity Fair* described himself as a "dressy man" (the first words heard by the 11-year-old Thackeray entering his school dorm were "come and frig me"). Captain Whiffle, a character in Tobias Smollett's *Roderick Random* (1748), had long hair "in ringlets, tied behind with a ribbon".

Whiffle and Fribble would have loved the Macaronis, a set of late 18th-century fashionistas who teased their hair into beehives and acted in an extravagantly fastidious way. In 1770 *The Oxford Magazine* described them as "neither male or female, a thing of the neuter gender lately started among us ... it talks without meaning, it smiles without pleasantry, it eats without appetite, it rides without exercise, it wenches without passion". (Homosexuality was clearly an Italian vice. Dryden, in his 1668 play, *An Evening's Love*, had this interchange between two characters: "I imagined them to be Italians." "Not unlikely, for they played most furiously at our backsides." If not Italian, then sodomy was continental. In Dryden's later play, *The Duke of Guise*, same-sex coupling is dismissed as "a damned love-trick new brought over from France".)

Not all queers were so limp-wristed. The cross-dressing Mary Frith, alias Moll Cutpurse, pimp and fortune-teller, was, her biographer affirmed, "very tomrig or rumpscuttle ... [as a child she] delighted and sported only in boys' play and pastime; many a bang or blow this hoiting procured her, but she was not to be tamed". This pipe-smoking woman died of the dropsy in 1659.

In the next century a Mary Anne Talbot, calling herself James Talbot, joined the navy as powder monkey and cabin boy. Not just a tomboy, she "made a conquest of the captain's niece". The fan-fluttering, frizzed-hair Princess Seraphina, who "takes great delight in balls and masquerades", was a rough-handed butcher during the day; James Stevens, a waterman on the Thames, caused uproar "by going about in women's apparel in a very impudent and insolent manner".

Toughness was required because punishment could be severe. Thomas Doulton, we learn, was obliged to fill the pillory "for endeavouring to discover the 'windward passage' upon one Joseph Yates". The pillory could be a death sentence because the mob did not just fling rotten fruit, excrement or even dead cats, but would whip and punch its occupant. There was the noose too: sodomy was a capital offence until 1861. In 1835 John Smith and John Pratt, two poor men found in a derelict boarding house on the south bank of the Thames, were the last in England to swing for it.

The sources Ackroyd has to describe the "queer" experience are a rum mix of court reports, plays, song and usually disapproving pamphlets. That makes it hard to divine what the private and inner lives of these men and women were like: did they think of themselves as being wildly different from the run of society? It's not Ackroyd's fault, but they remain elusive, just as the everyday life of a modern gay would be if a future historian had to rely on *RuPaul's Drag Race*, Christian Institute screeds or prison records.

And while throughout there is plenty of Ackroydian wit — medieval "schoolmasters paid as much attention to the buttocks as the brains of their little pupils"; the Renaissance appeal of young men was that "there were fewer unfortunate consequences in the nursery way" — it feels as if he loses some of his vim when he enters the 20th century. That a gay woman became president of Unison is less interesting than Mother Clap's molly house.

Then there is that vexed word "queer", with its connotations of radicalism, which ought to be sent back to cultural theory departments. Ackroyd notes a 1619 memorial in Caius College, Cambridge that celebrates the union between Thomas Legge and John Gostlin — a heart in flames has a Latin inscription that reads: "Love joined them living. So may the earth join them in their burial. O Legge, Gostlin's heart you have still with you." That's not so much queer as touchingly normal and domestic.

Still, what is in a name? The men spotted at a molly house, near St Paul's, by a prodnose witness, "calling one another 'my dear' and hugging, kissing and tickling one another", probably did not bother considering whether they were queer, gay or — as the Victorian euphemism had it — temperamental.

WATCH OUT — HERE COME THE BRIDEZILLAS

David Emanuel interviewed by Hilary Rose

May 18 2017

It is fair to say that the Confetti & Lace bridal shop at Lakeside in Thurrock, Essex, is out of my comfort zone. So far out, in fact, that you could keep heading due east until you get to

Moscow and even then I would be no more of a fish out of water than I already am.

I have never worn a wedding dress. I have never given any thought as to what mine might look like, which is frankly just as well. So when I hear Danielle, a sales assistant in a fly-on-the-wall TV programme, filmed at Confetti & Lace, say to a customer, "So tell me about your bridal gown journey", and the woman knows what she's talking about because she actually has a bridal gown journey, my head starts to spin. Bridal gown journeys? Who knew?

I am here because of *Say Yes to the Dress*, an American TV import that has become a global phenomenon thanks to its simple premise: brides try on various dresses in front of assorted family members — at the end they're asked, "Will you say yes to the dress?" and everyone bursts into tears.

"You're trying to find the dress of their dreams, to fulfil their fantasies," says the fashion designer David Emanuel, the show's host, who is renowned as the man who designed Princess Diana's wedding dress. "A lot of girls want the big crinolines, but not many can get into them. I say, 'Darling, we'll have a go.' Or bigger girls come in thinking they can get into that," he says, pointing at a size 6 strapless, figure-hugging sheath dress. "I say, 'Darling, there's not enough support. You can't wear a skimpy little thing if you've got big bosoms.'"

Indeed not. Emanuel is a charming man, who looks like a cross between Barry Manilow and the Queen Mother. He's honest but not judgmental, encouraging but realistic. He won't let someone leave with a dress that he thinks looks awful on them: "Not on my watch. I've got a reputation." Instead, his standard line is "It's a contender" before nudging the bride towards something more appropriate. His task is not helped by the grannies, sisters, aunts, bridesmaids, matrons of honour and, in some instances, future mothers-in-law who are brought along to give their two penn'orth.

"There's huge pressure today and the bride wants reassurance," he says. "But she'll come out in the gown and the mother goes, 'I don't like it', and the mother-in-law will say, 'I love it.' "

In one episode, asked about the inspiration for her wedding, the bride replies "plimsolls", her preferred choice of bridal shoe. A sales assistant confirms later that most of her customers want to get married wearing Converse trainers. Emanuel complains that those who want to wear heels never think to consider how tall their husband is. One bride perplexed him by announcing that she was a big Harry Potter fan and wanted something Harry Potter-ish. "I'm thinking, 'You're 23, darling, you can't be obsessed with Harry Potter.' "

Another insisted that the main criterion for her dress was size, the bigger the better. The first crinoline wasn't big enough, or the second, so eventually he put an enormous hooped petticoat underneath and queried why size was so important. "She said to pin money on. It was a Greek wedding. I said to the mother, 'How much did you have pinned on yours?' and she said £20,000. I said, 'I want £40,000 for your daughter.' "

One wants to look like Kim Kardashian on her wedding day and recounts how she met her fiancé in Magaluf and they're having a ten-tier wedding cake. Another has something of a crisis of confidence, not unreasonably, when her aunt tells her that she has thighs like a rugby player.

Mothers invariably think the dress shows too much cleavage; brides invariably don't. The American version of the show almost brought down the government of Angola when the daughter of a hardline Marxist cabinet minister was filmed spending hundreds of thousands of dollars on nine outfits for herself and the bridal party.

One of Emanuel's bugbears is when brides don't look like themselves. "Exaggerated hair, exaggerated make-up. You want your husband to recognise you," he says. "They suddenly pile all their hair up and put on tons of make-up and the guys must be really shocked. A lot of girls think, 'This is my moment. I want to look like a movie star.' They think by putting more on it's going to work. Less is more."

It makes for compelling viewing, not least because of the sales assistants at Lakeside, who have more personality than half the brides. Rina Metaj, 20, from Colchester, has been working at the store since she was 16 and says that every one of her clients thinks they're at least one size smaller than they are.

"Especially if they've had a baby, because if they were a size 8 they still like to call themselves a size 8. Realistically, they're a 16. They can get a bit funny, a bit bridezilla-y on you, and 90 per cent of the time they don't leave with what they thought they wanted. They think fishtail, but they leave with ballgowns," she says, as her blonde colleague Danielle rushes past laden with them, dead on cue. So how does Metaj tell someone that a dress isn't working?

"I'm the worst here for giving my opinion and telling them they look awful. I feel like if I'm not honest then I'm not doing my job."

Her stock of 300 dresses ranges from princess ballgowns to sheaths with feathered bodices, their price tags from hundreds of pounds to more than £5,500. Like Emanuel, Metaj wishes the brides would just bring their mothers, and a fair bit of her job is managing expectations. If their best friend cried when she found her wedding dress, they want to be moved to tears too. "They think if they don't cry then it's not the right dress, but they might not be someone who cries all the time."

The brides on the show, in their twenties and thirties, recognise Emanuel from his outing on *I'm A Celebrity ... Get Me Out of Here!*, but their mothers know he designed Princess Diana's wedding dress. "She was so fun, she was young, she was excited, she was so in love," says Emanuel. The resulting dress was not to everyone's taste, but he stands by it.

"That dress had to do a lot of things: it had to be young, but it had to be grand. She had to be every little girl's dream of what a princess should look like. And the scale of it! St Paul's is enormous. She rang me that evening and said, 'Prince Charles loved it, everyone loved it. I just wanted to say thank you.' There was a lot of trust from Buckingham Palace, no red tape, no directives. And we talk about entourages but Diana came with one person: her mother."

Emanuel was seen at that wedding smoothing the dress out on the steps of St Paul's. Some of his more recent clients have invited him to their big day, but he declined. "People get very emotional and there's a lot of, what's the word? Not tension, but people get very highly strung at weddings. They're worried about the car coming, will the hairdresser turn up, will the make-up artist do it wrong? Calm! Relax. Have a glass of champagne. It's perhaps the most important day of their lives but if you have a child that's probably quite an important day, I would have thought."

He pauses for a long time before saying what he thinks of the Duchess of Cambridge's more streamlined number, as unlike Diana's as it was possible to be, and notably lacking in creases.

"It was ... lovely," he says eventually. "What amazed me more was her confidence. She was very much a bride in charge. And the other thing which I thought a little odd was she walked down the red carpet and there's her sister sashaying behind holding the train up! I was shouting at the TV — put the train down! It's a train! Put it down!"

If Emanuel was doing Pippa Middleton's dress, he says he'd go for the opposite model: something soft and pretty with a scooped neck, a little sleeve and lots of chiffon. "She'd look adorable."

But that wouldn't show off the famous rear. "We've seen the rear. We don't need to see any more rear. That was on show last time." Meghan Markle, on the other hand, he thinks could suit figure-hugging "because she's got a great little figure but again it has to be appropriate. Too figure-hugging can look like you're trying too hard. And remember she's divorced. There's no guarantee it'll be a cathedral wedding."

Perish the thought. If and when Harry does put a ring on it, Meghan could do worse than hop on the train to Lakeside. Rina and Danielle would be only too happy to help.

THE 10 WORST CRIMES IN HORTICULTURE

Ann Treneman

May 20 2017

There are certain things in gardens that should be illegal or, at the very least, require planning permission. Over the years I have inherited gardens in which several horticultural crimes have been committed, plus a host — not to be confused with hostas — of lesser calumnies, many of which can be put down to the delusion that infects almost all gardeners, an attachment to hope over experience.

Remember antisocial behaviour orders, the alternative to jail for delinquent teenagers? Well, I am developing a list of horticultural antisocial behaviours (Hasbos?) that everyone should try to avoid in their garden. This is because eventually your garden will be someone else's garden.

Most people, when buying a property, concentrate on the house, but I am sure that most gardeners, like me, are far more interested in what's outside than in. This was certainly the case with the place that my husband and I saw for sale four years ago in Bakewell, Derbyshire. I remember walking by in late winter and spying a drift of snowdrops through the bare beech hedge and thinking: "I want to own those."

Soon I did. And about 20,000 other plants. Did I say 20,000? Make that 200,000. We soon discovered that our new acquisition was a nontropical jungle, a plantsman's garden that had been created over decades by the husband of the previous owner. But Malcolm, as I will call him, had died some time before and, by the time we came along, his garden had developed into a thickety madness.

What had once been ornamental plantings had become thickets so dense that a hermit could have lived in them happily, undisturbed. The laurel had grown into something the size of a blimp, the raspberries were on a mission to take over the world.

However, I knew from experience that you shouldn't do

anything in an inherited garden for a year. First reactions are not to be trusted. Yet gradually we have set out to tame the madness and, along the way, I have developed a list of don'ts for gardens.

So here, then, are the ten things to try to avoid — some personal, others that should, in my opinion, become law.

Pampas grass — unacceptable in the UK

My first reaction as I wandered up a path and saw the fronds of *Cortedaria selloana* was: "What was he thinking?" Pampas grass may look perfectly normal in the high plains of Argentina, but they are, can I note, 7,240 miles from Bakewell. I dislike everything about it: the giant dense tussock, the waving, alien-like fronds ... It's like having Cousin Itt living with you. Apparently pampas are having a bit of a moment, having been spotted waving fondly, or even frondly, at trendy hotels in London. Fine. But not in my back garden.

Leylandii — just NO

No, no, no. I don't want to hear your shady excuse — there is no acceptable reason for putting these in your garden. "It's marked out my territory," said a friend as I sat in her back garden surrounded by walls of towering hedge that had created, basically, a prison cell that photosynthesises. They grow to 50ft in 15 years. That's not normal. To me, anyone who plants these deserves what they get: endless aggro from the neighbours and twice-yearly bills from the hedge-cutter.

Hostas are madness

One hosta is lovely, two will do, but any more require a lasting enthusiasm for anti-slug and snail measures that borders on the obsessive, not to say vigilante. I have at least ten hostas and, if I really wanted to keep them pristine, every night would be on "hosta patrol", headlamp on, salt in hand, looking for the enemy. But, of course, you never dó win against the slugs, do you? Hostas to fortune, I say. Neighbourhood Slug Watch patrol, anyone?

Don't grow anything poisonous — obviously

I am not sure why Malcolm felt the need to plant quite so many specimens of *Helleborus foetidus*, "stinking hellebore" to you and me, but the stuff is everywhere, with its huge light green flowerheads nodding away in the wind. It smells and all parts of it are poisonous. What's to like?

Don't grow anything orange

On the whole, Malcolm's garden includes mostly pastels, lovely purples and pinks, shades of green. But just when I'm thinking I can transform a corner into a mini "White Garden" (Sissinghurst unleashes dreams that don't die), I see something pop up that is, er, orange. There are lillies and crocosmia. There's also a plant known as "spurge", a fiery-topped euphorbia that I know I dislike and that I might actually hate. Purge the spurge, I say. Then, in autumn, cuckoopint will rise up to greet the day. Clearly, orange was his "accent" colour. Sigh.

Single-mindedness has no place in a garden

These are gardens created as love notes to one thing and one thing only. So every inch is bursting with begonias or petunias. I also include any garden involving anything more than three gnomes and what I call "zen" gardens, those Japanesey ones that involve koi, a too-small bridge and gravel that has to be raked one way, and then another. Just say no.

Invasive snowberries and bamboo must go

I am sure that, at some point, the ornamental bramble that arched over a corner of the garden, taller than me, with its horrendous thorny stems, seemed a good idea. By the time I arrived, it had claimed so much territory that I felt a treaty was in order. Getting rid of it (*Rubus cockburnianus*) was murder. Snowberries are the same. So is some bamboo. Give them an inch, they'll take a mile.

Don't grow big things in small places

Yes, I am sure that whoever bought that little conifer at the garden centre and planted it in the front bed, right next to the house, did not know that it was, in fact, a towering pine that really wants to live on the hills of Scotland. Still, it's just about checking the label. There's no point pretending that you can grow a sequoia when you live in a terraced house in Scunthorpe.

Climbers and clingers can break your house — consider carefully

Years ago, I bought an Edwardian house, its picturesque brick walls resplendent with a wisteria on one and on another, a pinky clematis. Then, at some point, the wisteria got so heavy that it almost broke the porch. The clematis was much more creative, wrapping itself round 1) the phone wire and 2) the TV aerial cable. I snipped through both of them while pruning. The moral of the story is: plant climbers with care.

Burials in your garden — bad idea

It is, apparently, possible to bury a person in a garden, but, truly, that is a bad idea, at least worthy of a Hasbo, not least because new buyers may want you moved. (This happened to Sir Arthur Conan Doyle and his wife, keen spiritualists, who were buried upright in their garden in East Sussex in the 1930s, but then had to be moved, body and soul, in 1955.) But I also think pet burial is not a good idea. It is so much more thoughtful to scatter ashes, and good for the soil too.

SHOCK POLL PREDICTS TORY LOSSES

Sam Coates

MAY 31 2017

THE CONSERVATIVE PARTY could be in line to lose 20 seats and Labour gain nearly 30 in next week's general election, according to new modelling by one of the country's leading pollsters.

YouGov's first constituency-by-constituency estimate of the election result predicts that the Tories would fall short of an overall majority by 16 seats, leading to a hung parliament.

The central projection of the model, which allows for a wide margin of error, would be a catastrophic outcome for Theresa May, who called the election when polls pointed to a landslide result. Her support appears to have plunged after the poor reception of the party manifesto, including plans to make more elderly voters pay for home care.

YouGov's model puts the Tories on course to win 310 seats, down from the 330 they held when the election was called. Labour would get 257 seats, up from 229, the Liberal Democrats ten, up from nine, the SNP 50, down from 54, the Greens one and Plaid Cymru three. This would leave the Tories 16 seats short of the 326 they need for an overall majority in the Commons.

The projection allows for big variations, however, and suggests that the Tories could get as many as 345 seats on a good night, 15 more than at present, and as few as 274 seats on a bad night.

YouGov acknowledged that the predictions were controversial and pointed to significant "churn" in voting intentions. But Stephan Shakespeare, its chief executive, said that the model had been publicly tested during the EU referendum campaign last year, when it always had Leave ahead.

The model is based on 50,000 interviews over the course of a week, with voters from a panel brought together by YouGov.

This allows the pollster to assess the intention of every type of voter, from where they live to how they voted in the EU referendum, their age and social background, to weight the results.

The estimates were met with scepticism by Tory and Labour figures. One prominent Conservative said that the party was expecting a majority of 50 or more, despite an "atrocious" campaign, and insisted that anger over the manifesto was fading.

A Labour figure in the Midlands said that while the Tory social care blunder had helped, Jeremy Corbyn's unpopularity continued to deter natural Labour voters and the party would be losing rather than gaining seats in the region.

Other pollsters predicted a convincing victory for the Tories. Andrew Hawkins, chairman of ComRes, said: "If voters behave in the way they broadly did in 2015 then the Conservatives remain on track for a 100-plus majority. This seems, on present assumptions, the most likely outcome."

An ICM poll released yesterday gave a 12-point lead to the Conservatives, on 45 per cent, with Labour on 33 per cent, the Lib Dems on 8 and Ukip on 5. If this swing were replicated across the country, it would mean a Tory majority of 76. The spread-betting company IG Index suggested that the Tories would win 378 seats, Labour 148, Lib Dems 14 and SNP 46. The latest Elections Etc combined forecast by Stephen Fisher, of Oxford University, suggests a Tory majority of 100.

YouGov used data from the Office for National Statistics, the British Election Study and past election results. It then estimated the number of each type of voter in each constituency. Combining the model probabilities and estimated census counts allowed the pollster to produce what it hopes is a fairly accurate estimate of the number of voters in each constituency intending to vote for a party on each day.

YouGov's final poll in the 2014 Scottish independence referendum put "no" to independence on 54 per cent and "yes" on 46 per cent. The final vote was 55 per cent "no" and 45 per cent "yes". Today's YouGov election model is based on voting intention data collected in the past week. It puts the Tories on 42 per cent, Labour on 38 per cent, Lib Dems on 9 per cent and Ukip on 4 per cent.

Mr Shakespeare said that the figures could change dramatically before June 8: "The data suggests that there is churn on all fronts, with the Conservatives, Labour and the Liberal Democrats likely to both lose and gain seats."

Sterling fell in late London trading. Against the US dollar the pound was 0.5 per cent down at $1.279 and against the euro it fell 0.4 per cent to €1.144.

SUMMER

INVESTORS PRICED OUT BY THE BANK

Alistair Osborne

JUNE 7 2017

WHAT A BUNCH OF killjoys. Just when the entire nation needed cheering up, look what's happened: Royal Bank of Scotland's irate shareholders have only gone and settled their legal action over April 2008's dodgy rights issue.

The upshot? Pretty much no chance of a court appearance from Fred Goodwin, the man who blew up the bank with his ABN Amro antics. Shred will now get to stay on the golf course, free from all obligations to explain what he knew when he was tapping up investors for £12 billion just months before RBS went pop. No chance either, m'lud, of seeing him squirm over that £45.5 billion taxpayer bailout. And that's just for starters. What about the historical detail that the trial would have thrown up, what with the rights issue being sandwiched between March 2008's fall of Bear Stearns and Lehman's collapse in September that year?

How, for example, Mr Goodwin's domineering style extended to designing the company Christmas card. Or how he personally selected the colour of the RBS executive cars — a Pantone 281 Mercedes S-Class — to match the bank's corporate blue, with their interiors the exact beige of the office carpets. Or how boring banking stuff, such as risk and credit, wasn't really his thing.

And, of course, no one can blame the bulk of the 9,000 retail investors in the RBS Shareholders Action Group for caving in at 82p a share: a settlement worth £200 million. Represented by Signature Litigation, they were part of the final 13 per cent of disgruntled shareholders holding out for compo. Four other investor groups have already settled for much less, most at just 41.2p. And the 82p would have been off the table once the case came to trial.

No, the main reason Fred's almost certainly off the hook is

the actions of the present management, led by the RBS chief Ross McEwan. He's spent an obscene sum in legal fees, ensuring that hardly anyone could afford to take on the bank: pretty rum for a lender 72 per cent owned by the taxpayer.

RBS's legal costs already top £100 million. And they weren't going to stop there, as the bank gleefully put about. It was ready to spend another £29 million merely on part one of the three-phase trial. So, if shareholders had lost, incurring RBS's costs in the process, they'd be in for a gargantuan bill. Indeed, RBS's tactics were designed to deter action from individual investors who still don't want to settle, such as Neil Mitchell of Torex fame.

True, the case was complex, apparently involving 25 million documents. And Mr McEwan, who set aside £800 million for the rights issue litigation, must protect the interests of all shareholders. Yet the result is that the biggest failure in UK banking history doesn't get the proper legal interrogation it deserves, instead having to make do with 2011's bland report from the now-defunct Financial Services Authority. Moreover, Mr Goodwin emerges as the main winner. No wonder people are cross.

ELECTION 2017

Leading Article

June 10 2017

The slow drive from Downing Street to Buckingham Palace is supposed to be a ritual triumph. Preceded by outriders and tracked by helicopters, the winner of a British general election seeks leave to form a government from the monarch. It is almost painful to imagine what the Queen might have offered by way of small talk in her meeting yesterday with Theresa May.

Mrs May has triggered Article 50 of the Lisbon treaty. The

clock is ticking on a two-year Brexit timetable that was already tight before this week's election, as more than one European leader noted yesterday. The prime minister understood the need for a large parliamentary majority in the circumstances. Instead she has lost her small majority. The Conservatives' calamitous showing in the election has left Britain effectively leaderless at a moment when its fate depends on leadership.

This crisis has been years in the making. Mrs May's party believes government is in its DNA. Yet it has failed to win a majority in five of the past six general elections and it has left the UK all but ungovernable as a consequence of two extraordinary miscalculations: David Cameron's decision to proceed with a European referendum and Mrs May's to call a snap election, against the advice of her chief political consultant.

She is now fatally wounded. If she does not realise this it is another grave misjudgment. More likely, she is steeling herself to provide what continuity she can as her party girds itself for an election to replace her.

It is easy for her enemies to be wise after the event, but it is clear that the Conservative Party's political instincts have, for now, deserted it. This would not matter so much were the country not committed to leaving the EU, and saddled with a Labour opposition under Jeremy Corbyn that has been cemented in place by a campaign that proved as successful as it was irresponsible.

By their actions, the Conservatives have not yet broken the British system of democracy, but through hubris and incompetence they have managed to make a mockery of it. The task of restoring orderly government to make sense of Brexit is now a national emergency, and it falls to them.

But in her speech on the steps of Downing Street yesterday, Mrs May showed why she lost her majority. There was no hint of self-awareness, let alone gallows humour, and no attempt to acknowledge the gravity of the predicament into which she has led the country. The omission recalled her failure to admit U-turns on national insurance contributions after the last budget and on social care funding during the campaign. In her determination to stay in control of her message, she has developed an unfortunate habit of insulting voters' intelligence.

In her earlier remarks at the Maidenhead constituency count she promised one thing: stability. Her decision to stay on and form a government dependent on the Democratic Unionist Party of Ulster may have been taken out of a sense of duty, but beyond the next few weeks it will not provide a basis for stability any more than the election did.

The logic leading to Mrs May's departure from Downing Street is remorseless. She said during the campaign that if she lost six seats she would have lost the election. She has lost 12. In practical terms this means her government cannot be relied upon to assemble a majority for its economic agenda, let alone for the series of bills that will be necessary to make Brexit a reality. Her personal authority is in any case already draining away.

But Mrs May is not the only leader guilty of miscalculation. The same can be said of Nicola Sturgeon. The prospect of a second independence referendum, with all the uncertainty that threatened, has been shelved. The Scottish National Party has not only lost 19 seats, it has seen the defeat of some of its key figures — the former leader Alex Salmond and its deputy leader Angus Robertson among others. That sends out an unmistakeable signal to the party, and the first minister is right to say that she will "reflect" on the new climate in which it will operate.

The SNP must now focus on policies of more immediate concern to the people. This election may not have been about the bread and butter issues in Scotland — education, health, social welfare and the economy — since these are matters reserved to Holyrood and this was a UK election. But there is no doubt that this was as much a judgment by voters on the SNP's role in government in Scotland as it was about Brexit, immigration or the single market. When, at the very outset of the election campaign, Ms Sturgeon announced that a second referendum lay "at the heart of the campaign" she misjudged the mood of the electorate almost as fatally as Mrs May misjudged the mood of the UK as a whole.

The Scottish Conservatives in particular, ably led by Ruth Davidson, played the referendum card against the SNP and played it effectively. As the campaign progressed, the Nationalists tried to pull back — but they were painted into a corner. The dream they had been able to present in 2015 of a better future as an independent nation has collided with the harsh reality of grim economic figures and a poor performance in government.

What then should its new role in Scotland be? Over the past weeks the SNP government has had to defend poor results in key areas such as the performance of Scottish schools, waiting lists in hospitals and the performance of an economy that hovers on the brink of a recession.

Traditionally, and in the past, it has fallen back on the argument that it governs in Scotland with one hand held behind its back: if only it was given the full powers of independence, all would be changed. That position has become less and less tenable as the economic situation has deteriorated. With a substantial deficit on the horizon, there is a growing view that a future Scottish government would face at least a decade of privation outside the UK as it attempted to rebalance the economy. Even its position in Europe is undermined by the election.

Instead, what the party must now do is turn its attention properly to governing Scotland, and accept that it can no longer claim the dominant position it enjoyed after the 2015 election. It must focus instead on the difficult and often unrewarding business of effecting change and improvement in the domestic issues for which it is responsible. Unless it changes, the party will face a verdict of no confidence from the Scottish people when it comes to the next vote at Holyrood in 2021.

Meanwhile, for the Scottish Conservatives, and Ms Davidson in particular, this has been a hugely successful election. It can genuinely claim to be the principal opposition party, and what that means is that the political argument in Scotland can be properly joined: the case for a low tax, enterprise economy, with the emphasis on creating jobs rather than simply increasing the public sector burden, can at least be heard. For far too long, politics in Scotland has lacked the central ingredient of a genuine ideological debate.

Now that debate can begin, especially with the rebirth of Scottish Labour. This too is a healthy development, since the SNP can no longer take for granted the notion that it is the only voice speaking up for the unemployed, for deprived areas and for those on the margins of society. Yet while change is to be welcomed in Scotland, a daunting deadline looms in Brussels. The Brexit talks scheduled to start on June 19 can be delayed, but EU leaders have been united in insisting that the 2019 deadline cannot. The more rushed the Brexit process proves, the less likely it is to yield even an interim agreement. Despite the turmoil at home, the talks need to start soon.

The prime minister's decision to stay on is therefore the right one in the short term, but it is untenable in the longer term. Her party needs a new leader. That leader will need an enhanced majority even more urgently than Mrs May believed she did. Britain is in the midst of a prolonged electoral upheaval that will almost inevitably involve another election well before the Fixed-term Parliaments Act requires one.

Mrs May's pledge to ensure a period of stability must be her parting gift. If she can start an orderly transition to a bolder, more imaginative, more candid and more optimistic Conservative leadership she will have plucked a victory of sorts from the jaws of defeat. If the Conservatives fail to pick up this gauntlet Mr Corbyn will, and his mission is to take Britain back to the last century.

SAVED BY FRIENDS FROM ACROSS THE WATER

Patrick Kidd

JUNE 10 2017

THERESA MAY spread out the map of Northern Ireland on the cabinet table. "So let me see if I've got this right," she said to Nickanfi, her double-headed chief adviser. "The green bits are held by Sinn Fein?" Nickanfi nodded and hissed a little. "And the reddish areas belong to our new friends and allies, the DUP, on whom our stronganstable leadership depends?" Another nod.

Then Mrs May saw a large blue area on the map. "Aha," she said. "And I suppose this is where all the Conservative MPs are to be found?"

Nickanfi cleared their throats. "Not quite, prime minister," they said. "That's Lough Neagh."

It had been a long and difficult night for Mrs May. She had been surprised by the exit poll showing her short of a majority. "But I am stronganstable," she protested. "The numbers must be wrong. Maybe John Curtice covered up Surrey with his sandwiches. Nickanfi, ring the BBC and demand that they add another 50 to our tally."

At her count in Maidenhead the paranoia grew. Was that tall man with the bucket on his head actually Philip Hammond, mocking her? That would be beyond the pail. She won her seat comfortably enough but it was clear that the rest of the party had let her down. They had *not* been stronganstable. She was surrounded by weaklings and fools.

Mrs May paid particular attention to the count in Hastings. There had been rumblings on television that she would have to go for this. How could she continue after fighting an election on the question of strong leadership and losing seats? When Amber Rudd clung on, Mrs May told Nickanfi to send the home secretary a message. "Tell her 'well done' and to be prepared to go out and resign on my behalf in the morning."

In the end, the sacrifice was not needed. The red bits of Northern Ireland agreed to lend a hand. Mrs May went to the palace to tell the Queen that she was stronganstable. "I am determined to go on and on," she declared. "You certainly do," Prince Philip grumbled.

In the car on the way back, Mrs May asked Nickanfi for a speech. "The one marked 'contrite and humble'?" Nickanfi suggested. "No," Mrs May barked. "Give me the 'whopping majority' one."

And so she delivered a speech that gave no indication of the events of the previous night. It oozed stronganstable. "I will now form a government that can provide certainty and lead Britain forward," she said. "We must fulfil the promise of Brexit."

In Brussels, Michel Barnier was wheezing like Mutley, while Jean-Claude Juncker opened a bottle of chilled schadenfreude. Mrs May had taken seven weeks to disintegrate a 24-point poll lead; this renegotiation was going to be fun. "Tell her she can take as long as she needs," Mr Barnier told an aide. "But remind her that the clock is ticking."

At the *Evening Standard*, George Osborne took a break from flicking V signs at the television to tell his comment editor to up the snark a shade in the leading article. He was going to enjoy tucking into a dish of revenge for lunch, served cold with lashings of May-on-her-knees.

The prime minister, however, did not appear humiliated. Trying to affect an Elizabeth-at-Tilbury look, she promised to deliver a brighter Brexity future. "That is what the people voted for last June," she said. What they voted for the day before had already been disregarded.

US BANNED TOWER CLADDING

Alexi Mostrous, David Brown, Sean O'Neill, John Simpson, Sam Joiner

JUNE 16 2017

THE DEATH TOLL from the London tower inferno was expected to pass 50 last night as it emerged that the United States had banned the type of cladding that allegedly encased the 24-storey block.

Scotland Yard said that it had begun a criminal inquiry amid calls from MPs for corporate manslaughter charges to be brought. Seventeen people were confirmed to have died in the blaze that swept through the building in the early hours of Wednesday.

Senior sources voiced fears yesterday that up to 100 people could have died in the fire but later revised their estimates. Grenfell Tower, in west London, was home to about 600 residents.

The difficulty of matching reports of those missing with the complex process of identifying the dead has hampered efforts to establish the scale of the tragedy. Many of the block's residents spoke poor English and there is concern that some who are safe have failed to report to the authorities. The police have warned that the ferocity of the blaze means that some bodies will never be recovered.

The criminal investigation and a public inquiry launched by Theresa May will include the materials used in an £8.6 million refurbishment of the block, which was completed last summer amid warnings from local people that it had become a firetrap.

Hundreds of aluminium panels called Reynobond are believed to have been fitted to Grenfell Tower by Harley Facades, a small firm subcontracted as part of that refurbishment. Reynobond makes three types of panel: one with a flammable plastic core and two with fire-resistant cores. It is thought that contractors chose the cheaper, more combustible, version for Grenfell.

A salesman for US-based Reynobond told *The Times* that this version, which has a polyethylene core and is known as PE, was banned in American buildings taller than 40ft (12.2m) for fire safety reasons. "It's because of the fire and smoke spread," he said. "The FR [variant] is fire-resistant. The PE is just plastic."

The PE version is used for small commercial buildings and petrol stations, he said, rather than for tower blocks or critical buildings such as hospitals.

Reynobond's fire-resistant panel sells for £24 per square metre — £2 more expensive than the standard version. A rough calculation suggests that panels covered more than 2,000 sq m on Grenfell, meaning that contractors could have acquired the fire-resistant version for less than £5,000 extra.

The PE panels conform to UK standards but are rated as "flammable" in Germany.

Camden, Croydon, Ealing, Newham, Greenwich and Redbridge councils in London are carrying out urgent reviews of fire safety in tower blocks and flats.

Of the 17 bodies recovered at Grenfell Tower, six were outside and are believed to be those of people who jumped from the building as the flames spread. A further 11 bodies were found inside but investigators have not yet reached the upper floors where some larger flats inhabited by families were located.

One of the dead was Mohamed Alhajali, 23, who fled the war in Syria and came to London where he lived with his brother in the tower. Among the missing was Mohamed Neda, 57, an Afghan minicab driver, who helped his wife and son to safety then ran back into the building for an elderly neighbour.

At least 45 people, including ten children, are missing. They include a six-month-old baby, a bride-to-be and entire families.

One mother, Genet Shawo, said that she had been unable to find her five-year-old son in the thick, black smoke. As they tried to escape, she said Isaac told his family: "I don't want us to die."

Commander Stuart Cundy, of the Metropolitan Police, said

that he did not know how many were inside and that the death toll would rise, but added: "I hope it isn't going to be triple figures. I don't think it's inevitably going to be triple figures. For those of us that have been down there, it's pretty emotional, so I hope it is not triple figures."

The casualty bureau has received 400 reports of missing people, but there has been extensive duplication, with one person reported 46 times.

Nick Hurd, the Home Office minister, said that the public inquiry would "leave absolutely no stone unturned". Sadiq Khan, the Labour mayor of London, said it should produce an interim report this summer and that its scope must include "whether the tower block was refurbished in a safe way".

Rydon, the firm that carried out the Grenfell regeneration, said its work had "met all required building regulations — as well as fire regulations and health and safety standards".

HELMUT KOHL

Obituary

JUNE 17 2017

HELMUT KOHL was nine when the Second World War broke out. The conflict "abruptly and mercilessly ended an almost ideal childhood", he recalled. His father, Johann, a civil servant who loathed the Nazis, was forced to join the Wehrmacht and sent to Poland. Eighty per cent of his home town of Ludwigshafen, an industrial centre near the French border, was destroyed by seemingly endless waves of allied bombing raids. His brother, Walter, was crushed to death when an allied bomber crashed into a pylon.

As a young teenager Kohl helped firemen to retrieve charred bodies from wrecked buildings. In late 1944 he was sent to a pre-military training camp as part of Hitler's desperate effort to save the Third Reich by enlisting boys and old men, and ended up in Bavaria. At the war's end he and three classmates walked 250 miles back to Ludwigshafen through a country in ruins. They scavenged for food, were attacked by liberated Polish prisoners, and saw the bodies of deserters hanging from trees.

Those searing experiences shaped Kohl's life. They inspired him to enter politics to rebuild his country and to pursue European integration to ensure that there would never again be war on the Continent.

He was strikingly successful. Along with Ronald Reagan, Mikhail Gorbachev and Margaret Thatcher, he helped to bring the Cold War to an end. As the longest-serving chancellor since Otto von Bismarck a century earlier he played a central role in ending the postwar division of Germany and of Europe. He forced the pace of European integration, primarily by championing the monetary union that created the euro. And he helped to re-establish Germany as a strong and positive force in Europe, Nato and the broader international community. Much of that he achieved despite enormous obstacles and substantial opposition. It was a remarkable record for a man who was a butt of jokes and fodder for comedians for much of his political career.

Kohl was no intellectual. He was not charismatic. He spoke only German, and that with a thick provincial accent. He was a poor public performer, prompting one rival to joke that his television performances gave "the impression that anybody could become chancellor". He was 6ft 4in, weighed more than 300lb, and was dubbed the *birne*, or "pear", because of his great bulk. President Clinton once told Kohl at a Nato summit that he reminded him of a sumo wrestler.

However, Kohl's provincialism, his lack of airs and graces, was an important part of his appeal. Germans identified with him, trusted him and liked the aura of stability and reassurance that he exuded. Rather than rely on advisers, he spent hours calling lowly officials around the country to find out what ordinary Germans were thinking. Even as chancellor he spent weekends at his neat, comfortable bungalow in a suburb of Ludwigshafen called Oggersheim, mingling with the townsfolk. He took holidays in the same Austrian village each year. He liked to wear well-worn cardigans and slippers in his office. "I am certainly not the embodiment of elegance," he readily admitted.

He was jovial, gregarious and loved to eat, especially hearty traditional German food, which he gleefully inflicted on visiting foreign leaders. "Lunch consisted of potato soup, pig's stomach [which the German chancellor clearly enjoyed], sausage, liver dumplings and sauerkraut," Margaret Thatcher recalled with evident distaste after spending a day with Kohl in Ludwigshafen.

By and large he got on well with foreign leaders. They appreciated his directness. He forged a special bond with President Mitterrand of France, with whom he held a memorable meeting on the First World War battlefield at Verdun in 1984. Their long handshake became a symbol of Franco-German reconciliation, and the two men subsequently became a powerful force for deeper European integration. Kohl shed tears at Mitterrand's funeral.

He also built friendships with the elder President Bush and Gorbachev, the Soviet president, that served him well when he required international approval for German reunification. He shared saunas with Boris Yeltsin and big meals with Bill Clinton, another notorious trencherman. He and John Major enjoyed each other's company.

The one leader with whom he never managed to establish a strong relationship was Thatcher. Their political differences were obvious: Kohl regarded European integration as the key to ensuring peace in Europe, while Thatcher saw it as a threat to British sovereignty and a back-door route to German domination of the Continent.

There was little personal chemistry. One of their first meetings was in Salzburg, Austria, where Thatcher was on holiday. Kohl tired of her company and cut the meeting short, claiming that he had another important engagement. Thatcher, with time on her hands, walked around the streets and found Kohl sitting outside a tea house eating a huge cream cake. "My God! That man is so German!" she exclaimed after another of their meetings.

Kohl, in his memoirs, said of his British nemesis: "It was very unpleasant to have her as an opponent. The enmity didn't finish at the end of the day. It carried on the next morning." He told her: "Margaret, the difference between you and me is that I live in a time after Churchill and you live in the time before him."

Kohl was far shrewder than he looked: "I have been underestimated for decades. I have done very well that way," he once remarked, and for a while he hung magazine articles predicting his political demise on a wall outside his office. His rather slow, clumsy appearance masked a ruthlessness, a sharp political brain and a hunger for power that matched his appetite for food. He built networks, dispensed patronage and seldom forgave those who crossed him. He perfected the policy of *aussitzen* — waiting till a problem disappeared or opponents gave in. Having spent a lifetime working his way up the political ladder, he also enjoyed total dominance of his party, the centre-right Christian Democratic Union.

That dominance contributed to his eventual downfall. Soon after losing his bid for an unprecedented fifth term as chancellor, Kohl was found to have accepted illegal donations to his party. He refused to name the anonymous donors. In 2000 he was forced to resign as the CDU's honorary president and criminal charges were dropped only after he agreed to pay a £100,000 fine.

That scandal was closely followed by a personal disaster. In 2001 Hannelore, his dutiful wife of 40 years, killed herself. Kohl had met her at a dance in Ludwigshafen when she was 15, although they did not marry for another 12 years. She was a refugee from Leipzig, which had been occupied by the Red

Army at the end of the war, and a Soviet soldier had raped her at the age of 12. Her suicide was attributed to a condition called photodermatitis, an allergy to sunlight from which she had suffered for many years, but some commentators also blamed his neglect of her and his political disgrace.

Kohl subsequently married Maike Richter, a woman 34 years his junior who had worked as an economist in his chancellery. Neither of Kohl's two sons by Hannelore was invited to the wedding. Walter Kohl, a businessman who is married to a Korean, and Peter Kohl, an author and entrepreneur married to a Turkish banker, were estranged from their father. They accused their stepmother of having had an affair with him before their mother's death and of keeping him "like a prisoner" in his Ludwigshafen bungalow in his old age.

Kohl was the most successful German chancellor of modern times and shaped the history of the late 20th century, but his family paid the price.

Helmut Kohl was born into a conservative, Roman Catholic family in Ludwigshafen in 1930. By the time he returned to his home town at the end of the Second World War he was a young man with a mission. "Materially and morally Germany was in ruins," he said. "The thought of being able to shape and help build something fascinated me."

He joined the newly formed CDU at 17, and in one youthful escapade with political overtones he and some friends tore down signs on the German-French border near Ludwigshafen. After studying law in Frankfurt, gaining a PhD in political science in Heidelberg and working briefly in the chemical industry that dominates Ludwigshafen he became, at 30, the youngest member of the state legislature in Rhineland-Palatinate. At 39 he became the youngest state premier, at 43 the youngest national chairman of the CDU and at 52 Germany's youngest chancellor — although not through an election.

As the CDU's leader in 1976 Kohl had won 48.6 per cent of the vote, but was denied the chancellorship when Helmut Schmidt's centre-left Social Democrats formed a coalition government with the liberal Free Democratic Party. In 1980 Franz Josef Strauss, leader of the CDU's Bavarian sister party, the CSU, was the centre-right's candidate and lost. Kohl became chancellor two years later only because the FDP abandoned the Social Democrats and formed a coalition with the CDU instead. He governed without a mandate until the elections of March 1983, when he won a resounding victory — the first of three during his 16 years at the helm.

Kohl soon showed his mettle by accepting US intermediate-range nuclear missiles on German soil, despite huge domestic protests that reflected the anti-war, anti-American sentiment sweeping western Europe. It was a courageous decision that dashed Soviet hopes of splitting Nato and bolstered the resolve of the western alliance at a time when it was faltering. Kohl called the debate "one of the most dramatic in German postwar history". It helped, perhaps, that his family had received care packages from the US in the desperate days after the war, leaving him with an unshakeable affection for America.

Kohl was the first German chancellor since the war to visit Israel. He also visited Auschwitz in Poland, where he vowed that there would be no repetition of the "unspeakable harm" perpetrated by the Nazis. He sought to develop ties with eastern Europe generally, and was the first chancellor to invite an East German president, Erich Honecker, to Bonn when that city was still the capital of West Germany.

Kohl's invitation to President Reagan to join him at a German military cemetery in Bitburg proved a less successful symbol of reconciliation. The visit generated great controversy because the cemetery was found to contain the graves of 49 members of Hitler's SS.

The crowning achievement of Kohl's chancellorship was undoubtedly the peaceful reunification of Germany with Soviet consent, an outcome that was far from certain immediately after the fall of the Berlin Wall in November 1989. Thatcher spoke for many Europeans when she voiced fears of a huge, resurgent Germany dominating Europe — "We defeated the

Germans twice, and now they're back!" she famously declared at a Strasbourg summit that December, and convened a meeting of historians at Chequers to discuss the question of "how dangerous are the Germans?" Whether Gorbachev, as a reform-minded president, would permit — or could survive — the loss of a Warsaw Pact state to Nato was not clear.

Kohl seized the moment, or at the very least exploited a rapidly unfolding series of events that nobody could control. As other western leaders dithered he announced, with prior consultation, a ten-point plan for eventual reunification. The CDU's sister party in the German Democratic Republic trounced the old communists in the GDR's first free elections. The GDR's new parliament formally sought accession to the Federal German Republic. East Germany's economy collapsed and the deutschmark replaced the ostmark.

Kohl obtained Gorbachev's approval for reunification in return for economic and technical aid. He assuaged Polish fears by renouncing claims to territory that was historically German. George HW Bush, the US President, insisted only that the enlarged Germany remain a Nato member. Thatcher and Mitterrand found they had little choice but to acquiesce, and the prime minister later called her opposition to reunification an "unambiguous failure".

At midnight on October 3, 1990 — scarcely 11 months after the Wall fell — East and West Germany officially became one, with Berlin as the capital. It was a huge personal triumph for Kohl, who stormed to a third victory in the first federal elections to be held in a reunited Germany that December. The chancellor was well aware of the fears that an enlarged Germany raised in the rest of Europe. Indeed, he shared them. Reunification spurred his efforts to achieve greater European integration, even if that meant ditching the mighty deutschmark. It inspired a "rush to European federalism as a way of tying down Gulliver", Thatcher wrote in her memoirs. This, she added, "formed the background to the ever more intense battles on monetary and political union in which I henceforth found myself engaged".

The result was the Maastricht treaty of 1992, which paved the way for monetary union and the introduction of the euro in 1999 — with Britain opting out. The motivation was as much political as economic, as Kohl readily acknowledged. "We want the political union of Europe. If there's no monetary union then there can't be political union, and vice versa," he explained. In the event political union did not materialise to anything like the degree he envisaged, and a decade later the consequences for the single currency became painfully apparent.

Reunification had another consequence that Kohl did not foresee. Absorbing East Germany proved a huge drag on the entire German economy, causing sluggish growth and high unemployment. He won a fourth election in 1994, but rashly sought a record fifth term in 1998. By that time Germany was no longer Europe's economic pacesetter. It yearned for new and younger leadership. Kohl's CDU suffered its worst defeat in half a century at the hands of Gerhard Schröder's Social Democrats, losing even in Ludwigshafen. He wept openly as he stepped down as chairman of the CDU after 25 years.

Worse was to follow in the form of the funding scandal and his wife's suicide. In 2004 he had to be airlifted from a Sri Lankan hotel after the Asian tsunami. In 2008 his driver found him lying on the floor of his Ludwigshafen kitchen, a pool of blood by his head, having apparently suffered a stroke. By the end of his life he could not walk and had difficulty speaking, and the euro was in crisis. Yet the setbacks of his later years appear slight when balanced against his historic achievements. Kohl will be remembered as one of the most influential statesmen of modern Europe.

NICK TIMOTHY AND FIONA HILL: HOW CIVIL SERVANTS LIVED IN FEAR OF THE TERRIBLE TWINS AT No 10

Oliver Wright, Francis Elliott, Bruno Waterfield

June 17 2017

It must have seemed at the time like an innocent enough sentiment.

As the former shadow chancellor Ed Balls left *Strictly Come Dancing* last November a press officer working in Downing Street tweeted: "Alas it's over. Well done Ed Balls for getting this far & entertaining us." Robin Gordon-Farleigh knew he was being followed by Theresa May's chief of staff Nick Timothy. What he could not have predicted was his reaction.

Mr Timothy called aside the prime minister's principal private secretary, Simon Case, and demanded that Mr Gordon-Farleigh be reprimanded for breaking the rules on civil service neutrality. By the time the reprimand reached Mr Gordon-Farleigh it was more of a warning: "Be careful, they're watching everything you do." A few months later Mr Gordon-Farleigh decided to leave government.

He was one of the lucky ones. In their time in government, *The Times* has been told, Mr Timothy and his fellow chief of staff Fiona Hill forced out or sidelined supposedly independent civil servants, some after a period of alleged bullying, in direct contravention of Whitehall codes of conduct.

As far back as 2011 Ms Hill was officially reprimanded by Gus O'Donnell, the cabinet secretary, for her behaviour. On several occasions the senior civil service union was called in to represent those who had fallen foul of Ms Hill.

Now that they have departed serious questions are being asked about how two unelected political aides could ride roughshod over the civil service while exercising such an iron grip on everything the prime minister saw or heard.

The role of the cabinet secretary, Sir Jeremy Heywood, is

also under scrutiny, with senior civil servants questioning why he did so little to rein in the pair.

"He abdicated his responsibility as leader of the civil service," one senior former No 10 staff member told *The Times*. "You were on your own and the people you looked up to in the house — people like Jeremy Heywood — to give you that cover absolutely didn't."

Joey Jones, a former adviser to Mrs May, said: "Responsibility for the toxic dynamic in Downing Street was not Nick and Fi's alone. Senior people in the civil service should also ask themselves searching questions." *The Times* has been told that at least one senior official intimately involved in the Brexit negotiations was at one stage prevented from seeing the prime minister by Mr Timothy. Sir Ivan Rogers, who was then Britain's permanent representative to the EU, tried to alert Mrs May to what he believed were flaws in the government's understanding of Brussels.

"He was told that he couldn't write submissions to the prime minister and that everything had to go through the chief of staff," one insider said.

"He tried to get one-to-one meetings with Mrs May and was rebuffed. Everything that the prime minister saw or heard was controlled by Nick."

Senior sources said no attempt was made by Sir Jeremy to ensure Sir Ivan got access to Mrs May. Believing he had been frozen out, Sir Ivan quit. A former senior Whitehall figure said that had disastrous consequences for the initial stages of Brexit preparations.

"Losing Ivan Rogers at that point was really bad just as we were preparing our position on Article 50," they said. "He was ex-Treasury and knew about budgets and financial services and how Brussels works. They just lost that. You've ended up with yes men and they're bloody useless to everybody."

Sir Ivan's isolation was possible because the pair ripped up the previous practice in Downing Street that senior civil servants could directly put submissions and papers into the prime minister's nightly and weekend red boxes.

Under the new regime material seen by the prime minister had to be vetted first either by Mr Timothy or Ms Hill. That not only dismayed Whitehall but gummed up the process of decision-making by inserting a fresh layer of bureaucracy into the No 10 operation.

The pair shared an office directly outside Mrs May's and in a breach of usual practice they were given their own civil service private secretary in an attempt to smooth relations with other officials. It didn't work.

One senior figure in the government department outside Downing Street told *The Times* that a policy would be agreed by No 10 officials only to be ripped up when it was sent for sign-off by the "twins".

But it is the allegation that pressuring and ordering about of senior civil servants went unchallenged that is potentially the most damaging to Sir Jeremy.

In one instance Helen Bower, the prime minister's official spokeswoman, was banned on the orders of Ms Hill from travelling to America when Mrs May first met Donald Trump. It was the first time in 20 years that the prime minister had not been accompanied by her official spokesman on such a trip.

"Fiona took umbrage with Helen and decided she could get lost," was one insider's take on what happened. "It was shambolic." It is understood that Ms Hill was unhappy with Ms Bower, who had disagreed with decisions on media strategy. Ms Bower took up a new role in the foreign office.

Her replacement — in her civil service role — was James Slack, the political editor of the *Daily Mail*. While the £140,000 post was advertised, only seven people applied and none of them was internal. Unusually, recruitment consultants were not brought in to help to find a suitable candidate.

Mr Case, Mrs May's principal private secretary, was also said to have been put under considerable pressure by the pair to the extent that he looked for jobs elsewhere in the civil service.

Another senior civil servant who worked in the Ministry of

Justice was forced out of his job within days of Mrs May coming to power because he was seen as being too close to the prime minister's old enemy Michael Gove.

The official was put on gardening leave at the taxpayers' expense before taking on a role in the Cabinet Office, which suggested that instructions for his removal came from the Ministry of Justice. However, the civil servant believed that Ms Hill was involved in the decision.

Several of those who believe they were forced out, and who have spoken to *The Times* on the guarantee of anonymity, felt betrayed by their treatment. "One by one, May's team got Heywood to replace permanent secretaries and senior Downing Street officials across Whitehall, plus the head of the UK's delegation in Brussels, and brought in officials more compliant to Downing Street's complete hegemony," one source claimed.

Another said: "The prime minister's team ran a coach and horses through the civil service rule book and no one seemed interested in stopping them."

Sir Leigh Lewis, a former permanent secretary, suggested that the style of management in No 10 under Mrs May led to bad decision-making. "It seems to have been pretty common knowledge that Downing Street was characterised by powerful gatekeepers who were highly intolerant of anyone who challenged their view."

A Cabinet Office spokesman said: "Sir Jeremy Heywood takes his responsibilities as head of the civil service very seriously, including ensuring special advisers comply with their code of conduct."

The Times contacted Mr Timothy and Ms Hill. Mr Timothy declined to comment on "unsourced personal attacks". Ms Hill did not respond.

FOOD AND SERVICE IN A TIME MACHINE

Giles Coren reviews Assaggi

JUNE 17 2017

FOR A LONG time, I believed that Assaggi in Notting Hill was the best restaurant in London. Because that was what everybody told me.

Michael Winner certainly loved it. So did AA Gill (I think). The wealthy parents of friends of mine in my relative youth, who had houses in Italy and professed to love plain honest peasant cooking and revile all fanciness and pretension, simply adored Assaggi. And friends of my generation who were still living in Notting Hill into the present century (none does now) were always insanely proud of being able to get a table there and bestowed seats at it upon their friends with the beaming munificence of oriental potentates offering a grubby traveller his pick from the royal harem.

So I used to go along when invited — I could never get a table of my own — and observe how they enjoyed being hugged by the owner and brought little nibbles of this and glasses of that and I'd think, "That looks a nice gang to be in." The room was always very bright and airy, and it always seemed to be summer in there. The clientele was aged 30–60, very wealthy, very local, incredibly happy and usually drunk.

They loved the fact that downstairs was just a pub (the Chepstow, I think it was called) because this enabled them to say, "It's just a dining room over a pub." So you could tell they were just simple, honest folk. Totally unpretentious. And they were. After all, their houses down the road were then worth only £5–£10 million. Although I don't think any of them ever set foot in the pub.

And the food would come out: simple pasta dishes, a fritto misto, veal chops, a panna cotta. So simple, so plain, so marvellous. There would be three or four bottles of "simple Italian wine", coffee, and then the bill for six of us — that lovely table for six by the big window in the middle of the room — would be, ooh, maybe a thousand pounds. Honestly. Less than two hundred pounds a head. But then of course it was just a simple peasant supper in a room over a pub. You wouldn't expect to pay real money.

So there it was: Assaggi in Notting Hill. Best restaurant in the best part of the best city in the world. My jealousy of its initiati knew no limits.

And then a couple of years ago I heard it had closed. Which I thought was odd, seeing as it was the best restaurant in London. But then of course restaurants in areas like that are struggling now. Because the £5–£10 million houses of 2002 have been going for more like £40–£50 million in recent years. And the people who have that sort of money to spend on a house can't afford to live in it, because their tax arrangements keep them out of the country for most of the year. So the local restaurants do tend to struggle.

But then Assaggi reopened. And I gathered that it had all been about complications with the lease and that it was the same guy as before at the helm and he now had the whole building (this area really, really has no need for pubs), so that downstairs was no longer just a humble pub but a humble pizza restaurant owned by him.

The opportunity to try it arose when we invited our friends Katherine and Edward into town from their home in Berkshire for dinner. We needed somewhere close to Paddington station so they could get home afterwards, and of course Notting Hill is. Though I doubt the people who live round there these days know that.

I called to book using one of my usual crappy pseudonyms and had no trouble at all getting a four at 8pm the following Thursday, which was a little worrying. And then on the evening in question we drove quietly through the streets of Notting Hill, simply marvelling at the thought that 25 years ago these houses had normal people in them. English people. With jobs. And smiles. And children. Now they are immaculate multistorey palazzi with a permanent leaf-blowing guy and scampering Filipinas flitting past the windows, but nobody truly in residence at all.

Chepstow Place, the long residential road on which Assaggi is just about the only place of business, was completely quiet. Not a car in sight. Because although it is a residents' zone that goes on till 10pm, the residents all park behind their security gates on revolving platforms that stack the cars all the way down to the water table and beyond. By day, this part of town is ablaze with the screech of angle grinders and the hammering of drills as the houses expand endlessly in every direction, but by night it is as empty and silent as the Zombie Dawn.

The new downstairs pizza restaurant was fully staffed but completely empty on a warm Thursday evening at 8pm. No appetite for casual pizza round here, it seems. I guess the Polish builders all bring their own sandwiches.

Upstairs in the famous old dining room — which is unchanged, with its orange walls and monochromatic modernist art — there were some people. But not as many as there used to be. And they are older than they were. I guess because it's the same people. At 47, I am usually old enough to be the father of half the people in any given restaurant. Here, I could have been the son of any of them. Which from an inheritance point of view would have been most advantageous. Clearly they all live locally. You can tell from their red, angry faces that they are the very last of the old guard and feel lonely and embattled, like the final few Native Americans of the Old West, defiant in the face of smallpox, the 7th Cavalry, the Winchester repeater and "progress".

The staff are lovely, friendly and comically old-school. The menu being printed only in Italian, they are desperate to recite it in its entirety with simultaneous translation. Not something I need (being familiar with Italian menus), but I wouldn't have dreamt of preventing them from delivering what is clearly regarded as part of the "theatre".

There was delicious pane carasau on the table (the cooking

is broadly Sardinian) and I asked for an Ichnusa, a Sardinian beer. It came already in the glass, which is not how bottled beer should be served, and it was not cold. Beer that is not cold is as much use as a cat with no eyes. I sent it back and they brought a cold one in the bottle. Would have been classier to do that the first time.

The food that followed was okay. I had grilled fresh pecorino with rocket and San Daniele (£15.90), which I was directed to wrap in the flatbread provided. Quite jolly. Katherine's stuffed courgette flowers (£14.90) were very deep-fried, all brown and crispy like spring rolls down the chippy. Esther liked her three scallops (£16.90) with pea purée and bacon, but found her piece of turbot ("Fish of the day" at £31), which ought to be a mild, meaty fish, to be a bit sloppy and fishy, served on quite tough vegetables, with nothing of interest (like a caper or two) to lift it.

The fritto misto was light, crispy, fresh and copious but the proud denial of the existence of aïoli or mayonnaise in the whole establishment, which was practically sung at me when I ordered, just made me yearn for it. For anything to alleviate the dryness. I suppose there were the soggy vegetables: courgettes like they used to do it in the old days — chopped, boiled, slung in a bowl — some shrivelled peas, some spinach. But I wasn't impressed.

The wine list was short and expensive. We had the only gavi di gavi at £69.50, and a little tiramisu in a ramekin (£9) which was interesting only in that it was still on a menu in 2017.

I want to reiterate how lovely and attentive the staff were. I don't want to dance on this restaurant's grave. But the evening just demonstrated how much we have all moved on. This was food and service in a time machine. Not back to the red sauce and checked table cloths of the 1960s, but to the new bogusness of the 1990s, of Granita, Cibo and Conran's Cantina del Ponte.

The already underpopulated room thinned further during our meal as the local oldsters shuffled out into the empty streets — haunted no doubt by memories of fun-filled evenings now almost a quarter-century gone — until soon it was just us and our £400 bill for an ordinary Italian meal with one bottle of wine. Just us in the empty restaurant in the empty street in the emptiest neighbourhood in England.

SOVEREIGN WEALTH

Leading Article

JUNE 24 2017

AMID THE CHAOS and the fury of the EU referendum campaign, the recriminations and denunciations, the pleas from executives and counsel from presidents, one short shibboleth pierced through the noise. "Take back control", devastating in its simplicity, was once the clarion call of the Leave campaign. It is now the unofficial slogan of the government.

Yet a year after the vote, it is plain that to treat "control" as absolute, to view it as an end in itself divorced from its consequences, will not be in Britain's interests. Brexit will work only if the government is open to co-operation, too.

Effectively elevated to her office by the political success of Brexiteers, Theresa May quickly assumed their three central ambitions: to take back control of our laws, borders and money. All spoke to decades of well-justified irritation at the overweening interference of European Union institutions and its political ambitions. Yet after a year beset by the quest for sovereignty, the government has found that it comes with costs. Some are imposed by the EU. Others flow from the basic tenets of economics and public policy.

Control of our laws was cast not just as a total repatriation of legislative powers from Brussels to Westminster, but also an end to the involvement of the European Court of Justice in the legal system. Already this is emerging as a flashpoint in the negotiation over citizens' rights, as the EU demands a role for its own institutions in protecting its citizens after Brexit.

This may well be surmountable, but the government's attitude to law-making will create bigger problems when it negotiates on trade. Even after months of conversation about Europe, senior politicians too often give the impression that their understanding of the European single market is hazy. They talk as if it were a club where EU leaders work as bouncers, granting or denying access. In truth it is a rule book. Where one country's regulations line up with another's, there is no need for arduous checks to make sure that goods and services crossing the border are legally compliant. That allows firms to do business unencumbered. Co-operating on laws is the essence of free trade.

Ministers have also been working to take back control of our borders. Here the prospect of absolute sovereignty is more perilous still. The peace process in Northern Ireland relies on a soft border between the North and the Republic. That means a border subject to little, not extra, control. When border checks were administered, they were symbols of division and targets for attack. Meanwhile the ambition to bear down on the number of people crossing Britain's borders, cutting immigration to the tens of thousands, is routinely rebuffed by businesses leaders who need foreign labour. There are few Brits to fill the spots of EU workers since unemployment is at record lows.

The final aim, to take back control of our money, has perhaps proven the most paradoxical of all. Contributions to the EU budget were a major theme of the referendum campaign and it is right for the government to get them down. At the same time the British did not vote, as Philip Hammond said on Tuesday, to become poorer. Control of money will be bittersweet if there is less of it to control. That is all the more reason for the government to focus on free trade.

The prime minister has often been criticised for being too tight-lipped on Brexit, repeating slogans rather than going into detail. Since Mrs May's Lancaster House speech in January, this critique has been unfair. She gave answers. However, the election revealed that her answers did not convince people. That is why pressure has been building since polling day for the government to think not just about taking control, but also taking responsibility for the future of the economy. This was a difficult year. Unless the government learns from the election, next year will be harder still.

THE PRIMITIVE LOST SOCIETY OF LOVE ISLAND

Ben Macintyre

July 1 2017

In 1970 a group of intrepid anthropologists approached North Sentinel Island, a speck of land in the middle of the Bay of Bengal that is home to the most isolated tribe on earth, a hunter-gatherer society without fire or agriculture, untouched by modern civilisation. The Sentinelese brandished spears and fired arrows from the shore. The scientists, not daring to land, watched from a safe distance.

"At this moment, a strange thing happened," wrote one observer. "A woman paired off with a warrior and sat on the sand in a passionate embrace. This act was repeated by other women, each claiming a warrior for herself, a sort of community mating ... When the tempo of this frenzied dance of desire abated, the couples retired into the shade of the jungle."

This scene, baffling to the anthropologists, will be familiar to anyone who has been watching *Love Island*, the hugely popular ITV reality television show in which a group of young Britons in a villa on Mallorca have been cut off from the outside world and encouraged to mate.

Love Island is appallingly, compulsively watchable (one of the benefits of having a teenage daughter is that I have seen every episode). The contestants have beautiful bodies, extensive tattoos and, in some cases, very small brains. The coupling and recoupling takes place in a long dormitory, the equivalent of the shady Sentinelese jungle, where the islanders cavort beneath duvets in a strange half-light.

Love Island is manipulative, crass and oddly unerotic. But as an anthropological experiment it is quite remarkable: living evidence of how isolated communities swiftly evolve unique forms of behaviour. The culture of *Love Island* is artificial and ephemeral. Genuine island cultures shaped in seclusion, like that of the Sentinelese, are important, and in an increasingly homogenised world profoundly vulnerable. The very silliness of *Love Island* is a reminder of how real island cultures need to be preserved and protected.

The Love Islanders have already developed their own language, moulded by environment and community. "To mug someone off" (to take advantage of another's feelings without reciprocation); "grafting" (flirting with sexual intent); "put it on" (sexual congress); "salty" (angry); "pie-ed" (to ditch a partner).

The contestants may be unaware that they are proof of the Sapir-Whorf hypothesis that perception is moulded by language, and vice versa. As Wittgenstein put it: "The limits of my language are the limits of my world."

The phrase "He was being super muggy, grafting on Montana and trying to put it on Tyla, so I got proper salty and pie-ed him" would not be comprehensible in the next-door villa. But the same is true of the Sentinelese, whose language is unclassified and unintelligible to their nearest neighbours.

The Love Islanders have their own mating rituals, pecking order and a special form of Darwinian selection in which only the fittest survive (as in: "Kem is well fit, so I will shag him, innit"). By implication, these naturally selected couples will breed together after the show to produce the next generation of handsome morons.

The island is brutally self-policed, with established codes of behaviour that, if transgressed, lead to expulsion. The promise of survival that comes from securing the best sexual partner means that betrayal is endemic and ruthless. What is depicted as "romance" is really about enduring in an essentially hostile island environment.

On *Love Island*, as in most insular communities, procreation is the most urgent human need. The men preen and posture but the women perform the selection, securing a mate and seeing off rivals through sexual display, usually in the swimming pool.

Much time is spent grooming. Individuals able to beautify others (hairdressers, personal trainers, etc) fulfil the role of shamans, and thus get more sexual partners. Anyone with artistic skill is revered as a magician. In the current series this is Marcel, who was in the hip-hop group *Blazin' Squad*, and will therefore win the show.

These are all characteristics of primitive, insulated, pre-literate societies.

The inhabitants of *Love Island* have developed no tools because they don't need to do anything, except lie around primping and pairing off, or "cracking on". The same is true of the Sentinelese: with an easy diet of coconuts, wild plants and fish, their most advanced utensil is a harpoon.

Every attempt to contact the Sentinelese has failed. In 1880 a British expedition kidnapped a family and took them to Port Blair in the Andaman islands, where the adults immediately died. The last attempt to land was in 1974, when anthropologists brought gifts of aluminium pots, a live pig and a miniature plastic car. The Sentinelese responded with a hail of arrows.

Two Indian fishermen, illegally catching mud crabs, drifted ashore in 2006 and were killed. The Indian coastguard helicopter sent in to retrieve the bodies was driven off by accurate archery.

The Sentinelese may number as few as 40 or as many as 500. They may be left-handed. They want to be left alone, and so they should be, to live their unique way of life in complete isolation.

The world was once full of individuated cultures; the

Sentinelese are one of the few preserved indigenous island societies, a small surviving jewel of distinctive human evolution.

Viewers of *Love Island* — two million and rising — may have noticed the islanders' mounting hostility towards the outside world. A fitting finale would be to close the door and let them continue the "frenzied dance of desire", in their private language, physically perfect and perfectly alone on their island.

SMALL ACTS OF KINDNESS THAT CAN SAVE A LIFE

Libby Purves

JULY 3 2017

WE HAVE ALL known the experience. Our train stops, the delay lengthens until a careful announcement is made. Not signalling, not breakdown, weather, livestock or even the slightly comedic "passenger causing a disturbance". Instead the irritable murmuring is stilled by the words "a person hit by a train". It may be an accident, but probably isn't. Even the barest scrap of decency forces us to stop grumbling, acknowledge a human death and recognise the shock and misery. Somewhere ahead the British Transport Police are taking evidence, phoning a specialist funeral company, inspecting the train, caring for a devastated driver. So we sit quietly and say a silent prayer.

We won't learn more because careful restrictions surround reporting. Until a distant inquest the words "incident not being treated as suspicious" will cover it. But we know that last year there were 237 railway suicides, confirmed or suspected. The Underground sees them too, and research suggests that victims are disproportionately young. A few are psychiatric patients. On the Tube the announcement normally says "a person on the tracks", and it is a relief (as the other day at the Elephant) when it turns out to be just a retrievable wandering drunk. More often it is stark tragedy. We hear "lines are now reopened", but somewhere a skein of lives has been instantly devastated.

But here is a small, significant piece of good news. Despite the turbulence of news and economic stringency, rail suicides are down to the lowest level since 2010. This is partly because of physical measures such as fences and lighting, but also because large numbers of Network Rail staff and Transport Police officers are taking a Samaritans' prevention course. Already 15,000 have been taught to spot the signs, make an approach, know what to say and what to avoid saying. Last year there was a sharp increase in "potentially life-saving interventions". On average, four times every day a staff member was stepping in to talk to someone apparently at risk.

One man observed that after initial cynicism about the course — born of seeing many an awful aftermath — he was more confident when the moment came. Another said "it's quite a scary situation to be in" as he brought himself to approach a lone woman sitting on a bench, head in hands. He learnt that she, a mother of three, had indeed planned to jump.

Suicide is always a mystery: profoundly individual in its violent denial of every creature's self-preservation instinct. There is nothing simple or universal about it. I have thought a lot on the subject these 11 years, having lost that way not only friends and acquaintances but a son. I talk with many other parents and family survivors: most recently I helped the Clark family to launch the InFinnity Project, promoting art therapy in memory of Finn Clark, a brilliant illustrator who took his life at 25. I said there that "all good art is like a hand held out by a stranger, showing that you are never quite alone". It had resonated with the reactions we get from young men in particular who read my son Nicholas Heiney's poetry and sea-logs. Even when the artist is lost, that sense of a comradely hand can help.

I still, with sadness, suspect that there are suicides that can't be prevented: maybe when your very brain turns on you in rising psychosis it becomes too urgent a relief to resist. Many show evidence of careful, calm, determined planning. Yet there is equal evidence that others — overwhelmed by grief, betrayal, loneliness, and a deceptive conviction of failure and helplessness — take the violent moment, often using high buildings or railway tracks. And, time after time, accounts suggest that a stranger's warmth might call them back. So the fact that ordinary rail staff are being encouraged and helped to provide it is wonderful. Specialist police teams worldwide have long done this: one US trainer's site says: "Repeat simple phrases like, 'You are not alone. We are going to get through this together.' Don't interrupt, criticise or judge. Ask their name. Just get a promise of one more day. Some of these people have never reached out for help."

Even people who know themselves loved by their families are sometimes called back by a stranger: maybe we need that uncomplicated, basic sense of unity with all mankind. Accounts down the years of this extremity are unutterably moving in their clumsy, loving determination.

In the London Marathon Jonny Benjamin and Neil Laybourn ran together, nine years after they met on Waterloo Bridge where Benjamin was planning to jump. Laybourn, unsure but determined, weighed in half-panicked, repeating, "It will get better mate, you will get better." When the other man said something about no one caring he babbled "I promise, I care ... please don't jump, please." Benjamin says that "it burst the bubble of that world I was in. I felt faith." They found one another years later and remain friends.

It provokes reflection on that power of a stranger's caring even in less dramatic moments, or earlier in the cycle of despair. Distrustful, reserved, we tend to stay bowed over phones and tablets, digitally immersed in the affairs of absent people. In public spaces it grows ever easier to think that nobody would pick up even our most unmistakable animal signals of distress. And in this so-called "connected" age it is also harder to make that first move towards an unhappy stranger. But a gentle "You OK?" can change a moment. And sometimes a life.

PEOPLE THOUGHT I WAS MAD TO OFFER MY SPARE ROOM TO A HOMELESS STRANGER

Alexandra Frean

JULY 4 2017

May 17, 2017
"Dad wants to know why I didn't stop you," my brother says, amused. Chatting to my parents on the phone earlier, I had casually dropped into the conversation that Youssef, an Eritrean refugee I had never met, was coming to stay in my spare room. They asked me what I knew about him. Not much: he's 27 and has been in the UK since last year, I'm the third family to host him, he likes football, he's Muslim. That's it. But how did I know I would be safe, they want to know. Now my brother is asking the same question.

In fact, it's a question a lot of friends have asked. A week earlier Refugees at Home, a charity that matches homeless refugees with volunteer hosts, sent a representative to my home to check me out and make sure my two-bedroom central London flat was suitable. He explained that most people in Youssef's situation had faced unimaginable hardships to get here and were strongly motivated to do whatever it takes to make a good life for themselves and not jeopardise anything. Ultimately, he said, it's a leap of faith. You just have to trust him. I liked his candour.

May 18
The idea of having a refugee to stay now seems perfectly sane to me. Refugees at Home was formed in October 2015 after a summer of heart-wrenching news stories about refugees being drowned in the Mediterranean or stifled in lorries. I am moved by this, but this is not what inspires me. I have already worked with refugees in the US, where I lived until last year and where I volunteered to teach English to a family of Iraqi refugees. I also taught literacy to immigrant healthcare workers (mostly

orderlies and cleaners), who would take a one-hour bus ride after exhausting eight-hour shifts to study with me and still find the energy to joke about my English accent. I would leave feeling happy that I had done something worthwhile. Honestly, that feeling is hard to beat.

May 19

I survey my flat before Youssef's arrival. I wonder what this young Muslim man will think of moving into a home with a 55-year-old godless, independent, wine-drinking Englishwoman. What will it be like sleeping with just a paper-thin wall between us and having use of a shared bathroom? I rearrange the furniture so that our beds are against opposite walls, as far as they can be from each other. I drink what's left of the wine and chuck out some dubious-looking half-empty bottles of spirits. I order fruit, vegetables and hummus on Tesco.com, and stuff the non-halal meat in my fridge into the bottom of the freezer.

May 20

I have spoken to the lovely lady who is at present hosting Youssef. She tells me he is a delight, but very reserved. "What do you know about his life? How did he get here?" I ask. She says she didn't like to ask.

May 21

Youssef arrives, carrying all his possessions in a very small bag. I spread out a map of the world on the dining table and point first to Eritrea and then to London. "Please," I say, "tell me your story."

I have done my homework. A United Nations report from 2016 concluded that Eritreans have been subjected to "gross violations of human rights" for 25 years. Many Eritreans are forced into indefinite military service and subjected to horrific abuses. This is why so many people like Youssef brave one of the world's most dangerous migrant routes, across the Sahara and the Mediterranean to Europe, to escape. Suddenly, this project takes a new dimension.

In faltering English Youssef tells me about his journey, walking 550 miles from Eritrea to Khartoum and then to Egypt. Eleven terrifying days at sea, landing eventually in Italy. From there to Calais and then, finally to the UK, where he reported himself to the police on arrival. Despite all he has been through, he never criticises the Eritrean regime. He still has family there.

Over dinner we look at photographs of his six siblings on his phone and talk about his family. My sons are both abroad at college. I FaceTime them and introduce Youssef to them — at this point I am still nervous about having him in my house. I want him to realise that if anything happens to me, there will be people — two lovely young men like him — who would miss me.

May 23

I awake to news of a terrorist attack at an Ariana Grande concert and freeze when I hear the word "Manchester" (I had expected to hear some foreign place name). I explain to Youssef what has happened. He knows where Manchester is. It turns out that he has a pretty good knowledge of English geography based on a lifelong love of Premier League football. I worry about racist reprisal attacks and feel he should be prepared. "Do you know what racism is?" I ask stupidly. "Yes, I do," he replies with feeling. "I'm sorry," I say. "How many dead?" he asks.

May 26

Five days in and we are getting used to each other. Youssef studies English at college two days a week. He hopes to get a job soon and, when his English is better, to study to become an electrician. I can't walk around naked any more and I no longer hang up my underwear to dry in the living room, but neither is really a hardship. He is slightly confused about whether to call me Alex or Alexa, since I am always addressing my Amazon Echo speaker as Alexa.

May 27
I'm off to the Hay-on-Wye literary festival for the weekend and put Youssef in charge of the cats. He seems delighted to have some small thing he can do for me. The cats can't believe their luck at having an additional human around. He has even won over the standoffish ginger tabby. Without being asked, Youssef carries my suitcase downstairs. This has become a pattern. He observes all the time, to find small acts of kindness he can perform. He empties the dishwasher and sweeps the floor unbidden and makes me cups of tea. He replaces the milk before we run out. Sensing that I am a bit of a neat freak, he keeps his room immaculately clean and tidy.

May 30
I return from Wales. The cats are totally under Youssef's spell.

June 3
Something is not right. I arrive home late in a cab after a night out. There are police everywhere. I put on flat shoes, grab a notebook and head out again. An officer turns me back at the end of my street. Another yells: "Take cover, go back." "I'm a reporter," I say, "I need to get through." But they turn me back again. I watch news of the London Bridge terrorist attack on Twitter. I'm not entirely sober and realise there's not much I can do. I lie in bed listening to police helicopters circling all night and waiting for Youssef to come home. The next morning he tells me he had been seeing friends and arrived back in the neighbourhood at about midnight. By then our street, a stone's throw away from the attacks, was sealed off. He had no idea what was going on. The police made him wait three hours before letting him through the cordon to the flat. I tell him what happened. "How many dead?" he asks. I'm sick of having this conversation with him.

June 7

"You haven't thought this through, have you?" I'm having lunch with my friend James and talking about the other big project in my life: my decision to start dating. "How can you bring a man home with Youssef there?" James wants to know. It's five years since my husband died, suddenly, of a heart attack, and I don't like being alone. I think I am ready now to start seeing someone. But James is right, I don't feel I could bring anyone home with Youssef there. I still have no idea what he thinks of the fact that I am out most nights with friends and family and often don't come home till late. Does he ever compare me with his own mother and wonder what kind of crazy world he has ended up in?

June 8

At an election night party, my fellow diners tell me how "brave" I am. It's a common reaction. I tell them I got lucky with Youssef; he's quiet, considerate and respectful and helps around the house. He doesn't have a single annoying habit. He's figured out my routines and we've settled into a quiet companionship. There's often no need to talk. On evenings when we are both home, we sit in the living room — him working on his English homework, me watching Netflix — goodness knows what he makes of *Lilyhammer* or *Backstrom*, the two rather offbeat series I've been watching (I've been careful not to watch anything with too much sex — that would feel weird).

June 17

Youssef's arrival at my home followed a very dark time in my life. In February, on the fifth anniversary of my husband's death, I fell off an emotional cliff. It felt like I was going backwards. At the insistence of my sister, I agreed to see a therapist. Annette is wise and is wonderful at helping me to navigate my way back up to the surface. By the time Youssef arrives I am already much better. I tell her that having him in my home has contributed enormously to my recovery and she smiles knowingly. A couple of weeks ago she asked me: "How do you want to use the rest of your life?" It was an interesting way of looking at things and now I think I know part of the answer.

June 18
A friend from Pakistan tells me that with Youssef I am not just helping one person, I am helping a whole family, possibly a village. It's touching, but I feel an immense burden of responsibility.

June 22
"How are you going to transfer money to your family back home?" I ask Youssef. "Western Union?" He smiles at me indulgently. I've learnt in the past month that he is both smart and funny and he tolerates my, at times, uninformed questions with good humour. There is no functioning Western Union in Eritrea, he says. He will have to rely on informal ways of sending money home through London's Eritrean community. "But then you'd have to check it arrived there," I say. He looks at me kindly, as if I'm an idiot. "Yes," he says.

July 2
I am returning from a weekend on the Continent, but my flight is delayed by the knock-on effects of an interfering drone at Gatwick. It's late. A text from Youssef asks what time I will be home. It's the kind of thing my boys might do if I don't turn up and it's a sign, I think, of how far we have come in a few weeks.

July 3
My dilemma is what to do when my sons come home from college in mid-July. I tell Youssef he'll have to move out, but can come back in September. He is trying to find a room to rent, but first needs a job. I realise now how much support he's going to need long-term and, having got to know him, I'm happy to help in whatever way I can because I've been a winner in this relationship too. It feels like the very least I can do.

POCKET MONEY, PHONE, RAMBO KNIFE

Rachel Sylvester

JULY 8 2017

ITS 6PM ON A Friday evening when I join the police gangs unit on patrol in Hackney. Already, two teenagers have been arrested with knives — one of them is a 13-year-old girl, who hid the weapon in her school bag.

As we drive around the streets in an unmarked car, a report comes in on the radio of a stabbing in nearby Hoxton. A few minutes later, we hear that a knife has also been confiscated in Stamford Hill library. I am shocked. But for the two plain-clothed officers I am with, this is worryingly normal.

"We are taking knives off the street every day and they have doubled in size in the past three years," says Sergeant Dan Murphy, who runs the dedicated Hackney unit. "I recently arrested a boy of 14 with 5 kitchen knives and a meat cleaver — he was carrying for the rest of the gang. They have moved on to carrying bottles of ammonia, too. It's difficult for us to deal with. They carry knives but they're also kids, so it doesn't feel right to be too forceful."

Hackney is my neighbourhood. Murphy and his colleague, PC Heidi Akers, pick me up from home, which is around the corner from their office. It is also, they tell me, less than 100 metres from the headquarters of the notorious London Fields Boys, one of Hackney's oldest and most brutal gangs. We pass my 10-year-old son's primary school, the station that my 13-year-old walks to every day and the park where the children play football at the weekend. It is all so familiar but it feels different. Next to the tennis courts, the police smell cannabis, put on the blue light and pull over a car. Although they don't find any drugs, there is a baseball bat in the boot. The driver claims he plays with his godson, but Akers is sceptical. "Sometimes they don't even have a ball," she says. It seems I have stumbled into a terrifying underworld right on my doorstep.

There are, according to Murphy, 22 gangs in Hackney, each with between 50 and 100 active members. The average age is 15 but some of those involved are as young as 12. Instead of fidget spinners or loom bands, blades have become the new craze for these children. A recent knife fight broke out in an ice-cream parlour, with toddlers looking on. The local McDonald's has become a trouble spot — the kids gather there in their school uniform for the free wifi because their parents have put a data limit on their smartphones.

The members of the gangs unit — which includes probation officers, social workers and welfare advisers as well as the police — are working 12-hour shifts to try to stop the violence spiralling out of control. In the week before I joined the patrol, 17 gang members had been arrested and 30 knives recovered in Hackney.

"Knives are a status thing for these kids," Murphy says. "They're showing off to their friends. The latest things are Rambo knives with 10in blades. The kids can be pretty wild. Last week they were letting off fireworks in McDonald's in the middle of the day. They just do anything for attention and, unlike the older boys who used to be in gangs, they don't have boundaries."

Tonight, there is a grime music talent show at the Hackney Empire. The last time I came here it was to watch the Christmas pantomime with my family, but now a large crowd has gathered outside the venue and the police are expecting trouble. Extra officers have been deployed and youth workers are also patrolling, but there is tension in the air.

As darkness falls, dozens of young people are standing in groups on the pavement. A few are circling on bicycles. Almost all have their hoods up, and some are wearing scarves over their faces revealing only their eyes. Most do not look more than 14. One girl in a pink hair band is sucking on a lollipop. The boys seem wired, they are shouting and jostling, buzzing with nervous energy and aggression. Murphy points out the 14-year-old he recently found with the knives and machete. "Be careful," he calls over to him, with a combination of fatherly concern and headmasterly authority.

A scuffle breaks out in the churchyard and there are reports that a knife has been produced, but by the time the police arrive the agitators are running away and the weapon has been dumped. A boy dashes up. "Is there a fight? Have I missed it?" he asks, disappointed.

The kids wave at the police, taunting them, but one is more aggressive, coming up to Akers and shouting in her face, "Stop f***ing looking at me." She is about a foot smaller than he is — and just back from maternity leave — but she holds his gaze. The children don't often attack the police, she tells me; they are more interested in each other. "I've watched some of them going through the ranks and then the younger brothers joining, but it's different now," she says. "In the old days, there was a hierarchy to the gang. The 'elders' would keep the 'youngers' in check because they didn't want us involved in their business, but now it's groups of kids getting together on social media."

Almost all the teenagers on the street are black, but in Tower Hamlets they would be Asian and in Dagenham white. This is, the social workers say, about poverty, not race.

"A lot of these boys have started out with nothing, so they see this as a chance to feel better about themselves," Murphy explains. "We understand why they fall into this life. But so many lives are wasted. Some of these kids are really intelligent. If only they were directed into something productive."

We bump into PC Gary Collins, one of the Metropolitan Police's "super-recognisers", who works for the gangs unit. He has a photographic memory for faces and spends every day studying police mugshots, Instagram posts and YouTube clips. When a crime is committed, he examines CCTV footage to identify possible offenders. After the London riots in 2011, he picked out 180 of the looters.

Now, as he scans the crowd outside the Hackney Empire, he begins to recognise suspects. A 15-year-old boy, who had been caught on CCTV beating up a 59-year-old man after he told the gang to stop messing around, is arrested for GBH. A 14-year-old, suspected of a recent stabbing, is picked up for attempted murder. As he is led in handcuffs into a police van, he is smiling and his friends are filming him on their phones so they can post a video of the arrest online. There is no sign of remorse. When the police search the boy, they find a small plastic bottle filled with what they call a noxious substance, maybe Domestos, ready to throw in somebody's face. It is the contrast between domesticity and violence, the clash between innocence and experience, that is so disconcerting.

I find myself standing on a street corner with Collins. A group of boys crowds around us, trying to intimidate us, but Collins defuses the situation by naming them one by one. Occasionally, he also tells them the name of a brother or cousin. Having worked in the police for 22 years, he knows some of their parents. They come closer, horrified to be recognised but also thrilled by the notoriety. One boy begs him to forget him and walks away, but within seconds he comes back, asking, "What's my name?" There is vulnerability as well as cruelty in these children's eyes. "If I know them, they feel as if they've become somebody," Collins says. "A lot of them have nothing at home, so the gang is like their family. They want to belong."

There has always been an edginess to Hackney, although the borough's "Murder Mile" has in recent years been overtaken by macchiatos and MacBooks. Its interlocking cultures exist side by side, but the gradual gentrification has deepened the social and economic divides. When I moved to the area 15 years ago, there were no cappuccinos available anywhere. Now Hackney has its own coffee bean roastery and you can get prosecco on tap in the canal café. Sourdough bakeries and hipster breweries have opened up next to the Turkish kebab shops. It is possible to spend £10 on three vines of organic tomatoes in fashionable Broadway Market, or buy a plastic bowl of them for £1 in nearby Ridley Road. With elegant Victorian terraces fanning out around the tower blocks, it often feels as if different communities are living parallel lives.

Occasionally, you see signs of a violent subculture bubbling beneath the surface — a shooting in the park, reported in the local paper, accounts of an attempted mugging by the church — but it is usually easy to look the other way and suppress the anxiety. Recently, though, I've found the danger impossible to ignore. A few months ago on the way to drop my younger son and his friend at football training, I saw a teenage boy being chased by two others waving carving knives. I dialed 999 and the police later told me that a young man had turned up at the nearest hospital having been stabbed. Detective Chief Superintendent Simon Laurence, the borough commander, compares Hackney to a pressure cooker. "With gang violence it's about keeping the lid on, and how firmly it's on," he says. "When crime starts escalating, that's when we need to push the lid down in lots of different ways."

On the day I meet Hackney's most senior policeman there has been another stabbing in my postcode. It looks like a gang-related crime: the victim has lost some fingers in a street fight but doesn't want to talk to the police. A 13-year-old has been arrested. The day before, a 12-year-old had been picked up for another knife crime.

In the chief inspector's office there is a case full of weapons, giant samurai swords and bright green "zombie slayers". These are just some of the hundreds of knives that have been taken off the streets in the borough over the past 12 months — 585 in 2016 alone. That year, nationally, there were 32,498 knife crimes recorded in the UK, an increase of 14 per cent on 2015, according to Office for National Statistics figures. Hackney police carry out regular sweeps of local estates, looking for weapons hidden under bushes and bins, as well as proactively using stop and search powers to recover knives. Despite the number of blades seized, there were still 91 stabbings involving people under the age of 25 in the area in the past year, a 16 per cent increase on the previous 12 months.

There is what the police call a "matrix" that includes the names of 150 young people associated with gangs in Hackney.

Across London, 3,600 people are on a similar watchlist. Not all have committed offences, but they are judged to be at risk and are regularly visited at home. It is not just about punishment, but also about diverting people away from crime: there is help with housing and benefits as well as jobs advice. The oldest person on the matrix is 30; the youngest is 12.

There have been gangs in Hackney for years, but what worries Laurence is that younger children are getting involved at the same time as knife crime is rising. The police now go into primary schools to warn eight and nine-year-olds about the risks. "The level of speed to extreme violence is far younger and far quicker than we used to expect," he says.

Nobody quite knows what explains the shift: it may have started when some of the older gang members were in prison after the riots, leaving a gap for younger siblings and their friends. There is also a suggestion that new controls on stop and search, introduced by Theresa May when she was home secretary amid fears that the power was being used disproportionately against young black men, have hampered police efforts to tackle knife crime. What is certainly true is that social media sites such Facebook and WhatsApp have created new networks and ways of meeting up for a younger generation.

As the age profile of those involved changes, the gangs themselves are evolving. In the past, they were organised crime syndicates, running drugs lines to the counties as well as selling Class A narcotics in the capital. They had hierarchies and demarcated geographical areas. There were violent territorial disputes, but the gangs also competed to have the best business models and brands. They made professional videos to market themselves, sometimes even wearing a certain colour to indicate their allegiance. Although they were dangerous criminals, a sense of equilibrium had developed.

A couple of years ago one of the gang leaders was arrested. "It's like chess," he told the officer who was reading him his rights. "You've made your move and I will now make mine." There was almost a feeling of mutual respect, an order to the criminality.

These days the groups are much more fluid and less disciplined. They are often just kids messing about on the streets. They are more interested in playing with knives than selling drugs — although these children are also often recruited by the established gangs to run errands. Laurence calls it, "The paper round of drugs — it's, 'Here's a pair of trainers. Can you go and deliver this for me?' "

What makes the younger cohort difficult to police is that they are unpredictable. "They're chaotic and their grievances are so low-level," says Detective Superintendent Claire Crawley, who worked for the Met's Trident Gang Crime Command before joining Hackney police last year. "It could be something from school that seems so minor to an adult — a 'He said, she said' thing — but that then provokes an extraordinary level of violence."

Increasingly, she says, girls are being used to carry weapons because they are less likely to be searched. Many are under age but give sexual favours to gain acceptance. "Some of the girls are 13 and are caught in that lifestyle. That is normalised behaviour for them; they don't recognise that they've been exploited."

With children now embroiled in gangs, the police believe it is not enough to see this simply in terms of crime. "Enforcement does have its place," says Crawley, "but a lot of these kids have had such terrible backgrounds and been exposed to such trauma themselves. It could be domestic abuse, or territorial violence. If you've seen extreme violence at a young age, and you may not have any parameters at home, carrying a knife becomes commonplace."

David Lammy, Labour MP for Tottenham, who is conducting a government review of the treatment of black and ethnic minority people in the criminal justice system, has thought about the drivers of youth violence. Raised by a single mother himself, he says the absence of a father is a recurring theme among those in gangs. "That's a major issue. Boys need responsible male role models."

He also worries that the young are being desensitised to violence by a "Grand Theft Auto culture" in video games, rap lyrics and TV. "I've seen cases in my constituency where teenagers have lost their lives over Facebook posts. There are exaggerated notions of pride that can exist in impoverished communities."

The children who are being recruited into gangs at an ever younger age are, in his view, victims rather than perpetrators of crime.

Gwenton Sloley was 12 when he joined Hackney's Holly Street Boys, arch-rivals of the London Fields gang. By the time he was 18, he was involved in gang crime and ended up spending time in ten different prisons for armed robbery. Then, ten years ago, he had a son and decided he had to change his life. Now he runs a football academy for boys who have escaped from gangs as well as advising the police and the Home Office. When we meet in a café, he insists on sitting at the table facing the window and the door. "I know no one's coming to kill me any more, but it's instinct, like a soldier," he says.

Although he has been "out of the street" for more than a decade, he sees in the young people he now works with the same emotional issues that attracted him to gangs as a boy.

"I lived with my stepmum and my stepbrother and I didn't know whether my mum was dead or alive. I was walking around in pain. I got sent to this boys' school that had gangs in it, so it was survive or get bullied. You have to up your dangerousness."

The Holly Street Boys "became a family", he says. "We knew that if we didn't stick together, we would get terrorised by the older boys. Once we saw the power we had we started beating up the other schools." In that world, he explains, knives are a way of gaining respect. "If you stab someone you immediately become one of the main people in your gang. You look as if you are dangerous. That's good — you get a promotion. Even if you're a little kid you're a boss. You have to be wild. If you're not, your area is seen as not putting any work in. If you're not noticed, you're invisible. Who wants to be invisible in a gang?"

The boys I saw outside the Hackney Empire were "performing on a stage", he says. Often they will carry a man-bag slung across their body, which they will pat ostentatiously to indicate there is a weapon inside, even if it contains only tissues. Many of the children who are sucked into gangs have mental health problems or have been diagnosed with ADHD. "They are given Ritalin [a stimulant]. That's like giving them crack. So you've got a group of young people who are self-medicating. They want to release the tension that has built up in them on someone else. If I'm a young person who's been told I'm stupid and I'm crazy, then a group picks me and starts looking after me, I've been activated. And when you activate young people, you can't turn them off."

Sloley says that in every prison he went to, he lied and said that he was on drugs because he knew that was the only way he could get therapy. "Violence is an addiction. The first time I pull out a knife and everyone gasps, I'm going to get addicted to that feeling. The first time I stab someone, I might go home and vomit, but the next time I'm going to learn that, if you don't push that much of the blade in, the person won't die. The power of knowing that I could take your soul at any minute is addictive. My addiction was to the excitement that I got from chasing someone down the street or jumping over a counter and leaving with £10,000. That hasn't left me; I just use it to do different things. Two days ago I was in Thames Valley, training police commanders. That's what's exciting to me now. You have to work on the addiction instead of focusing on the crime."

Back in Hackney, I walk across London Fields. The sun is out and the hipsters are lying on the grass in the heatwave with their barbecues. Children are playing football and mothers are sitting chatting beside babies in buggies. There is a yoga class going on next to a taekwondo session, as well as basketball and baseball games. On their usual bench near the entrance to the park sit the London Fields Boys.

Within one small neighbourhood, people are living close together and yet far apart. We exist in bubbles, but it is not really possible to escape from the parallel universes all around us. I think back to the young people on the street outside the Hackney Empire, pumped up and looking for a fight, searching for recognition and a sense of belonging. Of course some of them are dangerous criminals — or will become so — but these are also our society's lost boys.

THE DUNKIRK MYTH NEVER TOLD OUR REAL STORY

David Aaronovitch

JULY 20 2017

BY JANUARY EVEN Britain should be Churchilled out. In June it was Brian Cox's turn to shake his wattles as the Greatest Briton in the movie *Churchill*, and in the new year Gary Oldman will discover new jowls as the lead in *Darkest Hour*. In between you can have your senses blitzed by *Dunkirk*, which opens tomorrow and which I saw in preview earlier in the week. Stranded men, gallant Spitfire pilots, small boats, wobbly (but ultimately firm) chins and some bars from Elgar. The movie ends with Churchill's "fight on the beaches" speech, and it seemed to me by the end that 1940 was not just our finest hour, it has increasingly become our only hour.

I think this matters because the overwhelming nature of this, our national myth, has an effect on the decisions we make. My evidence for this is largely impressionistic, but you can't have incontrovertible stats every week.

During and after the referendum last year I spoke to a number of voters on either side of the big question. Naturally some people talked about immigration or the economy, but more important in the conversation of many of the Leave voters was an idea of Britain as they imagined it had once been. In the past this Britain had run itself and had been in hock to no one. It hadn't depended on anyone else and no outsider had told it what to do.

It was easy for me to recognise this image. It is *Dad's Army* and *Goodnight Sweetheart*, a myth of ourselves alone, unencumbered at the last by foreign weakness, forced back on to our own reservoirs of steadfastness and discovering a capacity to innovate.

By "myth" I don't mean that all of this is untrue. The Dunkirk evacuation was something of a miracle and the fall of France left Britain existentially exposed, yet we prevailed. But what preceded Dunkirk was not just the unhappy policy of appeasement, supported in its day by a plurality of British voters, but nine months of a war conducted for the most part with stunning incompetence. In the immediate aftermath of Dunkirk, far from the "well done!" the returning soldiers get in the movie, Mass Observation reported that civilian morale in many places was at rock bottom.

There is one other aspect of the finest hour myth that is more pernicious than all the others. And it was given an odd illustration this week in the Adonis affair. If you recall, Lord Adonis gave a controversial interview to *The House* magazine. Viewed historically, he said, leaving the EU was a gigantic national strategic decision. It was right up there with "decolonisation in the 1950s and 60s and appeasement in the 1930s". Then he added: "We got it right on decolonisation; we got it wrong on appeasement".

The reaction was predictable. Iain Duncan Smith, for example, was double a'd (astonished and appalled) that Adonis "should have selected such a comparison, given all the appalling violence and death that Hitler visited on Europe and the rest of the world".

It is an irritating feature of the age that even our leaders no longer understand the difference between an analogy and a comparison, let alone an equation. But then I suppose that if everyone did, much social media and some radio programmes would collapse for lack of outrage.

But what intrigued me was the entire absence of objection to one half of the Adonis analogy: decolonisation. It was 50 per cent of his examples, and no one mentioned it. Just as, on Tuesday, we passed the 70th anniversary of royal assent being given to the Indian Independence Act, and if anyone talked about it, then I'm a Nicobar islander. That day in 1947 was the day the Queen's dad declared himself no longer to be the Emperor of India. It had been on the stamps, it had been on the coins, and then it was gone. Seventy years ago this June Lord Mountbatten had abruptly announced the date for independence and the setting up of India and Pakistan, for August 15. The maps weren't even ready, but the British authorities withdrew and tens of millions of people began migrating to either side of the new borders. Maybe a million died. No Harry Styles film.

But in the preceding eight years 190,000 Indians had died, were wounded or were captured in the service of the British Empire, from Burma to Italy and North Africa.

So we were never alone. Not even in the period between independence and our joining the EEC. From Ghana in 1957 to Brunei in 1984, and taking in places like Malta and the Maldives along the way, we divested ourselves, necessarily, of our great global obligations. For centuries in some cases we had manipulated our global reach to serve our own interests and now this was ending.

Yet, culturally, you would never guess it now. You know those odd early scenes in *The Crown* involving verandas and black people? Empire. We managed to get through six series of aristocratic doings in *Downton Abbey*, set at empire's zenith, practically without mention of it. The era of empire, when we were not a defiant, self-sufficient island (as we never were) has been whitewashed over as surely as the frescoes in a Puritan church makeover.

After seeing the film I took this to my daughters for generational comparison. And received a secondary shock. Neither of the two older ones — both graduates and both historically literate — knew what Dunkirk was. I was double a'd. Cue a Govian outburst about schools and the history curriculum?

Wait. I realised that I hadn't been taught about Dunkirk either. But I didn't have to be: my childhood and adolescence was suffused with the finest hour. My first German words I learnt half a decade before I was taught the language at school. They were Gott im Himmel, Donner und Blitzen, Achtung, Spitfeuer! And "For you, Englander, the war is over." I made Hurricanes, threw grenades into pillboxes and shot down Heinkels. When I was 16, *Battle of Britain* topped the film charts for 14 weeks. Our parents had all been there, just as no one's seemed to have been part of the empire. After all, how do you explain a small group of white people ruling over a very large number of black and brown ones?

And, despite the Winston flurry, I think Dunkirk may be passing too; the last knockings of a myth of containment that has both sustained us and held us back. What will replace it is much harder to imagine. Something possibly much more fragmented: a Scots myth, a London 2012 diversity myth or, I fear, a negative myth of inevitable national decline.

Whatever it is, it'll be something that is not susceptible to pedagogy, but will be created by popular culture itself. We will note it, but we can't easily create it.

MY CAREER'S IN REVERSE AND I COULDN'T BE HAPPIER

Emma Duncan

July 22 2017

There are many disadvantages to middle age. There are the little folds of skin that appear around your armpit and suggest, gently at first but increasingly insistently, that your sleeveless dresses' days are numbered. There is your keys' annoying habit of migrating from wherever you last put them to somewhere you're absolutely sure you didn't, or at least you would be sure if you were certain of anything at all that had happened in the past two minutes. And there is the creeping realisation that, although you can't actually face doing the sums, the time since you started at university is probably longer than the time until you're dead.

But there is a lot to be said for being aware of your own mortality. The sound of death's hooves thundering towards you focuses the mind wonderfully. You start realising that time is precious, so you should use it wisely, doing less of the stuff that you don't like doing and more of the stuff that you do. For me, that means spending less time with people I feel I ought to see and more with those whose company I genuinely enjoy during my leisure hours. And in terms of my career, it means going back to the shop floor.

I set out to be a journalist 30 years ago because I thought it would be interesting snuffling round the world finding stuff out and writing it down. I spent some years reporting in Britain and some scurrying around the world, and I enjoyed it all enormously. After a decade on the shop floor, I was offered more money to take a promotion to an editor's job. Instead of reporting and writing myself I had to get other people to do it, to improve their work if they weren't very good and hire new people if they were awful.

In time I acquired a house, two husbands and three children (not all at once), so the money came in handy. I also enjoyed some of the perks of power, like getting invited to parties by people who thought I might be useful to know, and being listened to in meetings. But I missed the snuffling round and writing stuff down.

Now I've decided to go back to where I started. At the beginning of next year I'm returning to the shop floor. I'm giving up editing *1843* magazine and I'm going to be a reporter again on *The Economist*, its sister title. I'll be taking a pay cut and there are other downsides: I'll get invited to fewer parties, people won't listen to me in meetings and I'll get told what to do by people 20 years younger than me. But I reckon it'll be fine. My life is less expensive than it used to be because the house is nearly paid for, the husbands are long gone and the children are peeling off. (One of them is even getting married, which could be pricey, except that he is male: tradition dictates that the bride's parents pay for the wedding, and when it is convenient I am a staunch traditionalist.)

I no longer want to go to networky parties, because I'm not scrabbling up the career ladder any more, and the people who actually like me will still invite me round. It doesn't much matter if people don't listen to me in meetings since I'm planning to skip lots of them, and even though whipper-snappers will be ordering me around I'll do as I'm told because I'll be having fun — doing the real stuff of journalism, the stuff that attracted me to the profession in the first place. My career will acquire the shape of a bell-curve: I am on the downward slope, sliding cheerfully towards senescence.

I don't pretend that I'm doing this for anything other than entirely selfish reasons. As it happens, though, my new trajectory is highly socially responsible.

The traditional idea of how people's careers should work is unsustainable. We can no longer expect our jobs to provide us with a long, straight, upward progression to a peak of earnings and status from which we plummet, clutching a fat pension, into a bed of dahlias that we spend the next couple of decades tending. An ageing society and lower returns to capital mean that the fat pensions are mostly gone, so we are going to have to keep working for far longer than our parents did. We can't cling on to well-paid management jobs, because there aren't enough of them, and anyway organisations need to give management jobs to younger people. So older people need to move out or down.

That's not just what the economy requires. It's good for older people too. As they get freed up from responsibility at home they can shuffle off responsibility at work, get pickier about what they do and swap money and power for freedom and job satisfaction.

Among my contemporaries I'm in the vanguard but I'm not alone. Friends are pursuing variants of the bell-curve. A couple have left big companies to set up on their own, touting their skills as freelancers. Lucy Kellaway, a columnist at the *Financial Times,* is returning to the shop floor but in a new profession: she is training to become a teacher and has started an organisation called Now Teach, which has persuaded an impressive bunch of similarly successful middle-aged professionals to do the same. They'll earn less but will get a new lease of life while doing something socially useful.

For this trend to spread, rules and expectations need to change. The bell-curve career requires workers, employers and government to be more flexible than they are now. A host of regulations get in the way, from the small — the requirement that, in order to train as a teacher, you produce exam certificates that have long been lost in the mists of time — to the large — the laws designed to protect employees. At present an employer who offers an employee a new role at lower pay, for instance, may be guilty of constructive dismissal. Such protections may sound good for workers but they're not: they make it likelier that employers will get rid of older workers altogether, instead of finding new ways to deploy them.

But the main thing that needs to change is our expectations about how our working lives will pan out. In the first stage we'll be scrambling up our careers. In the second stage we'll be on peak earnings and peak power. In the third we'll have less of both money and power and also less responsibility, more fun and more freedom. Join me on the downward slide: it's going to be fun.

PUPPY LOVE

Caitlin Moran

JULY 22 2017

"I HAVE ALWAYS been a dog person," people say. "You just are, aren't you? You're either born a dog person, or not." Sometimes, that's not true.

We were dog people, and then we were not dog people.

Our first dog was, scientifically, the best dog in the world — Christmas. "I called her Christmas, so you could have Christmas every day," Dad explained, mistily.

She was half-collie, half-spaniel — round as a barrel, silky, black with a honey and clover face and bib. She was as gentle and warm as Sunday morning. I would lie on my back, in front of the fire, reading a book, with her as a pillow under my head. When it snowed, we threw snowballs for her to catch: she would leap, catch them, then look endlessly surprised as they exploded into snowflakes in her mouth. She loved the sea, she would run into it, wriggle in the waves, drink it (gravel, tiny crabs and all) and then vomit it up as the Volkswagen headed out of Aberystwyth. She was the dog, the very dog — the best dog. She was a gentle, sure, ambient hum that made every day seem better. We were dog people, then.

When she died, aged 17 — worn out, curled up in her basket with her head on her paws; like a puppy again — my father sat on the back step with her and wept. I'd only ever seen him cry twice before: the first when his mother died, and the second, when John Lennon was shot. Those were the things you could cry about, as a man, then. Mums. Beatles. Dogs.

We buried Christmas under the apple tree, our hair full of falling blossom. We mourned for months. The house felt empty, without a dog. There was no ... pivot. My parents promised another dog. "And this one — this one will be yours," they told me.

I was 13. I was ready for my own dog. I was ready for a

personal best friend, in dog form. I wanted another spaniely dog because spaniels are the best dogs. They are gentle and merry, and their ears look like they have long, luxurious hair, and I had long luxurious hair, and I loved all other things with long, luxurious hair: mammoths, Cavaliers, the Beatles.

But, in those days, you didn't get to choose what type of dog you got. How dogs happen is that your dad goes to the pub, talks to some people and then, a week later, he comes home with whatever dog fate — the other men in the pub — hand you.

Saffron was a German shepherd. "A pure breed!" my dad said, delightedly. She'd been rejected from police-dog training for reasons my father glossed over, as he led her into the house.

A German shepherd was not the right dog for us. At least, not this one.

"She's a bit ... nervy," he said, as Saffron peed all over the hall carpet, then ran up the garden and cowered under a tree.

Her recent life history was vague, but I could tell it had involved trauma, and eating things out of a bin. When I went to retrieve her from under the tree, I could see half a butter wrapper, poking out of her bum. I fashioned tongs out of two sticks, and pulled it out. It was Country Life. I never ate Country Life butter again.

Dad decided the best way to "settle" Saffron's nerves was to get her pregnant. "Puppies will sort her," he said. As my mother had had eight children, and hadn't peed on the hall carpet recently, we couldn't argue with his logic. Next time he came back from the pub he brought Max, another German shepherd, who had also been rejected from the police training scheme, over "psychological issues". Who knows what was happening in the West Midlands police's dog training scheme at the time, but it seemed to be producing a stream of reject dogs who behaved as if they'd served a disturbing tour of duty in Vietnam.

Max was, from day one, an angry dog, a huge beast, primarily the colour of cheap, glossy pine furniture. His mouth was particularly horrible — slobbery but also crusty — and he seemed untrainable, to a family used to gentle spaniel crosses.

He got constant ear infections that made the house stink, and made him even angrier. Every evening, we would have to put drops in his ears while he tried to bite us. It was like living with an unhappy, pained bear.

You can tell much about a family by their personal lexicons: words only they use. We had the word "savving", short for "savaging".

If you took Max for a walk, he would "sav" — bark, snarl, strain endlessly at his leash until he choked. My mother was pregnant and my father disabled, so it was down to us children to walk Max — burning with shame as he "savved" at every passing person, dog, cat and car — twice a day. Everyone on the estate hated us. I totally understood why.

"Do you sometimes wish Max would die?" my sister Caz whispered one day. "Not in a bad way. But just ... fall asleep?"

"Yes," I replied. It was our biggest secret.

"They're your dogs," Dad would say. "Just give them a thump." That was how they trained dogs, when he was young. You rubbed their noses in their poo, and left their poo in the road, where it fell. There were no doggie treats or poo bags back then.

But we did not want to hit the dogs, and so we went back to our rooms, to draw pictures of spaniels, and cry.

When Max got Saffron pregnant — a distressing day: eight children watching two dogs mating, in the garden, and then becoming hysterical with fear when they couldn't separate and howled at each other for half an hour — the puppies seemed to make her even more nervy, and Max even more angry. You know, like sometimes happens with humans, when they have children.

The house was now full of dogs and puppies and parents and children, all of them making each other unhappy. When they got to eight weeks old, we sold the puppies, for £60 each. They paid for another caravan holiday, in Wales. While we were there, Max got loose in a field of pregnant sheep, and chased them for half an hour, as we screamed his name endlessly. The farmer caught him and threatened "to put an axe through his head". It was deeply traumatic. It was fair enough.

Six months after the puppies were born, Max ran to the door when my sister's friend came over and attacked her. She had 16 stitches in her hand. The "Welcome" mat was so covered in blood we had to throw it away. Max was put down. Saffron got ill and died a year later.

The day after, I sat in the garden with my siblings, on top of the grave that now had three dogs in it.

"When we grow up, we will never, ever have dogs," we vowed. "Never. Never. We will learn from our parents' mistake."

Everything about having those two dogs had been awful. Awful. They were the wrong dogs, and we were the wrong people, and we had done everything wrong, and something this bad could not happen again.

That is how we were dog people — and then not dog people.

Twenty-five years later, and my daughter wants a dog. She is a dog person. She is an "all animals" person. She has tropical fish, a cat, and two pet rats — Ringo and Bingo — that she has trained to sit in the hood of her coat, while she sits at the piano, playing them Billy Joel and the Beatles. They run up and down her arms, as she plays jazzy fifths. Sometimes, they land on a key.

"I have a band of musical rats," she says, as they arduously wade from "C" to "G". "And I love them. But I can't take them anywhere. I want to go walking. I want to go out."

For Christmas, I buy her two tiny rat harnesses, so she can take them for a walk. She spends half an hour putting them into the harnesses. The rats immediately wriggle out of the harnesses. You cannot take rats out.

"Why can't we have a dog?" she says, sadly putting the harnesses in the charity-shop bag. "Families should have a dog. That's what families do. You had a dog when you were 13. Why can't I?"

Why would we not have a dog? Because the dog might be a problem. The dog might make life worse. The dog might be unhappy. The dog might hurt her. The dog might break our hearts. The dog might be the wrong dog, and we the wrong people. We might do dogs wrong.

"We could take other people's dogs for a walk," I say, signing up to borrowmydoggy.com.

"But the point of a dog is it's yours," she says, quite correctly. "You love it, and it loves you, and it's happy when you come home, and it sleeps on your bed, and you go everywhere, on adventures. You wouldn't borrow someone else's child. A dog — a proper dog — is your dog."

Perhaps a very old dog is the answer. I don't say this to her, but maybe if we got a dog that was going to ... die soon? So however bad it got, the problem would be over in a year? We start looking on dog rescue sites, and then dog shelters, looking for something small, gentle and old. Ideally with a caption on it, reading: "Life expectancy: nine life-enhancing, yet short, months."

But all we see is boisterous Staffies and nervous greyhounds. Those are the unwanted dogs of the 21st century, in endless excess. We know people with both, who love them dearly but they are simply not the dogs for us. It would be wrong for them and us. I can't afford to make a mistake again. I am, simply, scared.

One very long day, we go all the way to Durham to see Bruno, who appears on the website to be a gentle, medium-sized hound, part-labrador, part-terrier.

When we get there, he's the size of a horse, barks incessantly and pulls so hard on his lead, he drags Nancy over.

"I'm going to teach you a word from my childhood. 'Savving.' That dog is 'savving'," I tell her.

The train journey home is four long hours. We eat crisps, and Nancy looks sad, and I think, "Oh come on, just f*** it. You know you're going to get a dog — people don't go to Durham if they're not getting a dog. So do it properly. Commit. Don't make this girl have an old, mad, unhappy dog — like you did. Don't accidentally repeat history! Give her a puppy. Start from scratch. Believe you can make a good dog. Put some effort into it."

She's called Luna. She's the size of a child's mitten and the colour of dune sand. Her eyes aren't open yet, and she sits on Nancy's hand as content as a baby bird. Luna is a week old. We're in a house in Norfolk, because Luna's mother is a silver and black spaniel with liquid eyes, who radiates such an intense aura of love that, in other countries, she would be worshipped as a dog god and garlanded with flowers.

"Always go by the mother," experts stress on their websites. "That is the greatest guarantee of your puppy's personality."

That is what I have done here. I have found the sweetest mother dog in the world — the spanielest spaniel of all time. The father, meanwhile, is a small, merry poodle.

There is a slight problem here, because this makes Luna, technically, a cockapoo, something I find difficult for two reasons.

The first is that the word "cockapoo" is simply a terrible word — it's the word "cock" and the word "poo", but for a dog. It might as well be called a "knobaplop", for all the dignity it has. When I find out that they call them "sproodles" in Australia, I decide that this is what I, stubbornly, will refer to her as. A sproodle sounds like a mad noodle, far more dignified. I will never say "cockapoo".

The second difficulty is that cockapoos are, apparently, regarded as the least cool dog you can possibly buy. They are the thunderously predictable middle-class choice of dog in the 21st century. Hypoallergenic, due to their poodle fur; small; gentle; easy to train; disinclined to bark or chase other animals. They are the Waitrose of dogs. The Boden. The Adele. Hipsters have pugs or French bulldogs; the properly posh have labradors; the dedicated dog lovers rescue Staffies and bring out their good natures. But cockapoos — they are the boring, safe, slightly smug choice of middle-class families. I rail against this for a while, before my husband points out that I have spent my entire life trying to become a boring, safe, slightly smug middle-class family, and that it's too late to suddenly fight this now.

I know cockapoos are not cool, because I know everything

about dogs now. As those with chaotic childhoods do, I've decided that total control is the answer: I have spent three months researching dogs, breeds, breeders, training methods, food, poo bags, collars v harnesses, crating and the astonishing range of snacks and chews available for the modern dog. In my day, dogs did not have "chews". They found a shoe and made do.

The modern dog, by way of contrast, appears to live in a chewtopia, with bull's pizzles, stuffed cow's hooves and sections of deer antler to gnaw on. It seems there is no animal on earth not offered up, in sections, to lucky pet dogs, by way of chewing gum. I'm surprised there is no Puppy Rhino Horn website. Perhaps there is. I would probably buy one, if there were. I've bought everything else. The house looks like a dog equipment warehouse. I am prepared.

"We're just going to look at Luna," I warned Nancy, before we left. "It's not certain we'll keep her. Maybe she's not the dog for us. We'll know when we see Our Dog. We won't just get the first cute puppy we see."

Looking at Nancy — sitting stock still, stroking the tiny golden dome of Luna's sleeping head with one finger; examining the miniature, pink, as yet unused paws and gingernut-coloured ears the size of a fingernail — there's only one thing left to happen.

"Can we keep her? Is she ours?" Nancy whispers.

"Yes."

We get the first cute puppy we see.

Seven weeks later, and we bring her home.

I'd like to pretend it's a simple, relaxed homecoming, but it's not — not really. Still fearful that I might be bringing chaos and awfulness into our lives, I've hidden every shoe in the house (because of chewing), erected training crates on every floor (to teach her separation), arduously planned the one square metre of paving in the garden the dog is allowed to toilet on (so she doesn't bugger up my beautiful lawn) and warned everyone, "This will be hard work. HARD WORK. We can't stint for a moment on training — or else she will end up a nightmare dog everyone will hate! EVERYONE MUST PILE IN!"

As a consequence of this, my elder daughter has spent the last two months warning us she will hate the dog. "I don't like dogs," she says, unhappily. "I will not have anything to do with it. I'm not going to feed it or touch it. It's your dog. I will have nothing to do with it."

When Luna arrives — exhausted after the three-hour drive from Norfolk, during which she has been sick three times on the beatifically smiling Nancy, who wipes it up with the unperturbed calm of an NHS nurse — she totters into the front room on her tiny rabbit legs and heads straight for a shoe.

"WHO LEFT A SHOE IN HERE! THE SHOE WILL BE EATEN!" I roar.

Luna simply climbs into the shoe and falls asleep looking like a tiny curl of fur, tail over her nose. She is absurdly small.

"Oh my God, I love her," Lizzie whispers. "Can she sleep on my bed tonight?"

"She's my dog, she's sleeping on my bed tonight," Nancy says, indignantly.

"She will sleep IN THE TRAINING CRATE — we will teach her INDEPENDENCE AND NON-NEEDINESS," I say. "THIS IS AN ABSOLUTELY UNBREAKABLE RULE."

The girls look at the training crate — vast and crate-y — and then at the tiny dog. I look at the tiny dog.

The tiny dog sleeps, that night, on Nancy's pillow making tiny puppy "Iff! Iff! Iff!" barks in her sleep. We all sit on Nancy's bed, staring at her, smiling, for two hours. Whispering, so we don't wake her up. "She's the most beautiful dog in the world," Lizzie says. "She is our dog. We found her."

The dog sleeps on Nancy's bed every night.

I had prepared for a psychological and practical battle: a momentous upheaval of our lives, a potential threat in our house.

Within a day, it's clear that this is not what this tiny dog is. This tiny dog is ... joy. She arrives on the first day of April, just as spring is filling the garden with a haze of tiny, unfurling, exquisite buds, and that's what she is, too: a tiny, unfurling thing. She totters around on her tiny, unused legs, looking like a miniature Falkor the Luck Dragon from *The NeverEnding Story*, and sits under the maple tree staring in wonder at her own paws.

When she does her first "Woof", it's a tiny, clockwork-mouse "Woof" that surprises her so much, she falls over backwards. We spend the rest of the day saying "Woof" to each other, in tiny voices, like Luna. All we want to do is woof now and fall over. She has replaced all our words with "woof". "Woof" means everything.

She falls into her water bowl and has to be scooped out; she falls asleep while she eats, head resting on a pillow of chopped meat. After her adventures — running away from a ball, alarmed; curiously chewing a puppy-training book — she likes to climb right up your body, while you're watching TV, and fall asleep on your shoulder. When she licks your ear with her tiny, pink tongue, you wonder why there is no such saying as, "Delightful as being licked on the ear by a puppy." There is, surely, nothing so purely happy.

She is not a tiny dog, really, but a whole new place instead: the house is utterly transformed. It's as if all the doors and windows have been opened, and blown our old, sadder, duller lives away. We have invited into it something that every ten minutes or so does something that makes everyone coo, or sigh, or laugh. We are like kings, with a new jester — an entire court in thrall to her tiny-dog life.

She shakes up our whole day, and the pieces settle in a better order. In the mornings, she is carried downstairs to do her business, and the whole family sit around, on the patio, drinking tea, bleary-eyed, and cheering, "Good girl to do wee-wee," when she does her proud, shaky squat. The lawn is absolutely buggered — she scorches all the grass with her wee — and I couldn't care less. I'm so proud of her toilet training that each straw-like circle looks like a gold star, for achievement.

In the evenings — long and golden now, as we head into May — the whole family take her for a walk, to Alexandra Palace Park. Two teenage girls! On a nightly walk! Willingly! Wandering along in the sunshine and the rain, casually chatting in a way I thought we'd left behind in their childhood. We've lived here 13 years, but it takes having a dog to finally give you all a ... reason to wander. We discover a lake we never knew. A wood. A meadow.

"God, London is beautiful," I sigh — something I should have known, but had no reason to, until a tiny dog needed to run around in it.

I thought she would make our lives smaller — bound by her schedule and needs — but, instead, she's opened us out to the world like a pop-up book. Everything that seemed like it might be a problem turns into a bonus. What happens next year, when we go to visit Pete's family in Greece? We can't fly with her.

"Let's drive there, instead — a road trip. With Luna!" Nancy says, starting to draw the route on a map on the wall. "We can show her the Alps!"

A child that previously had no interest in the Alps is now thrilled to show them to a dog. She starts learning the history of Italy, "so I can tell Luna, when we're there. I don't want her to be an ignorant dog."

What about the impact on our social lives: she can't be left alone, when she's so young? "Oh, I like taking her for walks," Nancy says, cheerfully. "Boys come up and play with her — and they're not trying to be 'street', like usual. They just squeal, 'Look at the cute dog!' — like girls — and then talk about their dogs. I like it. It's like joining a new club. Dog Club."

Of course, she's only five months old, and still learning, so there are still occasional puddles of wee on the landing, and walks where she sees another cockapoo — cockapoos love other cockapoos — and won't come back: running around like a lunatic as we call her name, before finally slinking over with a "Sorry guys, just had to sort out a bit of business" look on her face. But she's such an amiable, soppy, friendly thing that the idea of those uncontrollable, unhappy German shepherds seems like a bad, mad dream.

My siblings recently came over, to meet her for the first time. "Don't get a dog," they had warned, in advance. "You know what happens with dogs."

Ten minutes later, they were rolling around on the lawn with her.

"This dog ... This dog is nice," they marvelled.

After three months, I'm at Nancy's school concert, with the dog asleep in a bag at my feet — not stirring, even for the timpani — and I whisper to my husband, "There isn't going to be a hard bit, is there? This isn't traumatic at all! Having a dog can be ... easy."

"If it's the right dog," he says, kissing my head. "If it's the right dog, for you."

THE CONSERVATIVES ARE CRIMINALLY INCOMPETENT

Matthew Parris

July 29 2017

If you've a moment, research "Mike the headless chicken" (April 20, 1945 to March 17, 1947). Mike passed away 70 years ago but had managed to live headless (sort of) for 18 months, staggering pointlessly around to the amazement and horror of spectators in many fairgrounds, before finally choking.

Returning to Britain on Thursday I had been wondering what our Conservative government now reminds me of, when a friend told me of Mike's sad story. Can this really be Britain? Or has my homecoming ferry re-routed itself to a Central American banana republic where the *congreso nacional* has packed up for the summer holidays, the foreign minister has gone cavorting in Australia, the stop-gap president has departed to walk in Switzerland, the hairy Marxist resistance leader has started wrestling his own comandantes and the lugubrious Don Felipe, minister of finance, is staging a slow-motion coup?

Humour, though, is no longer a refuge from the disgrace. What have we come to? Like some dark moon below the horizon, a rogue force is wrenching us from our orbit, and nobody knows what to do.

But if you think the purpose of this column is to lament that crazy Brexit decision, you are wrong. Brexit or no Brexit, I have a different focus. A more precise focus than the scattergun commentary that has interested itself in "Britain's" embarrassment, "the government's" incompetence, "Whitehall's" ill-preparedness, "the prime minister's" inadequacy, "Labour's" disunity or even "Europe's" aggressiveness.

There is a main culprit here, and it isn't any of these candidates. Labour didn't cause this mess. Whitehall didn't frame the task, even if it is ill-equipped for its execution. Theresa May may not be up to the job but it's a job into which she has been forced. And "the government"? The government is a collection of individuals. Where do these individuals come from? Who nominated them? Who keeps them in their jobs? Search for the key word in the following text.

We live in a parliamentary democracy in which voters elect representatives attached to parties. The party as an institution has form, and voice, and policies. The party chooses a leader. The winning party's leader asks the monarch for authority to govern and if she is satisfied that the party can support its leader in commanding the Commons, she gives it. The leader then chooses every minister from the party's ranks, and leads a cabinet drawn, too, from the party. And if the party loses confidence in its leader or government, it can, by withdrawing support, dismiss both.

The word that keeps appearing in this passage is hard to miss: an entity, a real thing, the thing that's now in charge of Britain's direction. It's called a party. It's the Conservative Party. Do the voters even begin to understand how this mess is entirely of the Conservative Party's creation?

The Tories are turning Brexit into a humiliating shambles. They called a referendum when they didn't have to, they accepted the result, they willed Brexit, they promised Brexit, and now they're comprehensively failing to organise it. You can't blame the voters, who quite reasonably assumed that the Tories would never have offered a referendum if they hadn't thought leaving Europe could be arranged. The fingerprints for this crime of mismanagement are Tory fingerprints.

Thirteen months since the referendum and the Conservatives still can't decide even the broadest outline of the terms on which we hope to leave. The difference between a soft and a hard exit is greater than the difference between staying in and a soft exit, yet the prime minister is still insisting that government policy is for a hard exit, while the chancellor (in her absence) says the opposite.

Nobody really knows what the foreign secretary thinks and I doubt he knows himself. The Brexit secretary, meanwhile, seems to be trying to play it by ear, but with no guidance as to the melody at all. And the trade secretary seems recently to have reconciled himself to three (or, if the chancellor is to be believed, as many as four) further years without any job at all. Some ministers say we'll be taking back control of immigration when we leave in 2019, others that we will not.

And almost everybody has started to talk of a "transitional" period after leaving, without any hint of a consensus on what we would be transitioning to.

Every Conservative MP bar Kenneth Clarke voted in February for the triggering of Article 50. It now appears they and their leader started the countdown to Britain's expulsion without even the vaguest plan for what we'd be aiming to achieve, let alone realistically likely to achieve. Worse, they pulled the trigger knowing very well that "Brexit" still meant different things to different members of the party and its government, and there was no reason to hope that divergent aims were ever likely to converge.

I call this criminal: irresponsible to the point of culpable recklessness towards their country's future. The Conservative Party just thought they'd give it a whirl and all but one of them voted for the adventure.

Even in bad times, even when we Tories messed up, I used to feel a pride in the party to which I owe so much. Often too slow, sometimes too rash, sometimes wrong, sometimes mildly corrupt, often missing the public mood, occasionally cowardly, it was still possible to trace through the party's long history a line of worldly common sense, a distrust of extremism, and a deep sense of duty to the nation. There was a certain steadiness there. Has this deserted us? Do we yet understand, has it yet been born in on us, that it is we and we alone who have led the whole country into the predicament it now finds itself in?

How shall I look in the eye those householders through whose doors I've been dropping Tory leaflets all these years: years that will be seen as a permanent stain on the Conservative Party's reputation?

The prime minister has gone away. "Ladybird, ladybird," we might cry, "fly away home! Your house is on fire, your children are gone!" Except that we're better off without her flapping around, spouting implausibilities. Perhaps reality in the shape of Philip Hammond may gradually bear down upon fantasy; perhaps forlorn hopes may steal silently away and various fools, while not repenting of their folly, allow it to slip their recollection.

I hope so. I left Spain feeling ashamed to be British. I return to England ashamed to be a Conservative.

JUSTIN GATLIN REMINDS US THAT SPORT IS NOT A FAIRYTALE

Matt Dickinson

AUGUST 7 2017

FIRST CAME THE gun and what, by any measure, was mesmerising sporting drama. Then a confused, pin-drop silence. Next the boos cascading around the London Stadium as nasty reality bit that the blue riband event of global athletics, the 100m sprint, had been won by Voldemort in spikes.

And now? For weeks, months and for the rest of eternity, the confounding headache of how we deal with sport's cheats. That will take infinitely longer than the 9.92sec that it took for Justin Gatlin to give track and field its most unwelcome result since Ben Johnson ran juiced into infamy.

So, how to tackle it? By booing if you must. Boo if it makes you feel better. Boo if you think it increases the deterrence to drug-taking. Boo if you think anyone who dopes should be a pariah, banished from their sport for life (though try to be consistent).

Booing was certainly a loud message to Lord Coe that Gatlin's presence should not have been tolerated. He agrees, but while the president of the IAAF has a record of supporting life bans — unlike his predecessor, Lamine Diack, who is being investigated for taking bribes in one of sport's worst scandals — Coe's remarks on BBC radio yesterday were notable for an admission of impotence.

Life bans exist for the worst repeat offenders but very rarely stick because, as Coe said with words to kill the sporting soul: "These things are suffused in legality." And this was the real horror of Gatlin's triumph beyond the shock of those who could not believe that Usain Bolt had lost his farewell race, Harry Potter slain in the final scene.

Coe did not want Gatlin on the start line, the crowd did not want Gatlin (except to jeer him), the sport can do without him but throwing him out is "suffused in legality", so he can run away with the glittering prize.

For a first offence, even the most brazen case of cheating, few in anti-doping think that life bans are enforceable. Many question whether they are even fair when, say, a truly repentant young athlete bullied by a coach could be banished. Testing is rarely a world of black and white, especially once the lawyers get to work.

Gatlin reminded us of all this at the worst possible moment, when the world's eyes were meant to be transfixed by Bolt strutting his way into posterity. But then so much of the Gatlin story is horribly inconvenient, like the usual damning description of him as a "two-time doper". Not so fast.

A double-cheat? For his first ban in 2001, he was a 19-year-old student coming off exams when he tested positive for medication that had long been prescribed him for attention deficit disorder. The original panel called the failed test "inadvertent" and said it was "very concerned that Mr Gatlin's reputation not be unnecessarily tarnished as a result of this decision". But then, shamelessly, he surrendered any benefit of the doubt. Gatlin does still have the horrible stain of a 2006 positive for testosterone (complete with dubious claims that he was fitted up) but that case is also awkward and does little to foster public confidence.

His ban was reduced from eight years to four, partly because he helped the United States Anti-Doping Agency to wire-tap his notorious coach, Trevor Graham. This is the type of bartering that is necessary when anti-doping agencies are so compromised, allowing Gatlin to win another world title 12 years after his first.

It left us with a media conference late on Saturday that was about as much fun as being woken by a starting pistol. Gatlin, whose shows of contrition have been so poorly signposted that he was almost starting from scratch, sought to be humble. He expressed bemusement at how he had not been booed before — "not here in 2012 but now?" — and a sliver of contrition.

"I have done my time," he said. "I did community service. I have talked to kids. I have actually inspired kids to walk the right path. That's all I can do. Society does that with people who have made mistakes. I hope track and field can understand that too."

He had bowed at Bolt's feet and added: "It's still Usain's night." But of course it was not, with Bolt's usual playfulness having no place in this room as he was required to explain how he finished behind Gatlin and Christian Coleman, the young American, and his feelings towards the tainted winner.

Bolt has called for life bans for cheats yet said of Gatlin: "He has done his time. If he's here, it means it's OK. For me he deserves to be here." It was an inconsistency that pretty much summed up the whole horrible mess. But then how indignant is Bolt going to be on doping when his Jamaican team-mates Yohan Blake and Asafa Powell have served bans?

There are plenty of convicted dopers competing in London who do so without jeers, and plenty of performances that should leave us conflicted. Almaz Ayana smashing the field in the women's 10,000m came against a backdrop of scandalously poor anti-doping in Ethiopia. Mo Farah's association with Alberto Salazar means that even Team GB's star cannot duck tough questions.

But Gatlin, a convicted cheat and Bolt's rival, makes the convenient villain and, while he can run through the jeers, he is not immune to them. "It just seems like the media want to sensationalise and make me the bad boy because Usain is a hero and that's fine," he said.

"I know you have got to have a black hat and a white hat but come on, man. I keep it classy. I never talk bad. What do I do that makes me the bad boy? I just try to stay in my lane, literally."

It was a self-serving defence but he is right to remind us that sport is not a Manichean battle of good versus evil, that over-simplistic narrative famously peddled by Steve Cram at the 2015 world championships when he screamed that, in beating Gatlin, Bolt "may have even saved his sport". Because Gatlin won, track and field is not now dead, or even dying.

This was certainly not the result anyone wanted, and Bolt's third place made this the most anticlimactic sporting farewell since Sir Donald Bradman was out for a duck in his final innings.

But this is sport, not fairytales, and while magic is often part of it — Bolt has provided some of the most electrifying moments ever witnessed — conflict and cheating will always be part of the package. Stronger deterrents can help but Gatlin has reminded us what a wretchedly fraught process that is when he could be here, triumphant.

Coe said only days ago that doping was not his sport's biggest problem. It cannot possibly have felt that way as he heard that cacophony of boos on Saturday or, with a heavy heart, hung a gold medal around Gatlin's neck last night.

STARTING NUCLEAR WAR IS PRESIDENT'S DECISION ALONE

Rhys Blakely

August 12 2017

Many of the details are secret but if a US president were ever to order a nuclear strike, we know this: the order would be transmitted to the crew who would fire the missiles in a message 150 characters long, about the same as a tweet.

After this week's sabre-rattling over North Korea the launch procedures are the object of fresh scrutiny. A new generation is learning that America's nuclear arsenal is on a hairtrigger.

The decision to launch is the president's alone and there is no failsafe against an unstable commander-in-chief. This was what made Richard Nixon's "madman theory" — he pushed the idea that he might just destroy Moscow — credible.

In the early years the fear was of gung-ho generals; the system regards them as a far greater threat than an irrational president. This point was made by Alex Wellerstein, a historian of nuclear weapons at the Stevens Institute of Technology.

In 1946 the Atomic Energy Act put the power in the hands of the president. The law was thrashed out in the months after the Hiroshima and Nagasaki bombs. The Manhattan Project scientists who developed those weapons regarded the military officials they worked under as warmongers.

President Eisenhower later gave the military standing permission to use tactical nuclear weapons in certain circumstances: if, say, Russian tanks rolled west over the Rhine. Under President Kennedy, miscommunication almost led both the Soviet Union and the US to launch. It was time for more safeguards.

Before his inauguration President Trump would have been told how to launch a nuclear strike. Accounts of what would happen vary. This one is based on work by Bruce Blair, a former Minuteman missile-launch officer and research scholar at Princeton University.

A call is placed to the Pentagon war room, which must authenticate that the person giving the order is the president. Either Mr Trump or a military aide will be carrying a laminated card known as the biscuit. An aide will also be carrying the "nuclear football", a briefcase of strike options.

The war room will offer a challenge code: two letters, spelt out in the military's phonetic alphabet. Mr Trump will read the correct response from the biscuit — maybe "echo, Charlie".

The war room will then send a launch order to the submarine, air and ground crews chosen to carry out the mission; 150 characters including a war plan number denoting the targets.

Codes contained in the launch order must match codes locked in safes. On a submarine the launch order also contains the combination for another safe containing the keys needed to fire the missile.

For ground-based missiles the order goes to five crews, each with two officers. The crews are miles apart. Two crews have to turn their keys to launch the missiles. Even if three refuse, the missiles go. After the order is given land-based missiles can be on their way within five minutes; for submarines it is about 15 minutes. They cannot be called back.

The US has resisted automating the system. Indeed, after the decision is made by the president, each stage requires two people to act: on a submarine both the captain and executive officer must agree to launch. At the same time, however, the system is designed to neutralise mutiny. In the 1970s a Vietnam War air force veteran, Harold Hering, was in line to become a nuclear missile squadron commander. He asked how he could be sure that a launch order was lawful. He had been taught that it was his duty to resist unlawful orders. He was discharged for "a defective mental attitude towards his duties".

Members of Mr Nixon's cabinet were deeply uneasy with the system. James Schlesinger, the defence secretary, said years later that he had ordered military commanders to double-check with him before launching. Schlesinger was concerned that the president was unstable. His order had no standing in law, however. There is no saying what would have happened if Mr Nixon had ordered to launch.

In the 1980s the idea took root that there was a taboo against using nuclear missiles, and that this was a control on presidents. Don't be too sure: a Stanford University study published this week showed that a majority of Americans would back killing two million Iranian civilians to prevent an invasion of Iran that might kill 20,000 American troops.

There are no checks, no balances. As Mr Wellerstein puts it: the only way to keep any president from launching a nuclear attack would have been to elect someone else.

'WE'LL NEVER BE ABLE TO STOP THE HUNGER FOR REVENGE HERE'

Anthony Loyd

AUGUST 12 2017

THE SOLDIER SHOWS me two photographs on his mobile phone. In the first an old man, heavily bearded, stares back at me from beneath a set of thick black eyebrows, his head held upright by the hand of an unseen captor who clutches a fistful of his grey hair. The old man's eyes are in shadow but discernible. They look straight into the lens because that is what it appears he has been instructed to do. His captors want to show the old man's face to the others, to whom they send this photo. They want the others to check that they have got the right person; they want them to see the old man subjugated and captive; and they want to give him a sense of what is coming his way once he has been examined.

These are the courses in vengeance's feast, the stepped timeline by which a hunted man learns that he is about to become a victim. Killing is the final and least satisfying part of the process. There is only emptiness after that.

There are a few other details worth noting. In that first photograph the old man's hands are tied behind his back. He is sitting cross-legged beside the insignia of a military unit painted on a vehicle door. The skin on his captor's arm is that of a young man who is wearing Merrell trainers and black combat trousers, the favoured dress of Iraqi special forces units.

A short amount of time has passed between the first and second photographs being taken: maybe minutes, probably hours, but more time than merely the second needed to bang a bullet into the old man's head and send him backwards into the grit and dust of a concrete floor where he lies centre frame, his brains rolling out of his left temple.

The dead man's name is Abdullah Aboud, the soldier tells

me, and he was 60 years old, a Sunni from the Jubour tribe. Aboud was, so I am told, a prime architect in the slaughter of the soldier's own family; a killing recorded in one of the most atrocious Islamic State videos ever released. "I was owed my revenge," the soldier says. His expression is as washed and featureless as slate when he says all of this.

We stop talking for a while and break for lunch, sitting down on the cool stone of the floor to eat chicken and rice while the summer heat burns the midday sky white outside. Three other men come to join us. Cousins of the soldier, they are gracious and scrupulously polite in the way of tribal custom.

The atmosphere in the room is calm and codified, and when we stop eating and continue our conversation the soldier neither crows in the telling of his story, nor shies from it. His name is Saif and he is 27 years old. There is little emotion in his voice as he describes what happened, charting the links of cause and effect, the killing and counter-killing, so that he could be describing the stages of a regulated transaction rather than the circling steps of vengeance's waltz in the roil, the heat and hate of Iraq's war.

Saif is self-possessed but there is a tautness behind his eyes and around his mouth, suggesting restrained rage. His cousins' faces carry the same expression.

Perhaps I should be revolted by the violent killing of this bound and elderly captive in the pictures. Yet it is difficult to feel sympathy for this man. I have been told about Abdullah Aboud by Saif before being shown either of the two photographs. So, rather than see age and vulnerability in the captive, I suspect wickedness in his face. He looks like a bad guy, a cruel man, in that first picture, I think. And when I see the second photo, I think how quick Abdullah Aboud's death was compared with that of those I am told he has had killed.

Much later, I see the photographs of Aboud again, this time on Iraqi soldiers' Facebook pages. "Go to hell, you dirty dog," someone has commented beside a photo of his body. "Good job, heroes," a soldier has written. These bitter, angry words carry resonance and a sense of completion. Maybe I feel slightly satisfied with their conclusion too, though I never knew Aboud, and can judge him only according to what I have been told. Maybe I am wrong. But the hunger for vengeance is catching; and in Iraq mercy sometimes seems like an option available only for the privileged innocent.

I can't make any claim that this story is about justice. I didn't see much justice to write about. It is about intimacy and passion instead: the intimacy and passion of killing and revenge.

Saif's story epitomises the events and sentiments in the cataclysmic battle for Mosul, the apocalyptic struggle that went on for longer than Stalingrad and struck the death blow upon Islamic State's caliphate.

Touching all who were there, the spirit of revenge subsumed the fight's conclusion, so that there was barely time to set the laurels straight on the Iraqi army's mighty and righteous victory over Islamic State before "goodness" became the biggest loser of the struggle, slain at the hand of a vengeful spirit that was in turn born from the rage caused by Islamic State's own predilection for cruelty and murder.

There was no moral equivalence in the scale, intent or orchestration of what happened in the city's tale of crime and vengeance. Islamic State was an organisation soused in the ideology of atrocity and savagery, from the self-styled caliph, Abu Bakr al-Baghdadi, right down to the lowliest fighter. They acknowledged their behaviour and they advertised it, reasoning it as a necessary stage in political evolution. Their doctrine was enshrined in an infamous publication adopted by Isis as part of its ideological core: *The Management of Savagery: the Most Critical Stage Through Which the Umma Will Pass.*

First published online in 2004 under the alias Abu Bakr Naji, this work — promoting the necessity of absolute mercilessness and savagery in the creation of a pure Islamic State — was quickly adopted by al-Qaeda in Iraq, before later being incorporated into the belief system of its descendant organisation, Isis.

The Management of Savagery not only advocated pure terror and ultraviolence, but sanctified it. "Despite the blood, corpses and limbs which encompass it and the killing and fighting which its practice entails," the author wrote, jihad is God's "greatest mercy to man" and "slaughter is mercy".

This core ideological tract did not merely dictate Islamic State's behaviour but, by being central to its creed, it also made every Isis fighter culpable as a terrorist the moment they took their *bay'ah*, their oath of allegiance to Islamic State.

So there was a degree of inevitability to the vengeance that followed after Iraqi troops overwhelmed the final Isis positions. Even before the last of the shooting ended in Mosul's Old City on July 17, a week after Iraqi prime minister Haider al-Abadi had declared the battle for the city ended, the bodies of Isis suspects were floating down the Tigris, twirling slowly in the green currents, face down, their hands tied.

Other corpses appeared overnight, dumped on the desert tracks outside Mosul, shot in the head and sometimes burnt. One innovative death squad working the west bank of the river along the valley south of Mosul even took to using ambulances to move between hits, driving unhalted through checkpoints to the homes of their targets, men listed as Isis collaborators by local vigilante groups eager for retribution.

"We'll never be able to stop the hunger of tribes for revenge here," an Iraqi police captain told me one afternoon as we spoke about the deathly ambulances. "It's deeper and more powerful than government or law."

But with tribal leaders estimating that between 10 and 15 per cent of Sunni tribes had an Isis affiliation, in the absence of reconciliation this cycle of vengeance only seemed set to condemn a sizeable tranche of Iraq's Sunni population to further isolation and embitterment: the very dynamic that allowed Isis to flourish in the first case. Its victims also included those who were guilty of nothing more than being a Sunni male, or else were just the innocent relatives of Isis members.

Elsewhere around Mosul the widows and children of

Islamic State fighters were already being driven from their homes by mobs, and their land appropriated. "The seeds of Islamic State must go from our land" read the graffiti on burnt-out Isis houses. One woman I met told me her brother and four nephews had been abducted and murdered by a vigilante squad as payback for her two teenage sons having served in Isis. Both had been killed by an airstrike south of Mosul months earlier, but this did not prevent the vigilantes shooting the remaining men in her family, apart from one of her nephews, who had his eyes cut out.

The torture and abuse of Isis prisoners, already a firmly entrenched behavioural norm among Iraqi security forces, grew rampant, and in the final days of fighting and its aftermath pictures of suspected Isis members being murdered in Mosul filled social media sites. Facebook postings showed clips of men being thrown off a high rampart by the Tigris, before being shot as they lay crippled below. One clip depicted a man, his hands tied, who was filmed being stabbed repeatedly in the neck. The more moderate revenge postings showed badly beaten Isis prisoners with shoes in their mouths.

Vengeance percolated into the battlefield tactics, too. Losing patience with the many hundreds of civilians — most of them believed to be Isis families — still trapped in the final slivers of ruination held by Islamic State in the Old City, and urged on by impatient orders from Baghdad, Iraqi commanders in Mosul opted to obliterate these last streets with airstrikes and artillery, condemning fighters and civilians alike to be blasted to pieces, crushed by rubble, or entombed and suffocated in their basement shelters.

It was as well that the enemy was so hated, or else such methods of war would have been deemed unacceptable. In the meantime, Isis shot or mortared any civilians they saw trying to escape, while for their part throughout the final stage of the battle the coalition kept asserting that its own airstrike protocols were scrupulously designed to preserve civilian life. This may have been true on paper, but on the ground it looked as though Godzilla had been at work, and Iraqi heavy artillery blitzed whatever coalition airstrikes did not.

In this struggle over the battle's narrative — which essentially tried to reconcile the facts that a mighty battle was being successfully concluded but at a frightful cost — Britain's own Ministry of Defence decided to opt out of contextual realism altogether, asserting that during the hundreds of precision airstrikes RAF jets had conducted over Mosul there was no evidence of civilian casualties at all. The clipped banality of these ministry denials seemed incredible among the ruins, Whitehall words from suited pukes detailing the benefits of low-yield munitions while laden with the stench of megadeath.

Meantime the final victory came at a crawl. Scrambling over the banks of rubble in the Old City with troops from the Iraqi Special Operations Forces (ISOF) in those last days of fighting, as the concussion from exploding hellfire missiles bounced down the ruined alleys and over us, I saw the bodies of numerous Islamic State fighters scattered among the lunar landscape, still wearing their chest webbing, stiff in their firing positions, who had died fighting to the last. Some were Iraqi. Many were foreign, and included black Africans and white Caucasians. One dead fighter was Asiatic — "Chinese! Chinese!" the soldiers yelled as machinegun fire lanced overhead — and photographs of an infant child had been taken from his webbing and laid on his blood-crusted chest.

Although the Iraqi authorities refused to disclose official casualty figures among Iraqi units fighting at this point of the Mosul battle, they were extreme. For some ISOF units, the casualty rate already stood at 50 per cent just on the east bank of the city, way before they even crossed into the heavier fighting on the west. During one large Isis ambush in the Old City in June, which involved two waves of female suicide attackers hidden among escaping civilians and went on to include Isis assault teams, snipers and mortar fire, military doctors described to me how 140 Iraqi troops were killed or wounded in the space of a few hours.

The level of physical destruction in the Old City was so all-encompassing that even some of the Iraqi generals looked embarrassed by the time it was over. They became terser as victory neared, and Haider Abadi appeared outright miserable when he visited the city in the run-up to announcing the battle complete.

"Shit — did we really do that to Mosul?" their expressions suggested as they surveyed the vista of waste.

That final day of the battle, some soldiers asked me if I wanted to see the head of a woman suicide bomber who had detonated near by. "Not really," I replied, but they took me to see it anyway.

Her head was upright, blackened but intact; her long locks tangled and filthy. It was nothing I had not seen before. The heads of suicide bombers usually pop off like champagne corks while the torso shreds. (Once a friend found a penis wrapped in an improvised tinfoil codpiece as one of the few remnants left of a suicide bomber, a young man who, lost in the deep seas of devotion, had hoped to keep it intact for the celestial virgins in jannah, or paradise.) Someone had placed a hairbrush and can of hairspray beside the woman's head. It was the funniest thing I saw in the whole battle: the horror of it all transmogrified into just a bad hair day. I couldn't stop smirking whenever I thought about the joke. Maybe you had to be there to get it.

Amid this background of loathing, ultraviolence and ruination, just two days before Abadi announced battle's end, Abdullah Aboud was captured alive in the rubble.

The story really begins in June 2014, when Islamic State first rolled into Mosul, scattering two divisions of regular Iraqi forces before them in a victory that catapulted Isis into world attention and delivered the apparatus of a quasi-state — including hundreds of tanks, armoured vehicles and artillery, as well as banks, hospitals, oil refineries and two million civilians — into the terrorist group's hands.

Saif was already a decorated member of an Iraqi Swat team at the time, a ministry of interior unit, and was a veteran of various raids and firefights across Iraq against Isis and its al-Qaeda forefathers. (One thing I always notice in conversation with Isis-killers is that while many westerners tend to bracket the Islamic State story in Iraq between their capture of Mosul and eventual defeat there, Iraqi soldiers see the fight as part of a war against the same radical group, just with different names and guises, that has been going on since 2004.)

Saif was born in the village of Juruf, a Sunni farming community on the alluvial plane on the east bank of the River Tigris, 20 miles south of Mosul. Most of those living in the area were from the Jubour tribe, the largest Arab tribe in central and northern Iraq.

In the era before Islamic State, numerous men from Saif's family had joined the Iraqi army and police, and his father, Ahmed Khader Abdullah, was a first cousin of Major-General Najim al-Jubouri, an Iraqi commander who was to play a key role in the battle for Mosul.

The extended Jubour tribe also included Abdullah Aboud, a contemporary of Saif's father, who lived in a village on the other side of the river. "We knew Abdullah Aboud before it all began," Saif explains. "Relations were normal between our families. Aboud was himself a retired member of the security forces."

Yet the decade after the US invasion of 2003 had torn at tribal allegiances across Nineveh, opening deep divisions between the communities living in the governorate, home to Iraq's most complex weave of sectarian groups. Angered by the sectarianism of the Shia-led government in Baghdad, many men joined the growing Sunni insurgency, a disparate array of groups including al-Qaeda in Iraq. In the year before Isis swept into Mosul, Nineveh's provincial capital, the mood around the city became brooding and intense as the Sunni-dominated insurgency worsened and sectarian violence flared up across the whole of Iraq.

In Mosul itself, the Shia-led security forces were accused of numerous extrajudicial killings, while rampant government corruption and intimidation by militias extorted huge sums of money from businesses belonging to the city's Sunni majority.

Abdullah Aboud had joined Sunni protesters demonstrating against the government in 2013, Saif tells me, and he was sent to jail on several occasions under Article 4 of Iraq's anti-terrorism legislation, which at the time was widely abused by the Baghdad government to silence Sunni dissent. Aboud was near to completing a short sentence in Najaf's Tasfirat prison when the first Islamic State units arrived in Mosul on June 6, 2014, linking up with sleeper cells and attacking army checkpoints across the city.

Saif's own experience of those few days typified the confusion suffered by Iraqi units in which a mere 1,500 Isis fighters — outnumbered 15 to 1 by Iraqi troops — took just four days to capture the whole of Mosul. His Swat unit was based in an abandoned hotel in the city. Three days after gunfire began rippling across different city districts while the voices of panic-stricken officers jabbered with increasing urgency over military radios, an Isis suicide vehicle rammed into Saif's position, killing three of his comrades and wounding 25 others. In the coming hours many regular Iraqi army units disappeared altogether, the soldiers abandoning their uniforms and fleeing the city, leaving their vehicles and weapons behind them.

Taking their wounded with them, the Swat unit was withdrawn from the hotel to secure 250 Isis prisoners from a jail that was about to be overrun elsewhere in the city. The unit then moved on briefly to Mosul airport, before pulling back across the Tigris to the city's eastern side on the night of June 9. The army units they expected to link up with there were nowhere in sight, and so the Swat troops handed the prisoners to a police unit in a station that was overrun by Isis hours later.

"The east side was like a ghost town," Saif recalls. "The streets were empty. The army were gone. There were just loads of burnt-out military vehicles, which had been attacked."

In daylight on June 10, as Islamic State announced its complete capture of Mosul, Saif's unit completed its own retreat, crossing into the relative safety of the zone held by Kurdish peshmerga fighters east of Mosul.

As a final indignity, the Swat troops were only allowed to pass though peshmerga positions after first handing over their weapons to the Kurds. But it was not the shame of relinquishing his assault rifle that bothered Saif most.

"Many thoughts swirled through my mind that day," he tells me, "most concerning my family. They had remained in their village. I called them but they said nothing was happening where they were. The Daesh were not yet near. I told my brother, a policeman, to get out, but he said everything was OK."

It was a fatal mistake. Three days later, Isis arrived in Juruf.

It was a year later before Saif next saw his elder brother, his two uncles and cousins. He was in Baghdad at the time, newly appointed as one of General Jubouri's bodyguards, who in turn had just been named as the commander of Nineveh Operations Command, the Iraqi task force being formed to recapture Mosul.

Saif received a phone call one evening in June 2015. A family source still inside Isis territory had called. The man told Saif that most of his family, who had been arrested in their village a month earlier, had been killed. Isis had filmed their deaths in a three-part video, the man said. He sent Saif the link. The soldier opened it and watched what unfolded. Then he downloaded it to watch again, "to keep me strong, to keep me focused, to keep me vengeful", he tells me.

Nevertheless, Saif looks suddenly exhausted at the recollection of it all. "It was a night that cannot be imagined," he says. He takes out his phone and replays the video once more, explaining to me the identities of the orange-suited men dying before us.

The video is revolting, even by the standards of Islamic State's gallery of horrors. It opens with scenes of dead civilians being pulled from rubble by Isis fighters while a narrator condemns the US-led coalition and the local Iraqis spying on the coalition's behalf.

Various captives in orange jumpsuits, among them Saif's relatives, then confess to being recruited by an Iraqi officer, Lieutenant Mohammed Bassem, Saif's cousin and a fellow Swat member, to spy on Isis and set up resistance cells in Mosul. The confessions are intercut with killing scenes.

In the first of these, three male captives are escorted to a car by Islamic State. They are put inside and an Isis fighter with a rocket-propelled grenade stands to a flank while the camera lingers on the faces on the men inside. Saif explains a missing detail as we watch.

"Three prisoners are filmed being marched to the car," he tells me. "But four captives are filmed inside the vehicle. That is because the fourth man, my uncle, who had already lost a leg to an IED, could not walk. So they had to carry him and put him in the vehicle after the first part of the filming had been done."

The RPG is fired into the vehicle, which explodes and all the men die in a fireball. The cameras replay the explosion and fire several times from different angles. Next up, five men are marched into a cage, which is then lowered slowly into a swimming pool.

"That's my brother," says Saif, tapping the smartphone screen over the face of a bearded young man in the corner of the cage, Rabia Ahmed Khader, 34 years old, who is already chest-deep in water. So as to capture every last thrashing moment of their deaths, Isis installed two GoPro cameras in waterproof cases on the bars. In this way these men die.

For the finale, seven other captives, including Lieutenant Bassem's father, are marched in line along a sandy ridge. They kneel in a row and an Isis executioner links them together with loops of detonation cord around their necks. They have their heads blown off in unison. By the time the video ends, Saif's brother, two uncles and five cousins are all dead, killed in one or other manner. His father, terribly tortured and aware of the others' fate, died broken in an Isis jail.

Islamic State had seized them all from Juruf in the first week in May, just days after General Jubouri's appointment to head Nineveh Operations Command. Survivors among Saif's family allege that Abdullah Aboud played a central role in the men's fate. Aboud had apparently appeared back in Mosul in 2014 after his jail sentence in Najaf had ended, and quickly assumed a position of power within the caliphate, heading a local council of tribes in support of Isis and leading a recruitment drive, inciting local youth to join the terrorist group.

Shortly before their arrest, Abdullah Aboud had personally orchestrated a moment of acute shame for Saif's male relatives, in which he had forced them to renounce their kinship with General Jubouri.

"But that wasn't enough to save them," Saif says. "Four days later they were arrested. Abdullah Aboud is the main one who was responsible for what happened to them after that. Many others were involved, and there were locals who gave their support to the Daesh for whatever reason. But Abdullah Aboud was the main actor."

Seated in the room with us as we talk is another of Saif's cousins, 25-year-old Omer Abdulhadi Khader. This gaunt-faced young man is a key witness and a rare survivor of Isis jails, having been imprisoned and tortured on several different occasions during the caliphate's three-year era.

Omer's father and brother had been captives murdered by Isis, and he gives a chilling description of his own time in jail with Saif's family shortly before their execution. He found the men covered in blood, their fingernails torn out, and so badly tortured that guards dragged them around the floor on blankets because they could not walk.

No one could escape from the villages in the area, Omer tells me, because Isis were quick to seal off the zone with huge, improvised minefields that effectively kept much of the caliphate's population hostage. Among the trapped populace inside Juruf and the surrounding villages were numerous former soldiers and police officers, who had been forced to repent at local mosques in return for amnesty. Yet that repentance was never enough to guarantee survival.

"After the first few months, if Daesh wanted to make an example of someone, or needed some prisoners to execute somewhere, they would just raid a few houses of former policemen, take them away and kill them," Omer says. "It didn't matter whether or not you had repented. We lived our lives in permanent fear of death."

Yet the most penetrating detail Omer describes of Isis rule relates not to a well-known video atrocity, but to the banality of systematic execution. Omer's own father, a local council member in the pre-Isis era, was taken away from the village and executed in an Isis prison on May 5, 2015, four days before Saif's family were arrested. Two days later, Omer was told to collect his father's body from a Mosul hospital. Yet when Omer arrived at the mortuary he found the refrigerators were so full of execution victims that the administration office had stopped keeping records.

"So I had to wade through 200 bodies in a single refrigeration unit before I recognised the corpse of my own father," Omer says. "And they were just the most recent executions. Not people killed on video; we never got those bodies back. Just normal people the Daesh chose to execute in the daily routine, shot in the head and heart like my dad. There were two huge refrigeration blocks in that hospital, and they were both stacked full of bodies."

The fortunes of war ebbed and flowed after Mosul's fall to Islamic State. Word of their victory there caused the complete collapse of Iraqi units in the north of the country, who were pursued in headlong retreat towards Baghdad, thousands of soldiers dying or falling into Islamic State hands in a matter of days.

These battlefield gains were slowly reversed over the next two years with intense coalition airstrikes in support of Iraqi units defeating Isis in the cities of Tikrit, Fallujah and Ramadi, before the operation to liberate Mosul eventually began in

October 2016. Juruf, Saif's village, was liberated on November 3, but victory there seemed empty with so many of his family dead and the perpetrators gone.

Yet vengeance, so long promised, finally came the day Abdullah Aboud was found in the Old City eight months of fighting later.

I look again at the second photo of Aboud and notice more than just the details of his death. Other changes have occurred, too, since the first photo. He has been interrogated. The old man's hands, tied behind him in the first image, have been bound to his front in the second photo. His face, gaunt in the first picture, is swollen in the second. That could be the effect of being shot. Or it could be the result of being beaten. His right eye seems damaged. There are puncture wounds to his right cheek and upper lip. Someone had some time with Abdullah Aboud before they killed him, leaving him to stare out of the frame in death, mouth agape, blood pooling around the back of his head.

I never do discover exactly who killed him. Saif, with respect to his position as one of General Jubouri's bodyguards, does not want to discuss the specific details of Aboud's death, and I do not believe he was there when it happened.

"Forget about it," he says tersely when I ask him to detail the final moments of Aboud's life. I am slightly surprised. In other ways he speaks so openly about what has happened and his desire for vengeance. Iraqi troops are hardly shy in posting photographs of vengeance killings in Mosul; they are proud of it.

But there is no shortage of those who did discuss Aboud's death, posting images of the killing on Facebook, with telling comments written beside. Others spoke out in private satisfaction over what had happened.

It seems that immediately after he was caught in the Old City, Abdullah Aboud was taken for provisional interrogation by Iraqi troops at a screening centre just behind the front line, where males were whipped with cables as a matter of protocol while a row of military intelligence officers checked their identities against databanks on laptops.

Here, Aboud's name was registered as being that of an Isis suspect, sought in connection with the high-profile murders in the infamous Islamic State video. By then it was already well known across Iraq that the victims killed in the video included the cousins of one of the most respected and powerful Iraqi generals commanding the Mosul operation, so there was already an extensive cast of people wanting to avenge themselves against Abdullah Aboud.

The first photo of him, his head raised by a captor's fist, was taken as part of the identification process. Next, according to details that emerged from west Mosul just after the battle finished, a phone call was made by one of the interrogating officers to another member of the victims' family, who was told of Aboud's capture.

That man duly arrived, interrogated Aboud as to the whereabouts of others involved in the killings, then shot him dead. The second picture was taken straight after Aboud's death, to show that revenge had finally been taken.

This should be the end of the story. Yet it is still unfinished. Humans are seldom satisfied. Revenge is imprecise, and its greatest flaw is that it feeds a cycle, rather than concludes a matter.

Do you feel satiated by Aboud's death, I ask Saif. "The level of my desire for revenge is still the same in me," he replies. "I cannot forget it while there is still a single Daesh left alive in my country."

He still has the footage of his family's murder on his phone.